MYSTERY MARK OF THE NEW AGE

MYSTERY MARK
OF THE NEW AGE

Satan's Design
For World Domination

TEXE MARRS

CROSSWAY BOOKS □ WESTCHESTER, ILLINOIS
A DIVISION OF GOOD NEWS PUBLISHERS

Cover design: Britt Taylor Collins

First printing, 1988
Third printing, 1988

Printed in the United States of America

Library of Congress Catalog Card Number 87-72956

ISBN 0-89107-479-1

TABLE OF

Contents

INTRODUCTION

A deadly and evil cold wind is viciously blowing with magnum force across America and the globe. From whence does it come? The Bible reveals that Satan is the *hellish creator* of this rough and chilling air current. He is the "prince of the power of the air" (Eph. 2:2). But the gale force winds now ripping through man's weakened defenses and shaking the very foundations of the world also have an *earthly source:* the New Age Movement.

The New Age is the last age. It will culminate in the emergence of an astonishingly powerful World Teacher, the New Age false "Messiah," who will be worshiped by all the world as a supernatural God of Forces. This man of sin, the Beast with the number 666, will cause every man, woman, and child alive to take a Mark, either on the forehead or the right hand.

Only born-again Christians will be so bold as to refuse this Mark. They will be put to death for their disobedience.

Satan knows his days are numbered. He must do his evil work quickly while there is still time, for soon Jesus Christ, King of Kings and Lord of Lords, will arrive on Planet Earth. Like a mighty whirlwind from heaven He will seize the Kingdom promised Him by the Father from the beginning and destroy the Adversary and his legions of followers. God's will *shall* prevail.

Furious and frustrated over his blazingly imminent end, Satan is gearing up for a monumental, last-ditch effort to capture the souls of men and women. Raging psychopath, liar and mass murderer that he is, Lucifer's mind is consumed with his mad ambition to take as many captives as possible with him into the dark pit. Into this fiery pit he will be cast by our Lord and imprisoned for a thousand years, awaiting his final, everlasting and doomed fate.

The immediate future will be bleak for all of humanity. The

Christian community will especially be in jeopardy as New Age leaders, incited by their demonic overlords, ruthlessly and methodically carry out their meticulously prepared Plan for world domination. Satan has energized his followers with a special infusion of enthusiasm and ill will. The planet will experience uncontrollable spasms of violence and chaos. Widespread terror and rampant savagery will envelop the land, and blood will be shed on a massive scale.

Those who believe in Christ Jesus will be the earliest victims of the coming days of horror and brutality. The stage is already set for the purge of Christian believers to begin in earnest. All that is needed is for the Son of Perdition, the Antichrist, to appear on the scene. And appear he will. Millions of New Agers, many in positions of great influence in politics, law, medicine, education, religion, have been tipped off by their demon spirit guides as to his imminent appearance. They have been discreetly told in advance that the dawning of the New Age Kingdom of the Beast is at hand.

Very soon the one upon whom they have waited so long in eager anticipation will burst forth to grab the reins of world power and take dominion.

Breathtaking events and extraordinary hardship and suffering will soon overtake mankind. The Bible foretold these events and told us that fear and shock will so grip men in these days of terror that their hearts will fail them.

Things will be so dreadful that if it were not for the Second Coming of the Lord, the planet and every living person would be destroyed:

> For then shall be great tribulation, such as was not since the beginning of the world to this time, no, nor ever shall be. And except those days should be shortened, there should no flesh be saved; but for the elect's sake those days shall be shortened. (Matt. 24:21, 22)

Things to Come: The Plan

In my book *Dark Secrets of the New Age,* I exposed the thirteen-point, hidden Plan of Satan to bring to pass a One World Government and a One World Religion headed by a New Age Messiah or "Christ."

Now, in *Mystery Mark of the New Age*, I unveil startling facts revealing exactly *how* satanically-inspired New Age leaders intend to successfully achieve these horrendous objectives.

As I worked unceasingly over the past two and one-half years probing into the strange, often impenetrable labyrinth that is the New Age, Satan came up against me repeatedly. But "greater is he that is in (us), than he that is in the world" (1 John 4:4). Each time Satan came forth to stall my investigation and thwart my research, I called on God to bind the Adversary. Without reservation, I give God all the glory for what is revealed here and praise Him for His faithfulness.

PART ONE

And He Causeth All to Receive a Mark

The Gathering Fury

And they worshiped the dragon who gave power unto the beast; and they worshiped the beast, saying, who is like the beast? Who is able to make war with him? . . . And all that dwell upon the earth shall worship him, whose names are not written in the book of life of the Lamb slain from the foundation of the world.

(Revelation 13:4, 8)

My Army is ready for battle, My Masters of Wisdom and Myself at the head. That battle will be fought for the continuance of man on this earth. Rest assured that my Army shall triumph!

(Lord Maitreya, the New Age "Christ")

Satan has a Mark he wants to give you. If you take his Mark, he will own your own mind, your body, your spirit. He will be your father. And there will be no escape, no way out. You *will* be damned.

However, you are not alone. Satan intends to give his Mark to every man, woman, and child on the face of Planet Earth. He will not be satisfied until you and your entire family receive his Mark, and all your neighbors and mine have it. No, he won't be happy until *all of humanity* comes to worship *him* and *him alone.*

Satan is well on the way to success in his goal of enslaving the world. To accomplish his dark objectives, he has reestablished his Church, Mystery Babylon. Popularly called the New Age Movement, it is a perverse and diabolical institution founded on a web of lies and deceit. Spanning the globe and encompassing hundreds of millions of teachers and disciples, it has within its fold thousands of individual cults, churches, groups, and organizations. All oppose Biblical Christianity.

These many churches and groups constantly cooperate and collude. There *is* a conspiracy—a monstrous and hideous conspiracy. The conspirators themselves fearlessly call it an "Open Conspiracy."[1] One of its leaders, Jose Arguelles, mastermind of the worldwide Harmonic Convergence of August 16/17, 1987, when several hundred thousand satanists, pagans, and other ungodly people assembled to herald the dawning of a New Age, has frankly stated:

> We're almost at the completion stage of bringing all the thousands of New Age groups, oganizations and churches together.[2]

Arguelles says that the purpose of the 1987 Harmonic Convergence was to have "144,000 rainbow warriors" chosen—culled out worldwide—to become divine leaders of the emerging New Age Kingdom and planetary government. These are to be the elite who shall rule Planet Earth. According to Arguelles, what happened at this huge "cosmic festival" was that New Age participants united in "surrender to the higher intelligence that rules this planet."[3] Since our Bible identifies Satan as ruler of *this* world until Jesus Christ returns, we clearly see to whom these 144,000 rainbow warriors owe their unreserved loyalty and allegiance.

The New Age Five-Year Plan

We also are told by Jose Arguelles and others that the Harmonic Convergence kicked off a five-year plan during which the New Age is to gain incredible, irreversible momentum toward achieving its goal of world domination.[4] Among the revealing aims of this ambitious five-year plan, the New Age intends to:

(1) Bring all New Age groups, organizations and churches together in unity and strength.

(2) Establish a "mediarchy," composed of all television, radio, newspaper, and other media who will work jointly to set up a propaganda environment favorable to the New Age.

(3) "Destructure civilization," dismantling national governments and setting up a one world order based on global units, called "bioregions." *The United States of America will be dissolved as a national entity.*

(4) "Purify the earth," a hazy and vague concept which, when properly analyzed, clearly means the forcible establishment of a one world religion and the abolishing of true Biblical Christianity. Christian resisters will be killed.

(5) Merge humanity with "spirit guides" and "ascended masters" from the invisible spirit world. (Christians know this simply means the possession of human beings on a mass scale by demons from the pit of hell.)

(6) Exalt humanity to godhood. Citizens of the New Age Kingdom will be suddenly and magically capable of superhuman feats. The present weak and inferior Aryan race that populates the planet will give way to the new superior race of Aquarian Man. Those unfit to join this new, advanced race of superbeings will be destroyed, possibly to be reincarnated later.

(7) Seize and redistribute the world's resources and riches, through the principle of "sharing."

(8) Bring in the New Age Messiah, or "Christ," now in the wings anxiously awaiting the moment of international crisis when he can assume the reins of world power.

The Leaders of the New Age World Religion

Satan quite obviously has big, big plans for man's future. But he cannot bring those plans to fruition without an extensive global network of dedicated and effective leaders. Does he, in fact, have this type of broad, powerful network of human collaborators? The answer, regrettably, is *yes*.

Perhaps the most frightening aspect of the New Age is the world-class caliber of its leadership. Satan has been able to put together a formidable last-days team comprised of many of the world's most persuasive and charismatic men and women. The New Age World Religion has in its ranks prime ministers, diplomats and statesmen, international bankers and financiers, university presidents, corporate chief executive officers of some of the world's largest multinational firms, Oscar and Emmy award-winning actresses, Grammy award-winning musicians, renowned philosophers, educators, and scholars, publishers, best-selling authors, "Christian" theologians, and many, many more.

The names of the most dedicated New Agers may well surprise you. Some are household names. Satan is no respecter of persons. He prides himself on taking advantage of false pride and inflated human egos. And he has been successful in snaring people whose fame and glamor bring in many unwitting disciples gullible enough to believe in a false religion simply because a glamorous movie starlet or politician whom they hero-worship professes belief in the New Age.

The New Age is not some kind of minor, weird, post-hippie movement. It is not simply a strange philosophy or fun and games taken up by a collection of flighty actresses and entertainers. This is neither a Shirley MacLaine phenomenon, nor is it simply an example of mind games for the restless and affluent crowd. *This is an unheralded, almost unimaginable, religious, political, economic, social, cultural and scientific movement that has already dramatically changed this planet whether you know it or not.*

The New Age isn't on the way. It's *here, now,* as you read this book. Open your eyes and wake up. You *have* entered the Twilight Zone. But this time you can't make it go away by turning off the TV set. It's been preprogrammed to assault your brain nonstop, twenty-four hours a day, *until Jesus returns.* (Did you catch those last three all-important words? If not, read them again and again and again.)

Has the whole world gone insane? No, God is still in control. But because of man's disobedience and rebellion, the world and mankind have entered the slimy era when Satan is—for a time—practically given free rein. This is why everywhere we turn, we find prominent people in all fields endorsing the New Age and even immersing themselves in its philosophies and religious practices. To understand the incredible planetary transformation that has *already* taken place while so many of us were unaware, let's take a quick look at some of today's most famous and most influential New Agers.

The Great and the Small

In succeeding chapters of *Mystery Mark of the New Age,* I'll show how world-renowned financiers, corporation chieftains, diplomats, statesmen and politicians are now combining their efforts with New Age religious leaders to usher in a New Age

World Order. The list of influential world leaders buying into the New Age lie and becoming its proselytyzers grows daily. For example, consider J. Peter Grace, many times over a millionaire and head of W. R. Grace, a huge multinational corporation. Grace now conducts seminars at Windstar, a New Age community in Colorado founded by singer John Denver. Windstar actively pushes for global peace without Jesus Christ and for a "One World Consciousness."[5]

Another multimillionaire, R. E. "Ted" Turner, owner of the Cable News Network broadcasting empire, and head of an abomination called The Better World Society, called for the election of a New Age President in 1988.[6]

In Great Britain, Prince Charles and Queen Elizabeth have become devotees of New Age holistic health philosophies;[7] meanwhile, Austria's president Kurt Waldheim, former Secretary General of the United Nations, has long been a dedicated New Ager active in peace issues. The recent revelations that as a World War II army officer serving the Nazi regime he had knowledge of and may have participated in war crimes merely augments the blackened character of this world leader.

Such New Age politicians as Senator Claiborne Pell (Democrat, Rhode Island), Senator Terry Sanford (Democrat, North Carolina), and Mayors Kathy Whitmire of Houston and Don Fraser of Minneapolis are gaining momentum in their efforts to bring in a new era of political activism on behalf of their malevolent but often disguised agenda. One New Age disciple, former U.S. Senator Gary Hart, was considered a shoo-in for the Democratic Party's nomination for President before the Donna Rice incident destroyed his candidacy.[8]

Senator Hart is well-known among New Agers. He was *their* candidate, a man who believes in and practices Native American Indian shamanism (sorcery). Hart has publicly stated that he receives "spiritual advice" from an Indian woman teacher who delivers such advice daily to his office.[9]

Many very powerful men in government have become New Age advocates—men like U.S. Secretary of State George Schultz, who astonished a Washington, D.C. audience in 1987 with his comment that a New Age had already dawned and that a unified economic and financial world order, which he favors, is fast taking shape.[10]

West Germany's Willy Brandt, formerly the Chancellor—the

top political leader—of that powerful European nation, is not only a member of the World Federalists, but has lately devoted his life to the cause of the New Age worldview.[11]

Mikhail Gorbachev: The World's Top New Age Leader

However, the most significant and most frightening news story of our generation comes from the largest nation on earth: the Soviet Union. There, an incredible New Age transformation is under way. Termed "Glasnost" by the world press and "Perestroika" by its architect, Soviet Communist Party Chief Mikhail Gorbachev, this revolution promises to be a key element in Satan's Plan for a One World Order led by an Antichrist world leader.

After closely studying the momentous events underway in Moscow and carefully analyzing this "Perestroika" revolution, I have come to this astonishing conclusion: Mikhail Gorbachev, head of this bear of a superpower, perhaps the earth's greatest military machine, is no longer an atheist. He has been converted to the New Age World Religion. His is now the "god of forces."[12]

Soviet leader Mikhail Gorbachev is unquestionably *the world's foremost New Age teacher and leader.* I will provide documentation of the startling new worldview, or paradigm shift, by the world's top Communist official in Chapter 13 of *Mystery Mark of the New Age* and will present further definitive proof in a subsequent book soon to be published. The evidence is unshakable: Satan has accomplished a mighty feat in winning the heart and soul of the Soviet Union's highest official. The implications of this feat are mind-boggling to consider; but undeniably, everyone on earth will soon be eyewitness to profound decisions and international actions that will shock and surprise a world already inured to startling and unbelievable developments.

They Shall Take the Mark . . . Willingly

Why, though, should we as Christians be either surprised or alarmed that the world's most powerful leaders and statesmen are turning their souls over to the Devil in these, the last days? Revelation 13:16 prophesies that the Beast "causeth all, both small and great, rich and poor, free and bond, to receive a mark." In Revelation 17:15 we see that MYSTERY BABYLON, Satan's final, end-times religious system, will encompass "peoples, and multitudes, and nations, and tongues." Then in Revelation 17:13, we discover that the Antichrist who is to come will reign supreme as a global dictator. The world's ten most powerful national leaders will "have one mind, and shall give their power and strength unto the beast."

Yes, the Beast will cause *all,* both small and great, to receive a Mark. When we examine the world scene today, we discover an amazing truth: The billions of men, women, and children who inhabit Planet Earth will not have to be tortured, beat over the head, and forced to take the Mark. Their leaders will not have to use the tactics of Hitler's jackbooted Gestapo, nor employ any undesirable methods of suppression and terror.

The vast majority will cheerfully and of their own free will and volition receive the Mark. It will be the most remarkable of all developments in human history: an epoch in which the people themselves rise up as one and demand their rights to worship themselves as gods. They will all gladly *want* the Mark to proudly signify their coming-of-age as gods.

Winning the Masses

As I've illustrated, political leaders in nations around this globe are now agitating for a one world, New Age order. But they are certainly not encountering opposition from the average Joe or Jane, the man- or woman-on-the-street. The media convincingly report that this is a massive *grass-roots* movement.

The New Age has infiltrated and captured strongholds in every sphere of society. Evidence of this abounds. For example, a surprising number of stockbrokers now consult astrological charts and visit tarot card readers. In every U.S. city, various groups meet nightly to watch videos of "wise" spirits speaking through channelers and to study such New Age "Bibles" as *The Keys of Enoch, The Book of Urantia, The Satanic Bible, A Course in Miracles,* and the writings of the Lucis Trust's Alice Bailey.

Redbook, one of the most widely read women's magazines in America, last October carried an article telling women how to develop their psychic skills, read their auras, and use candles for occult purposes.[13] Another popular magazine recently quoted a woman as saying "The New Age stuff has offered me the freedom to believe what I want to believe as opposed to having to believe in Jesus, in the Bible, etc."[14] Yet another woman stated, "The New Age gives people tools through meditation and self-hypnosis, or some of the reprogramming consciousness, to help you . . . harness your own power, or tap into a power greater than yours."[15]

The New Age has made such tremendous inroads into society that such Fortune 500 companies as AT&T and IBM are now sending their executives to seminars to learn New Age concepts of visualization, thinking and creativity, and management.[16] Holistic (New Age) medicine is booming, and New Age music is all the rage. Crystal powers are "in"—popular rock star Julian Lennon, for example, sports a healing crystal earring. Actress Raquel Welch has introduced a Yoga workout video for the New Age market, and sultry rock singer Tina Turner credits chanting with helping her achieve personal and professional success.[17]

A supermarket counter tabloid profiles talk-show queen Oprah Winfrey as also crediting her professional success to her New Age spirituality: "It is because of this God-centeredness that I am where I am," says Oprah proudly. "It is also because I fear nothing and no one. Each morning I center myself to touch the God light I believe is in all of us. . . . I get boundless energy from that."[18]

Most people involved in the New Age—especially Hollywood stars and other celebrities—are unsuspecting pawns in a cosmic chess game played by Satan. Tens of thousands of everyday people dabble in the occult and adopt such New Age doctrines as reincarnation and communication with the spirit world and don't even recognize they are part of the New Age. They are unwitting accomplices of evil.

The Plan: Spiritually Rebuilding the Tower of Babel

But top New Age leaders *know exactly what they're doing* in deceiving the masses, and they know whom they're serving. They know the "Plan," and they're dedicated to helping Lucifer succeed in implementing it.

That Plan, called "the spiritual path" of mankind by the

highest echelons in the New Age, is in reality Satan's design to carry out what he began millennia ago in ancient Babylon when God ruined his attempt to construct the Tower of Babel. As one New Age authority has remarked:

> The spiritual path seems to have a special connection to the story of Babel since the builders of Shinar (like we of the New Age) sought to build a tower to reach to the heavens. In our attempts to transcend purely physical limitations, we too are reaching to the heavens.[19]

What part does the Mark and other symbols play in this rebellious New Age effort to once again build a Tower of Babel? This same New Age leader frankly admits that in the bright new era, "Our ability to communicate is based on a shared acceptance of the signs, symbols, feelings, and phenomena of what, together, we accept as reality." He goes on to stress that the masses now "least likely to understand us," through such manifestations as *signs and symbols*, will be able to explore and map the "regions of fire."[20]

In plain language, the Mark and other symbols are to become the universal *picture language* of mankind—a simple but demonic form of communication that all can easily understand and share.

Through the symbol of the Mark, to be physically and permanently inscribed on the forehead or right hand of every person on earth, all peoples will become One. As One, all will share in the dark blasphemies to be poured out on a deluded humanity by Satan and his legions.

The Feast of the Beast

In the demonically-inspired 1980 book *Michelle Remembers,* the authors make mention of a Feast of the Beast that was to take place in 1982.[21] During this Feast, Satan was to issue his Master Plan to his earthly followers. I do not know if 1982 was the specific date when Satan's Master Plan, his blueprint for chaos and destruction, was first distributed. Certainly the Devil's Antichrist spirit has been active throughout the Christian Church Age, rousing the world to be at enmity with the people of God.

However, there is in existence today an operational military plan outlining, in voluminous detail, how Satan intends to bring off his One World New Age Kingdom.

The New Group of World Servers is an organization that claims to be the "Custodians of the Plan." The members of this group, jointly headquartered in London, New York, and Geneva, affirm their goal as the building of a "New World Order." They claim to be the "Enlightened Ones."[22]

"There is a Plan for humanity," says the guidebook of the New Group of World Servers, given by the "spiritual hierarchy of the planet to train the minds of men more rapidly and to build towards a more Synthetic Unity."[23] These Enlightened Ones, the Custodians of the Plan, frankly admit to being a hidden body of men from around the globe, known by insiders simply as "the Brotherhood." In effect, they profess to be "the inner Spiritual Government of the Planet."[24]

We need not accept at face value the contention of the New Group of World Servers that its members are the hidden "inner spiritual government of the planet." Indeed, there are numerous New Age groups making similar boasts. Yet, in analyzing the speeches and writings of this and all other New Age groups, I find striking similarities in doctrine and goals. This is understandable because every New Age cult, organization and church of which I am aware has this single, unifying, common characteristic: they were all *without exception* founded on the direct orders of a demon spirit!

Satan's New Age groups come under many disguises, cosmetically concealed under many faces and with many a dark covering and mask. But they all have common roots, common origins, and a master in common. Therefore, when a major New Age event comes along, such as the Planetary Commission's annual World Healing Day, all of the thousands of networking, interrelated New Age factions come together as one. And as one, they celebrate the Feast of the Beast, devour *his* Master Plan, and feed their disciples the poisonous scraps from the banquet table of the Beast.

The Teachings of the Beast

Satan's Plan reveals that soon he will send his handpicked and groomed World Leader to a world hungry for his presence. In the interim, Satan works through his dark angels and their human disciples who are busily planting the seeds of chaos. As Lord Maitreya, the demon spirit whom Benjamin Creme and the Tara Center tout as "Christ," has expressed:

> My Plan is that my Teaching should precede my Presence and prepare My Way. My people will release it through their groups and group endeavor. . . . I shall send My Disciples to You, and they will show you the way, but you must act and follow Our Plan.[25]

What is this "Teaching" of the Beast that is already being given to mankind to prepare the way for Satan's false "Christ"? Undoubtedly you have already heard much about this teaching. Even some of the better-known Christian evangelists are preaching it to their flocks. Its major tenets have been announced and taught extensively from pulpits, platforms, and on television air waves in every nation on earth.

Here, listed below, are the Seven Major Teachings of the New Age. A study of the Bible reveals these same false teachings to be the Seven Marks of Mystery Babylon, Satan's last-days religion:

(1) Jesus was not and is not the only Christ, nor is he God.

(2) "God" is impersonal, cosmic, a God of energy forces.

(3) Man is himself God, for he consists of and is the creator of "the forces." Man already exercises the powers inherent in his divinity and needs only to *awaken* to this fact.

(4) Man should seek and accept spiritual instruction and direction directly from the spirit world.

(5) All religions and religious teachings lead to the same goal. All are equally of merit.

(6) The "ancient wisdom" of Babylon, Egypt and Greece— *not the Bible*—is the basis of all Truth.

(7) Sin and evil do not exist. Peace and love are the ultimate realities.

The teachers of the New Age World Religion firmly believe that these teachings will continue to conquer all obstacles in their paths. The New Age Kingdom will be! says Matthew Fox, the heretical Catholic priest whose life is totally devoted to his New Age, nature worship ministry. Fox preaches that there is coming "A New Pentecost, a New Creation, a spiritual awakening that all the world's religions might share in."[26]

This optimistic view is shared by other New Age leaders. Their hellish master has told them he will prevail over the true God, and they foolishly believe him. Satan's Plan envisions the whole world undergoing a fiery time of crisis and chaos. The actual takeover of Planet Earth will come as a result of this crisis. Out of crisis, chaos, and death will emerge the New Jerusalem, populated only by New Age gods whose foreheads and hands bear the Mark of their master and lord. According to New Age leaders, the New Jerusalem will be the culmination of the evolutionary process:

> We live in urgent yet wonderful times. . . . It is proving to be a very difficult transition, a time of deep spiritual crisis with grave dangers but with unique *opportunities* for evolutionary progress.[27]

To speed up this evolutionary process and more rapidly usher in the New Age Kingdom, Satan and his demons have founded thousands of cults, churches and organizations. The humans who head these groups are cued by demons so that they recognize one another:

> Already there are a number of groups—World Servers for the New Age, Planet Stewards, Warriors of the Rainbow, Children of the Dawn, etc.—who envision a unification of individual beings from all parts of the planet as an evolutionary nucleus. The parts are being called together. They will intuitively recognize one another.[28]

Why are the leaders of the New Age being joined together at this significant time-period in man's long history? John Randolph Price gives us the unabashed answer: "Now," he explains, by unifying our efforts, "we can co-create the future according to the divine Plan."[29]

The Unmovable Obstacle: Christianity

There is, however, one major obstacle to the Plan of the New Age to rebuild the earth. That unmovable obstacle is the body of

Christ, the combined faith of true Christian believers. What's more, we know from Bible prophecy (2 Thess. 2:7) that the Holy Spirit now restrains the Devil from launching his final, all-out assault. But the Holy Spirit of God will one day soon remove the barriers and give the Devil free rein to do his works of terror.

Satan sorely despises Christian believers, for we are the light of the world—human mirrors reflecting the greater light that shines from above. Over the centuries Satan has sent wave after wave of persecution on God's people, and things will not get any better as we head for the ultimate showdown, the final conflict between good and evil:

> Yea, and all that will live godly in Christ Jesus shall suffer persecution. But evil men and seducers shall wax worse and worse, deceiving, and being deceived. (2 Timothy 3:12, 13)

The awful truth is that Christians who refuse to take the Mark of the Beast *are marked,* but in a much different way. They are marked *for extinction* by New Age forces. Satan has already passed sentence. The verdict is guilty. The crime: serving Jesus Christ. The penalty is removal from earth: death. But the Christian knows who ultimately has jurisdiction over his life. Almighty God promises life—eternal life—with Jesus Christ in a gloriously blissful existence that has no ending for those who accept the free gift of His Son.

Satan has succeeded in convincing the New Age masses that this free gift of God is an illusion. His lie is that mankind must depend on its own resources and put together a new, man-centered religion. In a symposium in Asheville, North Carolina, with the theme "Toward a Global Society," New Age globalist leader Donald Keys trumpeted to an ecstatic audience:

> We're at the final stage now of putting it all together. It's a New Religion called "Networking." . . . The New Age Wave is now entering social change.[30]

"Unfortunately," Keys complained, "we're also experiencing the beginning of backlash." From whom? Christians. Fundamentalist Christians who believe only in Jesus as Lord and the Bible as His Word. Keys scornfully called such people "pre-humanistic" and "anti-humanistic." With these neanderthal types around, Keys suggested, the New Age World "is awfully hard to govern."[31]

What is the solution? Keys said it would be necessary to have the services of a great One World Leader:

> Don't anyone think for a moment that you can run a planet without a head. . . . These folks who think that they're going to be able to get off with some kind of sloppy, do-it-your-own relationships among nations, just casually checking in now and then, have got to think again. This planet has to be MANAGED.[32]

Things could get a little messy, Keys implies, once this New Age World Leader assumes power. For one thing, there are these dangerous Christian fundamentalists who pose a problem:

> When it comes to running a world or taking people into a New Age, it ain't neat! . . . There's another element here. Let's call them 'a.h.' These are difficult cookies because they are anti-humanistic. . . . They're rather dangerous! They do pose a problem.[33]

The Christian as an Outcast

We may be "difficult cookies," as Keys puts it, but Christians sadly are an incredibly small minority today. New Age leaders have been able to bring together and unite every false religion and cult on earth. Hindus, Buddhists, satanists, witches—all are welcome and are joining in New Age unity. Only Bible-believing Christians are excluded. We are anathema; we are pariahs.

Unity is everything to the New Ager—a unity that denies the exclusiveness or unique nature of God. Djwhal Khul, the demon "Tibetan Master" who discipled Alice Bailey and so many other New Age leaders, taught that Christians were "separative" and evil and are the stumbling-block to world unity. His appealing but deceptive plea is as follows:

> Let us drop our antagonisms . . . and our social and religious differences and think in terms of one family.[34]

Khul, whom the Theosophical Society credits as their founding father, provides the rationale for giving all of mankind a unifying Mark and for persecuting those "separationists" and rebels who refuse it. Through their common use of the Mark, plainly etched in the forehead or right hand, all who worship the Beast will experience a sense of unity and fellowship. As Khul explains:

"A new commandment I give you," can be summed up in "inclusiveness," the hallmark of the New Age, the universal spirit, identification, oneness with all your fellowmen.[35]

The New Age leadership has flatly stated that in the coming New Age Kingdom, Christians will have to change their lifestyles and their entire way of thinking and become good "Aquarians" or else. Barbara Marx Hubbard has threatened: "People will either *change or die*. That is the choice."[36] Foster Bailey, of the Lucis Trust, further reinforces this dogmatic stance:

The new civilization in Aquarius will inevitably develop a quality appropriate to what we consider most valuable. . . . Our children, and men . . . will have to live with the New Age standards. Those who do not will end up as irreconcilable outcasts.[37]

Bailey stridently points out that in the New Age theology, separateness is considered heresy. It is the root cause of all the world's troubles. Refusal to unify, to become part of the Great Brotherhood, Bailey argues, is an act of "heresy against the divine Plan."[38]

Global Mind-Link: A Preview of the Coming World Unity

World unity devoid of Jesus Christ and his followers is at the very threshold of being attained. On December 31; 1987, the New Age leadership was reportedly able to marshal a colossal worldwide force of 875 million people to participate in a single event, Global Mind-Link, also called World Healing Day.[39] On that day, these hundreds of millions of New Agers knelt to meditate and invoke their demon spirits and inner "gods" (their "Master" or "Holy" Self) to usher in a New Age Kingdom on earth led by a New Age Messiah or "Christ."

John Randolph Price, whose networking group, The Planetary Commission, organized this huge planetary demon-fest, subsequently published this thought-provoking proclamation for all New Age disciples:

> To the people and organizations in the 82 countries/ principalities/dependencies who shared their Light, Love and Spiritual Consciousness for healing and harmonizing of Planet Earth, we say to you . . . You are the Master Builders of the New Civilization, and our work shall not be in vain. A giant Energy Field, a massive Thought-Form, has been created. A Unified Consciousness of spiritually-minded Light Workers has emerged, which is even now transmuting the negative energy and forming a critical mass of Positive Good for this world.
>
> But we cannot be complacent. In the months left until the third Global Mind-Link on December 31, 1988, let's reach in deeply to reveal the Master Self in consciousness— and then reach out to the far corners of the Earth, at that precious moment in time, to embrace in mind the Holy Self of each individual—forming a glorious Force Field through which a New World will be revealed.[40]

Think of it! Eighty-two countries, 875 million people unified in purpose, all meditating together simultaneously, calling up the blackest forces from hell to be made manifest. These people see themselves as positive, as good, because their common father, Lucifer, has twisted and warped their minds to believe the lie. Millions of New Agers want to be powerful gods. They're willing to take a Mark if necessary to become gods and they'll kill anyone that gets in their way—if their master tells them that such an act is for the "Positive Good."

How many Christians today are willing to refuse the Mark even if it means torture and certain death? Jesus told us that men would someday put His disciples to death and think they were doing God a service. Would you choose to go to your death rather than take the Mark?

How many Christians will endure to the end? Certainly we cannot imagine a number as high as 875 million! Remember: only Noah and his family survived the Flood. Only Lot and his loved ones escaped the flaming catastrophe of Sodom and Gomorrah. Jesus cautioned that His followers would be few:

Enter in at the strait gate; for wide is the gate, and broad is the way, that leadeth to destruction, and many there be who go in that way; Because strait is the gate, and narrow is the way, which leadeth unto life, and few there be that find it. (Matt. 7:13, 14)

The New Age comes preaching another gospel: *wide* is the way and *many* there are that shall find it. Only renegades are excluded from the Kingdom—Christian renegades.

The Lure of the Mark

As I've intimated, after the New Age World Religion of the Antichrist fully encompasses the earth, all the world's population, except the few despised Christian holdouts, will believe in the New Age gospel. This is a gospel that comes in fancy and shiny, tinsel-laden wrappings. It is a positive, earth-bound gospel of prosperity, peace, and love, seductively pointing the way to personal power and one's own divinity.

The Mark will come to be seen as the capstone of the new religion. Everyone will want it. Anyone who refuses it will be thought of as a weirdo, a rebel. Eventually the whole world, under the hypnotic, mesmerizing spell of the greatest occult magician who has ever lived, will hold the Christian without the Mark as a disgusting example of human rot. Seeing an outcast Christian without the Mark will actually arouse anger and resentment in the heart of the New Age believer. The stage will be set for a holocaust.

The Mark

And he causeth all, both small and great, rich and poor, free and bond, to receive a mark on their right hand, or on their foreheads, and that no man might buy or sell, save he that had the mark, or the name of the beast, or the number of his name. (Rev. 13:16, 17)

The larger triangle was quite straight, delicately incised in just the outer few skin layers as if by the work of a skilled master surgeon. . . . They had changed me, done something to me. I could sense it clearly that night but I could not articulate it. Later I thought that they were taming me.

(Whitley Strieber, *Communion*)

All eyes fastened on Richard as he excitedly entered the room. The door closed and the young man looked at the astonishing scene that lay before him. He observed that there were seven men in all, sitting in a circle. Their eyes fixed on his and the blood quickly rushed to Richard's face. Oh, no! he thought. The time had come. It was his turn to receive the Mark.

"We have met here for a specific purpose, Richard," a man obviously the leader said in a reverent tone. "These, my brothers in Christ, have come from distant places to officiate at the ceremony for which you have been summoned . . . the one concerning the name which has been given you; for did not our brother, Dr. White, tell you that soon it would be made a part of your body?"

A sinking fear took hold of Richard . . . He blanched and felt a little faint.

"Why do you tremble, Richard? . . . These things must be endured because they are essential. . . . The name the Lord has ordained unto you will be cut into your skin . . . and the scar tissue will be pigmented so it will be brightly legible for the rest of your life."

The boy held perfectly still without being instructed to do so even as he felt the knife cutting into him. He perspired profusely. . . . The pain was unexpectedly intense and he was all the more squeamish as he felt the blood running down the side of his leg.

Finally, the leader announced, "It's done. Now things have come to pass which were required of this date according to prophecy. . . . You, Richard, possess the key of David, by which your continued works are given authority. Now to the extent that you are with us, we are with you. Give thanks to Christ who guides us all!"

I did not make up this story. It is the account of a New Age disciple and it is recorded in his best-selling book, *The Ultimate Frontier*.[1] It is not, however, the sole account of a New Ager receiving the Mark of the Beast. And it will certainly not be the last.

The Bible tells us that as part of Satan's grand design for world domination, he has prepared a *Mark* that will be given every man, woman, and child on earth:

And he causeth all, both small and great, rich and poor, free and bond, to receive a mark on their right hand, or on their foreheads, and that no man might buy or sell, save he that had the mark, or the name of the beast, or the number of his name. (Rev. 13:16, 17)

After many months of intensive study and exhaustive research of the New Age World Religion, its leaders, and their intentions, I have been able, with the help of Almighty God, to uncover a plot on the part of Satan of truly monstrous proportions. Shockingly precise and brutally frank in its aims, the dark dimensions of this plot stagger the imagination. The Kingdom of the Antichrist is at hand—make no mistake about it!—and soon, very soon, the whole world will feel the savage impact of the Beast with the fearful number: 666.

God alone can stop the onslaught of the New Age Beast. But in His Holy Bible He has given us His prophecy of what is to happen. God is always true to His Word, and so we can rely on the revelations given to us in Bible prophecy. In fact, Bible prophecy is considered so important by the Lord that He promised that those who read or hear and believe in His prophecies will receive a *special blessing*:

> Blessed is he that readeth, and they that hear the words of this prophecy, and keep those things which are written in it; for the time is at hand. (Rev. 1:3)

The frightening thing about the New Age Plan of Satan is that its provisions exactly parallel the events and occurrences prophesied in the Bible. Jesus Himself gave us a checklist of things that would occur just before His Second Coming. For example, Christ forecast days of bloodshed and sorrow during which Christians would be terribly persecuted: "Then shall they deliver you up to be afflicted, and shall kill you; and ye shall be hated of all nations for my name's sake" (Matt. 24:9).

Jesus also warned that in that day many will say in their heart, "My lord delayeth his coming," and so continue to do evil, bringing destruction and judgment down on themselves. "There will be weeping and gnashing of teeth" (Matthew 24:44-51).

Likewise, Peter prophesied that in the last days, even as the return of the Lord Jesus Christ drew near, liars would multiply and people would sneer at anyone who expressed confidence in the Lord's imminent return:

> There shall come in the last days scoffers, walking after their own lusts, and saying, Where is the promise of his coming? for since the fathers fell asleep, all things continue as they were from the beginning of the creation. (2 Pet. 3:3, 4)

Today we are inundated with scoffers. We even find within the Christian community prominent evangelists and pastors who deny the imminent return of Jesus Christ. Some even say that Jesus is *unable* to appear. They say that He is "held in the heavens" until mankind has cleaned up its own act and brought in the kingdom.[2] Their blasphemous doctrine attempts to make a mockery of Scripture and a liar of Jesus Christ.

These scoffers merely bring to pass Peter's prophecy of their unseemly conduct. Moreover, Peter described what would be the eventual fate of these unbelievers in God's Word:

> But these, as natural brute beasts, made to be taken and destroyed, speak evil of the things that they understand not, and shall utterly perish in their own corruption. (2 Pet. 2:12)

Jesus instructed us to *watch* for the signs of His coming and to *be ready.* We are not to know the exact hour but, said our Lord, "when ye shall see all these things, know that it is near, even at the doors" (Matt. 24:33).

The Beast *is* at our doors. Soon he will beat down the doors and take us by force unless we first prepare and are ready. This book will help you prepare. It is a revealing exposé of the hidden mysteries that the New Age has so far opened up to only a few. Here, in all its dark, grotesque ugliness is the Plan of the New Age to initiate every person into the Mystery of Iniquity.

Unless you know the Lord Jesus Christ as your personal Savior, *you will take the Mark of the Beast* and thereby enter a blood covenant with Lucifer. You cannot escape, for the Bible makes clear that in the last days a Great Delusion will fall on everyone who has rejected the Lord. You will believe the lie. You will accept the Mark. You will become one of the damned.

> And for this cause God shall send them strong delusion, that they should believe a lie, that they all might be damned who believed not the truth, but had pleasure in unrighteousness. (2 Thess. 2:11, 12)

Step-by-Step: Satan's Battle Plan

The Devil has mapped out a detailed Battle Plan and has passed it on to his demons and those elite men and women whom they have chosen as leaders of the New Age. This Battle Plan includes the following broad goals:

(1) Christianity will be discredited and Christians will become accursed. They are to be branded an ignorant and inferior human species.

(2) A planetary crisis will be precipitated by Satan's human world leaders. Out of this crisis will come the opportunity for the New Age Kingdom to be realized.

(3) A great world leader and statesman will then appear to bring order to chaos. He will be Satan's handpicked man: the Beast, or Antichrist, with the number 666.

(4) New Age leaders, especially those who control the world's TV and radio broadcast media, will mount a tremendously powerful campaign on behalf of this World Leader, causing all the world to believe in his perfection and infallibility.

(5) After assuming the reins of power, the great World Leader will usher in a period of universal peace and prosperity. His magnetism and charisma will enable him to establish himself at the helm of a One World Government, One World Economy, and a One World New Age Religion.

(6) Consolidating all power and might, the great World Leader will finger Christians and Jews as "public enemies" who are a constant danger to world peace, justice, and sharing. The arrest and imprisonment of Christians will commence. All the world will applaud their persecution.

(7) Every man, woman, and child who has not yet been initiated into the Mystery of Iniquity will take a Mark and receive the Luciferic Initiation. They will then discover the awful truth, but it will be far too late. Their fate will have been sealed.

(8) All who refuse the Mark and the Luciferic Initiation and who refuse to worship the image of the Beast will be put to death.

(9) The whole world will be deluged with Satan's demons, who will eagerly and hungrily possess human bodies.

(10) After the whole world has been conquered, Satan's final treacherous act will be to assault the very gates of heaven.

Will Satan's Evil Plan Succeed?

The Bible reveals that all of the Devil's Plan except Step No. 10 will substantially succeed. There will be a one world government under the direct authority of the Antichrist. There will be horrible persecution of Christians, and the entire world will be forced to receive the Mark of the Beast . . . or be killed.

But in attempting Step No. 10, the foolhardy assault on God's throne, Satan will have made a grave mistake. His mad lust for absolute power will have driven him to ultimate destruction. The Scriptures testify that God's wrath will fall on the creator of evil and on Planet Earth. The Lord will scourge the legions who follow Satan, and He will cast the Devil and his followers—human and demon—into the fiery pit. Then all the world will know that Jesus Christ is Lord of Lords, King of Kings (see Revelation 19 through 22).

Would God really be so cruel as to send millions to an everlasting hell? This question is often asked of Christians by people who seek to discredit the Bible and by those eager to avoid responsibility for the consequences of their own actions and decisions. God says He will do it, and He will. He is sovereign; His decisions are always just. "For he saith to Moses, I will have mercy on whom I will have mercy, and I will have compassion on whom I will have compassion" (Rom. 9:15).

God would prefer that no one perish. Therefore, He sent His own Son, Jesus, to die in *our* place for *our* sins. Those who rebel against Him and make light of Jesus' sacrifice for their sins *condemn themselves*. But God is merciful; His provision for salvation is simple yet profound:

> That if thou shalt confess with thy mouth the Lord Jesus, and shalt believe in thine heart that God hath raised him from the dead, thou shalt be saved. (Rom. 10:9)

God will have mercy on whoever comes to Him with a repentant heart and a sincere belief in His Son, Jesus, as Lord and Savior. For these He offers protection and the gift of eternal life. But if you reject God's mercy and His unfathomable gift, you will die in your sins. What's more, you will have chosen to serve your father, Satan. *He will then have the right to do to you whatsoever he will.* Call it unfair, call it unjust, call it whatever you wish. But all of us must choose the master whom we will serve. We are not our own gods, regardless of what the New Age teaches. Who, then, is *your* master?

"We Do Have a Right!"

Does Satan *really* have the right to possess you and do with you whatever horrible things he wishes? He does if you are not one of God's adopted children. Whitley Strieber discovered, to his utter horror, this startling truth. In his number one best-selling nonfiction book *Communion,* he recounts his abduction by strange beings from what appeared to be a huge crystal-like UFO.[3]

Now frankly, I do not believe most UFO stories I read or hear; but in Strieber's case, the facts seem to bear out that he did, in fact, experience what he describes. Yet I hasten to say that what Strieber experienced was in reality *a demonic vision* or apparition rather than a UFO contact. Satan is a master at implanting images and visions in the mind of those he possesses. And Strieber's account accords with that of a man totally possessed by demons who caused him to remember and to retell to millions his incredible tale.

Strieber makes clear in his book that though he was raised a Catholic, he is not a born-again Christian. At the same time, he admits to a long-standing interest in the occult, in Eastern religions and in mysticism and New Age "consciousness." He also was fascinated with the study of the ancient history of Babylon, Egypt, and Greece. Prior to *Communion,* Strieber was the best-selling author of bloodthirsty horror novels. These raw experiences left him vulnerable and defenseless to the demonic attack that was to later envelop him.

Three fascinating yet horrifying things happened to Whitley Strieber that awful night in his isolated home in upstate New York. First he claims that while held captive by the aliens, he underwent what can only be interpreted as a sexual initiation by an alluring yet despicable-looking female demon. Strieber evidently believes this being may actually have been Ishtar, the Mother Goddess of ancient Babylon (see Revelation 17).

> The closest thing I have been able to find to an unadorned image of this [goddess being] is not from some modern science fiction movie, it is rather the ages old glaring face of Ishtar. Paint her eyes entirely black, remove her hair, there is my image as it hangs before me now in my mind's eye, the

ancient and terrible one, the bringer of wisdom, the ruthless questioner.[4]

Strieber, New Ager that he is, asks, "Do my memories come from my own life, or from other lives lived long ago in the shadowy temples where the gray goddess reigned? Perhaps the visitors are gods. Maybe they created us."[5]

Why gods? For one thing, Strieber notes that while inside a large, circular room of the craft in which he was held prisoner, the beings told him and others there that they were "chosen ones." One captive, a woman in a white, floral-pattern dress, was apparently taken in by their announcement. "Praise the Lord!" she shouted as she was told what to her was the good news that she was chosen.[6]

Second, Strieber recalls that as he struggled, cried and screamed to his captors, "You have no right to do this to me. I am a human being," he was confronted with a firm rebuttal from this "Mother Goddess" who was the leader of the other UFO aliens. Staring at him with eyes that reached to the very core of his being, she sternly replied, "We *do* have a right!"[7]

Of course, they do have a right. Satan can do any hideous and frightening thing he desires to *his children*. He is *the* judge and jury, the torturer, the executioner. Rebels against the true God are, as Whitely Strieber found out, totally under Satan's control. Only the children of God are exempt from his lawlessness.

Third, we read in *Communion* that Strieber subsequently woke up to discover etched on his arm a Mark.

When I got up the next morning I found two little triangles inscribed on my left forearm. I don't know what happened, and there is no way at all to explain the event in a conventional manner. The larger triangle was quite straight, delicately incised in just the outer few skin layers as if by the work of a skilled master surgeon. The other triangle, very tiny, was pointing at the larger one.[8]

The triangle is a satanic symbol, the implications of which I'll discuss in some great detail in a later chapter. The point here is this: New Ager Whitley Strieber was apparently initiated and left with the Mark of that Luciferic Initiation.

We know from Bible prophecy that once the Antichrist is in firm control of all the world's churches and religions, he will require every individual to take a Mark either on the hand or the forehead. By his account, Strieber's Mark was on his forearm. It is likely, then, that Strieber's experience is a prelude or preliminary dress rehearsal to the type of initiations that are to come in the days ahead.

The Mark: A Badge of Distinction

It is important to understand how the Mark is to be received. The word "Mark" in the Bible comes from the Greek word *charagma*, a noun that denotes a graven image or stamp that mars the skin.[9] Dr. Spiros Zhodiates, one of the world's greatest Greek Bible scholars, has told me that in Revelation 13, where the Mark of the Beast is discussed, the word "mark" literally means to cut into the body, to physically etch or carve. Such a Mark would undoubtedly be observable to the eye and not hidden.

There has been a lot of speculation about the Mark recently with the invention of new computer microchips so tiny they can be programmed with numbers and other information and be inserted *under* the surface of the skin.

There has also been concern that the laser bar code now in common use at checkout counters is the precursor to the Mark and that everyone may someday be given a laser bar code on their forehead or hand with the number of the Beast.

Could a microchip be programmed with the number of the Beast and be inserted under a person's skin? And what of the bar code? Could the laser be used to "brand" people with the Mark?

In light of the meaning of the Biblical word "mark" as used in Revelation 13, I do not see this as a viable possibility. For one thing, I believe the coming New Age World Leader will promote the Mark as a spiritual status symbol that people will proudly covet. It will be a Mark of distinction. Like the commercial for a well-known credit card says, you wouldn't want to leave home without it! To hide or somehow make the Mark indistinguishable would defeat its purpose.

Satan will undoubtedly get a perverse thrill from seeing men, women and children proudly display his Mark. Much like a haughty and proud Texas rancher who looks out over the thousands of cattle grazing on his lands marked with *his* brand, the Devil can point to the billions who have been branded for *his* name's sake. Pompously he will exult, "These are mine, the Lord cannot have them!"

The Afterglow

A growing number of New Agers have already undergone an initiation ceremony and accepted the Mark. They almost universally report that although they approach the ceremony with dread and foreboding, after it is over—after they have the Mark—these extreme feelings of fear magically vanish. They are replaced by feelings of great joy, of warmth, of serenity and peacefulness. Most report that the newly acquired Mark makes them feel unique and special—even *chosen*.

> After the encounter, I discovered that the lines on the palm
> of my right hand had been altered, and a portion of them
> now formed a six-pointed star about an inch in
> circumference. It terrified me when I first spotted it, for I
> knew I was no longer looking at my own palm. But as time
> went on, I learned to accept the changes within my body, and
> I really felt quite special.[10]

These feelings, voiced by so many who have received a Luciferic Initiation, are significant. They point to two inescapable facts: (1) The initiate recognizes beforehand that he is coming into close contact with dark, evil forces, and a spirit of fear engulfs him; and, (2) after the initiation is over and Satan's demons have taken residence inside the individual, his mind is patently altered. This is what New Agers call the *Kundalini* or *Skaktipat* experience, technically termed a *Paradigm (Worldview) Shift*.

Christians know it as demon possession. As a result, the person's thoughts and beliefs take on those of the demons who inhabit his mind. He is thus made to feel special and chosen. No longer does he fear the darkness and evil; he hungrily longs for it, embraces it, befriends it. He is consumed with satanic bliss.

What the Bible Says About the Mark

It is undeniable that the Bible prohibits God's people from making any graven Mark on their forehead or on their hand or anywhere else on their body:

> Ye shall not make any cuttings in your flesh for the dead, nor print any marks upon you. I am the Lord. (Lev. 19:28)

This restriction in Leviticus was a warning against pagan practices. During religious festivals and funerals, pagan people would often inflict wounds on themselves, to show reverence to the gods or out of grief for a dead loved one. God therefore let His people know that He alone is Lord and that the dead are *His* business. God's commandment was clear: marking—that is, etching or cutting and disfigurement of one's body—is not to be practiced for any reason. (Also see Leviticus 21:5.)

Throughout the centuries, Satan-worshipers and other pagans have used marks on the body, especially on the forehead and hand, to identify themselves with their god or goddess or false teaching. Historians and symbology experts say that the tattooing of the body and face originally began as a form of initiation and sacred worship with the ancient Egyptians, who used hieroglyphic characters.[11]

In the days of the early church, the Roman and Greek worship of Mithra was a strong competitor to Christianity. Adherents of the Mithra Mystery Religion were given strenuous initiation rituals which included bird and animal sacrifices as well as mental and physical tests of strength. Symbology was employed to condition the minds of the initiate.[12]

Tertullian records that the Mithra neophyte, or candidate, would be given a *secret name* (the name of the Beast?), followed by a *Mark on the forehead*. The Mark consisted of being "signed" on the forehead with a hot iron. This event was followed by ecstatic dancing in a symbolic circle, offerings of incense, riotous drinking, and ritual free sex.[13]

The Mark and Today's Occult Explosion

Current fascination with a Mark among many New Age believers most certainly is inspired by Satan. The Western world and

America are in the grip of a tidal wave of satanism and witch-craft. There is an occult explosion in the land, its flames being fanned by new Age teachers and Eastern religious influences that have gained popular followings.

The *Satanic Bible* and other patently occult books are now among the top-selling books at secular retail bookstores. The bookstore chains—Waldenbooks, B. Dalton and so forth—have even created special sections in their stores for such books, to meet public demand. In many of these books, we discover refer-ences to the Mark of Satan.

An example is *the Complete Book of Magic and Witchcraft*, published in a popular paperback edition by New American Library, one of America's largest publishers.[14] In this horrid guide, in addition to learning how to perform spells, charms, and incantations and how to conduct rites and ceremonies of satan-ism and witchcraft, such as copulation with the Devil, we are told all about the Witch's Mark.

> This mark might be identical with the Devil's Mark, a small sign placed upon her by the Devil as a sign of his ownership. Both marks might be various sizes, colors, shapes, and locations.[15]

Who Can Escape the Mark?

Revelation 17 tells us that Satan's last days, One World Religious System will be a revival of Mystery Babylon. The Roman and Greek worship of Mithra emanated from Babylon. Now today, as we near the dawning of the twenty-first century, the religion of Babylon and the practices of the Mithra cult are being re-stored. The New Age Antichrist, or Beast, will require all to take the Mark as a sign of initiation, or acceptance, of un-Biblical doctrines and Lucifer as lord.

Who can escape the Mark of the Beast? Apparently every-one who refuses the Mark will be arrested as an enemy of the state and summarily executed. The Mark will certainly be repre-sentative of and signify the "Image of the Beast." We find that any who will not worship this image will be killed.

> And he hath power to give life unto the image of the beast, that the image of the beast should both speak, and cause that

as many as would not worship the image of the beast should be killed. (Rev. 13:15)

Even if a person should hide out to evade going to a New Age temple or church to be initiated, he will eventually be caught and punished. The Bible reveals that enforcement will be aided by a new law that forbids the citizenry to sell to or buy anything from any person who has not received the Mark.

And that no man might buy or sell, save he that had the mark, or the name of the beast, or the number of his name. (Rev. 13:17)

Death will be the penalty for anyone refusing the Mark; so those who stand up for the Lord in the coming fearful days will suffer tremendously. Yet, Jesus Himself taught us not to fear him who can kill the body but rather to fear Him who has power to kill the soul. Only God has the keys of eternal life and death.

God's Wrath on Those Who Take the Mark

In studying Bible prophecy, we glimpse the horrendous consequences that result when God's law against receiving the Mark is violated. The Scriptures pronounce this chilling sentence on all who receive the Mark:

And the third angel followed them, saying with a loud voice, If any man worship the beast and his image, and receive his mark in his forehead, or in his hand, the same shall drink of the wine of the wrath of God, which is poured out without mixture into the cup of his indignation; and he shall be tormented with fire and brimstone in the presence of the holy angels, and in the presence of the Lamb. (Rev. 14:9, 10)

Revelation 14:11 also reveals the frightening *eternal* fate of those who take the Mark; they will be tormented "forever and ever; and they have no rest day nor night." Clearly, it is a terrible thing in the sight of God to reject his Son Jesus Christ and instead to accept the Mark of the Beast.

THREE

Mystery Mark of the New Age

Beloved, believe not every spirit, but try the spirits whether they are of God; because many false prophets are gone out into the world.   (1 John 4:1)

Let the disciple learn to use the hand in service; let him seek the Mark of the Messenger . . . and let him learn to see with the eye which looks out from between the two.
                    (Djwhal Khul, the demon "Tibetan Master")

Does the New Age leadership propose to give all of mankind a Mark to signify agreement with new Age occultism? My research shows conclusively that this is the case. An incredible campaign is now under way to *condition* humanity and prepare every person on earth to receive the Mark of the New Age Beast. We see this campaign in operation in every aspect of society, especially in the printed media, on television, in the movies, and in public schools. In Chapter 5, I'll provide graphic, incontrovertible proof that an explosion of occultic symbols are invading our culture . . . and our minds. I believe that one or more of these symbols will be the one used by the Beast as his Mark.

It is a proven fact that the New Age is a religion based on occult symbology. The key question, however, is this: Is there proof that the New Age advocates the taking of a Mark? The answer: Yes, and yes again. The use of a Mark is becoming a more frequent teaching with each passing day as New Age leaders build the theological and ritualistic foundation needed before the taking of the Mark can someday enjoy universal acceptance.

Recently, in America's largest New Age bookstore, I purchased a remarkable book that caught my eye with its frank title: THE MARK.[1] What also caught my eye was the color of its cover: purple, which has dark spiritual meaning in occult doctrine. Prominently featured on the cover was a symbol: a small circle inside a triangle, all enclosed within a much larger circle. In fact, this symbol was the only artwork on the front cover. The bookstore's cashier told me this book was one of their most popular New Age sellers.

This is the satanic symbol featured prominently on the cover of the New Age book THE MARK, by Maurice Nicoll.

As it turned out, the book is mostly full of mysteriously garbled esoteric nonsense. Yet, a careful reading enables the reader to glean what the author, Maurice Nicoll, was attempting to convey to his New Age readership concerning the Mark. Nicoll, a British psychiatrist and student of occultists Carl Jung,

Revelation 13:16 prophesies that the Antichrist will cause all to receive a Mark in their forehead or right hand. This strange illustration, showing a mark in the left hand, is from the popular New Age book CHILDREN OF THE DAWN.

Gurdjieff, and Ouspensky, emphasized his belief that if a person is not "transformed" into a New Age man through a fiery evolution of the mind, he "misses the Mark." What is necessary, he says, is that a *new will* be acquired by the inner man *independent of any external God.*[2]

How is this "new will" to be acquired? Nicoll provides the standard New Age answer:

> The ancient mysteries taught at Eleusis and Attica and elsewhere were called finishings, perfectings. Their significance was to complete man through gradual instruction in the knowledge of divine truth.[3]

Nicoll's teaching is that the New Age man can only become transformed into a divine being through initiation into the ancient mysteries that first originated in Babylon. This should not surprise us because Bible prophecy pictures Satan's wicked and perverse last-days religious system as mystery religion and as a whore or harlot. Sitting astride the Beast, she has a name written on her forehead: MYSTERY, BABYLON THE GREAT, THE MOTHER OF HARLOTS AND ABOMINATIONS OF THE EARTH (Rev. 17:5).

This name written on the forehead of the prostitute Goddess most certainly has a connection with the "name of the beast" of Revelation 13. Therefore, it is significant that today's New Age theology conforms to the prophesied last-days world religion that will, the Bible says, encompass "peoples, and multitudes, and nations" (Rev. 17:15).

The Mark: A Sign of Spiritual Maturity?

Bible prophecy affirms that the whole world will worship the Beast. He will not have to force the vast majority to take his

This startling picture is used in magazine ads for AS-TARA, a New Age cult.

Mark. They will *want* the Mark because it will signify their "arrival" as an exalted man-god and full-fledged member of the great and noble Aquarian Race.

Already New Age propaganda touts the Mark as a sign of the spiritually and mentally advanced person. An ad in New Age magazines inviting people to write in for information about ASTARA, a New Age cult, addresses its appeal to the person who is "different," and "unique." It asks: are you an adventurous seeker of "advanced ideas," do you want to "grow in spiritual understanding?" and, finally, do you want to feel and possibly experience *in yourself* "what the great sages and seers of all time have known?"[4]

The individual who gets hooked on all this high-sounding spiritual propaganda and writes for ASTARA's free booklet, *Finding Your Place in the Golden Age,* will undoubtedly discount the picture that first focused his attention on the ad. It's a picture of a man, obviously an advanced thinker type, with a glittering, lighted *star* emblazoned on his forehead!

The Mark of Saint Germain

Elizabeth Clare Prophet's false "Christ," Count Saint Germain, also has been said to have a name written on his forehead. One of the principal advocates of the teaching of Saint Germain, Guy W. Ballard, founder of the "I AM" movement, first wrote of this "Mark" on the forehead of the mystical Saint Germain.[5] Later, Prophet related the account to her supporters in a book about the evolution of the New Age Movement through the centuries.

Calling Saint Germain that great "Cosmic Master," Prophet describes him as having "the word VICTORY written on his brow."[6] The Cosmic Master, she comments, reminds people "of the ancient command to obey the Law of the One," of karma, and of the importance of his "Ascended Masters of Light."[7]

The mystical spirit who comes as the "Count Saint Germain" is also recognized by a number of other leaders as the new Age "Messiah." Some claim that it is Saint Germain, along with Djwhal Khul, the Tibetan, who is responsible for the newfound interest among New Agers in crystal powers.

The worldwide reawakening of awareness of the benefits which accrue from the use of quartz crystals is largely due to

the combined efforts of two of these Illumined Souls . . .
Count de Saint Germain and the Master Djwhal Khul, also
known as The Tibetan Master.[8]

One New Age authority, Edmund Harold, provides information that this same Saint Germain has been reincarnated before
as the Chinese philosopher Lao Tse, as the legendary Merlin at
King Arthur's Court, and as English scientist Roger Bacon.[9]
Elizabeth Clare Prophet says that Saint Germain is now assisted
by Master Jesus in his work on earth and in the invisible spirit
world.[10]

According to Elizabeth Clare Prophet and her Church Universal and Triumphant, Saint Germain is the "Hierarch of the
Aquarian Age." He supposedly began his most recent campaign
to usher in the New Age Kingdom on January 1, 1987. His
purpose is to bring to pass an earthly kingdom of "great peace,
happiness and prosperity," ruled by him personally with "supreme justice and wisdom."[11]

Prophet teaches that Saint Germain comes to *initiate* us:

He comes to the fore as the Lord of the Seventh Ray and
Age. He comes to initiate us in the gift of prophecy and the
gift of the working of miracles—that we might foresee by the
Spirit of the prophets what is coming to us and turn the
tide.[12]

What's more, as part of his initiation, this false "Christ,"
Saint Germain, is said to be *sealing* enlightened human beings in
their foreheads.[13] Stumping across America in city after city in
1987 to promote "the coming revolution in higher consciousness," Elizabeth Clare Prophet invites the public to come hear
messages from "the saints and adepts of the East and West,"
especially to hear the exalted Saint Germain:

Don't miss this rare opportunity to experience a dictation
from an Ascended Master and to receive Saint Germain's
transfer of light—personally to each one present—by the
emerald matrix, the "sealing of the servants of God in their
foreheads." Revelation 7 (in the third eye). Be there! And
enter the Aquarian Age.[14]

It is important we go to the Scriptures for an understanding of this "sealing of the servants of God in their forehead" reference by Prophet. Revelation 7 refers to the sealing of God's 144,000 chosen, to be saved out of the nation of Israel during the Tribulation period in the last days. These are Jews, not New Agers, who are to be sealed. What's more, they are not to receive a literal Mark, as the New Age implies, but instead these 144,000 (12,000 from each of the twelve tribes of Israel) will believe in Jesus Christ and receive His Holy Spirit. In context, the *Holy Spirit* is the Seal of God in man's mind, as Paul so aptly described in Ephesians 4:30:

> And grieve not the Holy Spirit of God, by whom ye are sealed unto the day of redemption.

The "sealing of the servants of God in their foreheads" in Revelation 7 is clearly understood when we go to the original Greek root word used in the New Testament for seal, *sphragizo*. This word means "security or preservation, by implication to keep or seal up."[15] Therefore, those whom God infills with His Holy Spirit are secure and preserved by Him until the coming of the Lord Jesus.

This is said to be what Count Saint Germain, the New Age "Christ," appears like in visions to his New Age disciples.

If someday in the future a New Age pastor or teacher attempts to convince you to take a Mark on the forehead, the Biblical response is to tell these false deceivers that you are already sealed, having received the Holy Spirit *within*. Reject the Mark which is permanently inscribed on the *outside* of the body. And if they lyingly refer to Revelation 7 to persuade you, reply that this seal is the Holy Spirit to be given to the 144,000 Jews converted to Christ during the Tribulation period.

Saint Germain: Yet Another False "Christ"

It should be noted that Saint Germain is said to come from the Central Sun, where Sanat Kumara, the Great One, lives. Saint Germain and all others in the spirit realm worship this Sanat Kumara as their "God." As I pointed out in *Dark Secrets of the New Age*, Sanat is simply the name Satan, spelled with a slight transposing of letters to confuse the uninitiated.

What we have here is simply another false "Christ" who comes direct from the spirit world to initiate us. Just as the Bible prophesies, he comes not as an ordinary man but as a *miracle-worker* (Rev. 13:14; Dan. 11:28, 36; 2 Thess. 2:8-10) to *initiate* mankind.

The teaching by his New Age disciples that on Saint Germain's forehead is written a name, VICTORY, is blasphemous because it signifies Satan's insane goal of achieving victory over God. Whether or not the real Beast of Revelation will have this particular name marked on his forehead or require it to be etched on *everyone's* forehead or hand we cannot say. Most probably this is just an idle victory boast on the part of a demon.

The New Age Manual of Initiation

The Lucis Trust also teaches of the Mark of the false New Age savior. The Lucis Trust (formerly Lucifer Publishing) has actually published an 819-page manual detailing the coming initiation of mankind. Entitled *The Rays and the Initiations,* this complicated text uses language strange and unfamilar to all except the most sophisticated of New Age students. However, its understanding is essential for us to truly decipher the dark plans of Satan's demonic forces, because this manual unfolds specific instructions on the initiation and Mark that is to be given all mankind.[16]

Masking the identity of Lucifer by portraying him as "the One initiator whose star shone forth," this atrocious manual declares:

> Let the disciple learn to use the hand in service; let him seek the mark of the Messenger . . . and let him learn to see with the eye which looks out from between the two.[17]

The Rays and the Initiations also reveals that the disciple being initiated may learn the "inmost mystery" only after he comprehends "the first letter of the word which has been imparted, or the hidden name."[18]

Alice Bailey's spirit guide, who dictated to her this New Age initiation manual, arrogantly remarked that it was safe to openly expound upon these plans and details for the initiation ceremony and the Mark and to publish the manual. The general public won't understand it anyway due to the concealed meaning and hidden language:

> These instructions . . . will, therefore, go out to the general public who will not understand, but thus the needed teaching will be preserved.[19]

The demon author of *The Rays and the Initiations* also revealed that his manual is being given out now so that it will be in the hands of future New Age disciples around the world and ready for widespread use "towards the end of this century."[20] If this demonic timetable holds true—that is, if God allows this chronology—the Luciferic Initiation could be ushered in universally on a mandatory basis within a decade or so.

The Fiery Five-Pointed Star

We also find references to the Mark by a number of other New Age authorities, usually veiled beneath a flood of confusing esoteric language so that hopefully only the informed insider is able to understand the meaning. For example, Geoffrey Hodson's *The Hidden Wisdom in the Holy Bible*, mentions that a "white and fiery pentagram (a five-pointed satanic star symbol) flashes out about the head of the hierophant (initiate) when a valid initiation rite is to be performed."[21]

Djwhal Khul, the "Tibetan Master," also speaks of a five-pointed star, the pentagram, being used as an initiation sign to signify that the individual *becomes one with the "force."*[22] I will discuss the significance of the pentagram and other symbols in Chapters 5 and 6 and especially in Chapter 14, when the Luci-feric Initiation is described and its chilling mysteries are uncov-ered and laid bare.

Trendy Tattoos: Conditioning the Minds of Youth

Satan is laboring mightily now in all quarters to condition man-kind so that when his false "Christ" gives the order, the whole world will willingly and enthusiastically volunteer to receive the Mark. One small but striking example is in the current fad among teenagers of having permanent tattoos needled onto their skin. Some of these tattoos are hideous representations of Luci-fer and his demons. Many kids today have been brainwashed through satanic rock music to accept tattoos of bats, dragons, the ram's head, the satanic pentagram and triangles, fiery de-mons, beastly claws, and lotus blooms.

One young lady told me that she and her girlfriends have had tiny rose and lotus designs tattooed on their breasts and inner thigh because they think that's "sexy." Just a few years ago this same teenager would not have considered for a moment permanently marring her body with a tattoo. Today it's the trendy "in thing."

Someday soon this young lady and tens of millions of others conditioned like her will be fed a lie by the government and by their churches. They will be led to believe that the permanent Mark on their forehead or hand symbolizes the admirable goals of world peace, religious harmony, and brotherhood. Who in their right mind, people will reason, would refuse to take a Mark that stands for world unity and love? Only a miserable misfit, the answer will come back.

Mother Mary and Her Mark

While many of our young people are being encouraged to accept tattoo marks as the fashionable thing to do, thousands of Roman

Catholics around the world are being indoctrinated on the necessity for taking the mark by a spirit who masquerades as the Virgin Mary, Mother of God.

An apparition calling itself Mary is appearing with regularity these days. Elizabeth Clare Prophet claims that Mother Mary came to her in a vision and even gave her a New Age rosary for today's Catholics.[23] In Yugoslavia, Mary is said to have appeared to six young children with the startling message that her son was coming soon and that all the world's religions are to unite and prepare for this momentous event. Mary assured her listeners that God can be found in all religions, not just Christianity.[24] I understand that millions of Catholics worldwide actually believe that this spirit in Yugoslavia is the real Mary.

The most shocking visitation by the spirit that says it is Mary was in Marienfried, Germany, where it was reported that she came in a vision to a girl, Barbara Reuss.[25] The Mary who showed herself to Barbara Reuss spoke of "dark incomprehensible events" to transpire. She cautioned that *only through her* could you find intercession with her son, Jesus. Finally, she reportedly delivered this intriguing declaration:

> I will make preparations for peace.
> I am the Sign of the Living God.
> I place my Sign on the foreheads of my children.[26]

Now the Bible says that Mary was blessed among women because she was chosen to give birth to Jesus, the Christ-child. As Christians, we rightly hold Mary in high esteem. Surely her chaste example is one that should be praised and followed by women today. But nowhere in our Bible do we find that Mary is a goddess or that she resides in heaven today honored as the Mother of God or the Queen of Heaven. That she was saved as a *disciple* of Christ *is* in the Bible, for she regarded Jesus as her Lord and Savior. We also read in Scripture that Mary recognized her own *low estate* as a mere human being mightily blessed by the Lord (see Luke 1:46-55). No wonder this wonderful and good woman exclaimed, "My soul doth magnify the Lord" (Luke 1:46).

The Bible also makes clear that there is only *one* mediator between man and God: Christ Jesus (1 Tim. 2:5, 6). Not Mary, not a dead saint, no matter how glorious were their achievements while on earth or in heaven. Only one mediator: the Son of God.

Once we understand this unarguable Biblical truth, we must reject the many "Marys" that are buzzing around the globe, in Yugoslavia, Mexico, Spain, France, Germany, the United States and elsewhere. These are demons come to lie and deceive. We must keep our eyes fixed on the Jesus of the Bible and not accept either a counterfeit Jesus or a fake Mary.

Regrettably, in the days to come many Catholics will line up to receive the Mark, convinced that Mary, the Immaculate Mother of God, has so ordained this ritual. They will believe the lie: that the Mark is to be given the true people of God while those who refuse it are people of evil. Thus will Satan turn truth on its head.

The Third Eye as the Mark

The Hindu gurus so prominent in the New Age first brought into America and the West the belief that each person has a hidden, *third eye* located in the middle of the forehead just above the central point where the eyebrows meet. The Greek myth of the one-eyed Cyclops creature was an ancient variation of this teaching, but the real foundation of the third eye doctrine is in the Egyptian Mystery Religion of the Goddess (again we return to Revelation 17 and to Mystery Babylon, Mother of Harlots!).[27]

The Egyptian priesthood taught first that Maat, the Goddess of truth and judgment, possessed a third eye. Later the central text of the Egyptian Mystery Religion was revised and a male god, Horus, son of the Goddess, was given the all-seeing eye. It is the mysterious all-seeing eye of Horus that is pictured inside the capstone of the pyramid found on the U.S. dollar bill. Horus was an armed warrior deity known as the great Sun God. Some mystical and occult teachers in the New Age preach that Horus is the bringer of the Aquarian Age, that he is a living god who will restore peace, light, and love to mankind.

In today's New Age and Hindu philosophies, the body is made up of certain energy points or *chakras*. Two important chakras are the one in the forehead and the other in the palm of the right hand. Note that these are the same body sites revealed in the Bible as where the Mark of the Beast will be taken.

What's more, the New Age body chakra points are considered *initiation sites,* with the individual receiving additional psychic and other godlike powers as each energy point on his body is "opened up" to allow the flow of energy from the universal *force* field.

New Age teachers call the forehead chakra the third eye, or the *Ajna Center.* This energy point on the forehead is thought to be the "passport to higher consciousness," or godhood, for a person. The Ajna Center is also said to be the site of the "sacred fire."[28] Today's Hindu monks, swamis, gurus, and spiritual seekers literally mark themselves over the forehead with a bit of red, yellow, or white powder or paste on this center as a sign.

The New Age and Hindu teaching of an energy point between one's eyes on the forehead is a precursor of the Mark of the Beast.

The Mark as a Sign of Awakened Godhood

In *The Hidden Wisdom in the Holy Bible,* Volume 1, it is argued that man has now advanced *racially* to a point where he is able to use the third eye lying beneath his forehead.[29] New Age men, the author suggests, are spiritual giants now "awakening from their long slumber."

> Modern man, becoming giant once more, if only as yet in mind, finds his closed third eye opening once more. Man's inherent psychic faculties, his innate seership, is no longer a dimly remembered racial power. . . . It is now recognized as

an almost universal and an active power which has been christened "extra sensory perception," or ESP.[30]

One can easily envision a future day when religious authorities spread the wonderful news to their congregations that this new Mark on the forehead or on the hand will open up incredible vistas of psychic, godlike opportunity. It would be proposed that a person initiated into the mysteries of the New Age religion and given the Mark will have his forehead or hand chakras opened so that he will begin to receive a mighty flow of energizing power into his spirit.

When that terrible day arrives, society will be taught to revere the man with the Mark and despise the man without it. A man who has the Mark will rank high in social status. He will be respected as an advanced thinker, a person of higher consciousness, and a fully qualified member of the superior Aquarian Race. He will be marked as a spiritual giant of the New Age.

FOUR

His Number Is 666

Here is wisdom. Let him that hath understanding count the number of the beast; for it is the number of a man; and his number is six hundred threescore and six.
(Revelation 13:18)

The number 666 has to do with the triangular balancing of forces towards the close of the cycle. . . . It deals with the Greater Initiation. (Alice Bailey, *A Treatise on Cosmic Fire*)

Bible prophecy tells us that the Beast will have a number, 666, and that by this number he will control and ravage mankind. Once the Beast, or Antichrist, has complete supremacy and power over all on the planet, he will institute a commercial system so that no one can buy or sell unless he has allied himself with the established religion of the Beast:

And that no man might buy or sell, save he that had the mark, or the name of the beast, or the number of his name. (Rev. 13:17)

For centuries, people have pondered over the mysterious meaning of Revelation 13. In Chapter 13, verse 18 we are alerted that few will be able to understand and interpret the meaning of this passage. "Here is Wisdom . . ." the verse begins, "Let him that hath understanding count the number of the beast. . . ."

What is needed for understanding is the wisdom that only

the Holy Spirit can impart to man. God *is* wisdom. He is gracious to His servants and provides *understanding* to them that is withheld from the world at large. The natural man will never be capable of comprehending Revelation 13:18; only the child of God imbued with His wisdom might unravel the mystery that is unfolded.

666 Is the Number of the False "Christ"

We start our examination of the dreaded number of the Beast by noting that 666 is the number of the counterfeit, or false, "Christ." This is the wicked man whom the whole earth shall worship (Rev. 13:8), the satanically energized world leader who will go up against the people of God and eventually conquer them. He will establish a One World Order where Lucifer is exalted and where everything that is godly is debased and expunged (Dan. 11). He will be *the* Antichrist and he will be a man: "for it is the number of a man. . . ."

To the warped minds of the Antichrist and his deluded New Age followers, the number 666 will be magically transformed into a *holy number* of great spiritual significance. It is of paramount importance that we understand this. Until the New Age World Religion recently began to flourish, there was a common understanding even among the unsaved that the number 666 signified something abhorrent and utterly evil. However, in the New Age this number will be given a fresh image. Its loathsomeness and pall shall be covered up; it will receive a fresh coat of glittery paint and be adorned with honor. The number 666 will be seen as a powerful symbol of man's ultimate ascendance to godhood.

Already, we can observe this ongoing transformation of the number of the Beast. New Age leaders have already begun to condition and reeducate their disciples and students on the "proper" understanding of the number 666 for the Aquarian Age.

6 = the Number of Divine Light

Alice Bailey and Lucis Trust have put out the word to their hundreds of thousands of followers that the number 6 is the number of light. It is the number of Shamballa, the supposed heavenly city or realm where the New Age "Christ," Lord Maitreya, and his hierarchy reside and from where they operate on Planet Earth:

> To this Centre we give the name Shamballa, the component letters of which are numerically S.H.A.M.B.A.L.L.A. or 1.8.1.4.2.1.3.3.1. This word equals the number 24 *which in its turn equals 6.*[1]

Bailey adds the revealing information that the number 6 is "the goal of the initiatory process." She writes that this number is a medium through which man can be *initiated* by "Deity," or "Sanat Kumara," who is said to be the divine superior of the New Age "Christ," Lord Maitreya.[2] The number 6, Bailey notes, is therefore:

> The number of idealism and of that driving force which makes mankind move forward upon the path and in response to the vision, and press upward toward the light. It is in reality *devotion to an unseen goal,* and an unswerving recognition of the objective.[3]

Like most of the material that Lucis Trust publishes, the above exemplifies the strange phraseology one finds in occult writings. After all, the word *occult* means "hidden," "dark," "secret," "mysterious" and "enigma." But it is easy to decipher what Bailey is telling her disciples here. She is saying that the number 6 keeps the initiates on the path toward their eventual godhood and that they must press on in devotion to their "unseen goal," which is merger with Lucifer, the true but hidden god of the New Age. This is their ultimate, hidden objective: to unite with Satan.

Thus, Bailey alleges that the number 6 has "divine qualities."[4] She remarks that "In an ancient book on numbers, the initiate is defined as the one who has experienced and expressed 666 and found it naught . . . and has thus found himself upon the WAY."[5]

Translated, this simply means that once the individual *totally and without reservation accepts the number 666 as an integral,*

inseparable part of his spirituality, he is transformed into a god.
As a god, he no longer needs assistance from the New Age
"Christ" and his hierarchy to discover the way to perfection and
godhood. He has made it! In the popular phrase of Werner
Erhard's est, the initiate who accepts and embraces the number
666 as his own can exuberantly exclaim, "I found it!"

What he has found, of course, is Satan. Anyone who is
initiated and takes the number of the Beast will become one
with the darkest being who has ever traveled the airways: the
"prince of the power of the air." Satan is the "Deity," the "God"
of the New Age; so Alice Bailey is entirely correct when she
states that the taking of the number of initiation—666 according
to Revelation 13—enables the person "to blend his individual
will with the divine will."[6]

6, the Number of Dark Angels and the Cosmic Force

Djwhal Khul, the Tibetan Master, adds further New Age clarity
to the meaning of the number of the Beast in the revealing book
A Treatise on Cosmic Fire. In this publication we find that the
triangle, a satanic symbol, and the "Force" are both linked to the
number 666.[7] Khul also informs us that "the number 6 is the
number of the deva evolution (Deva Kingdom)."[8] To the Hindu
and New Ager, a deva is an "angel" and the deva kingdom is
where angels reside. To the Christian, the word deva also means
angel—a *dark angel of Lucifer.*

Though he perverts God's truth, Khul is not ignorant of
Bible prophecy. He states that "black magicians work with certain great entities, 6 in number, who are spoken of, for instance,
in the Christian Bible as having the number 666." "They came
in," he adds, "on a stream of cosmic force."[9]

The Number 666 as a Destructive Force

But what exactly does the number 666 signify for the future of
man and the Planet Earth? In answering this question, Djwhal
Khul explains the laws of karma, reincarnation, and rebirth. He
says that at the end of the present age (or cycle), in order to
bring in the New Age, certain "destructive forces" will be unleashed on the world. These forces—which take a *triangular*

shape—constitute "heavenly karma," or cosmic justice.[10] There will be a Great Initiation of all mankind, Khul reveals, and the number 666 will be instrumental in both carrying out cosmic justice (it will be destructive!) and in initiating mankind into the New Age:

> According to DK [Djwhal Khul], the number 666 has to do with the triangular balancing of forces towards the close of the cycle . . . it deals with the Greater Initiation. DK forecasts a planetary Kundalini (transformation) which will work destruction on the world.[11]

We can see the transparent workings of Satan in the smooth, deceitful words of this demon messenger to the New Age named Djwhal Khul. It is crystal-clear that, first, the Plan calls for the number 666 to be used in the initiation of man by the New Age "Christ" into the Mystery of Iniquity. Second, those who refuse the Mark and do not have the number of the Beast will be destroyed. Initiation is therefore the process in which the Antichrist will weed out his disciples from those Christians who worship the true God.

6 = the Number of the New Age "Christ" Who Wages War Against Christians

This is well explained in the classic book *Coming World Changes* by Harriette and F. Homer Curtiss, founders of The Order of Christian Mystics.[12] They speak first of the arrival on earth of the "long-expected Great Teacher" (i.e., the Antichrist). This spiritual giant, the New Age "Christ," will make war with the forces of evil (Christians) and overcome them:

> The battle has already begun. . . . For this is the time of struggle to overcome the evils which the Race as a whole has outlived, yet which it has not fully conquered and redeemed.[13]

Note the Curtisses' statement that the evils which the Great Teacher wages conflict against are "evils which the Race as a whole has outlived, yet which it has not fully conquered and redeemed." What they are saying is that all the world is to be of the higher consciousness Aquarian Race except a few hold-backs—the Christian minority. This Christian minority is the enemy who must be challenged and overcome.

The campaign of the New Age to battle and conquer the people of God and to use the number of the Beast, 666, to cull out or separate these victims will fulfill Bible prophecy. Daniel prophesied that the last-days World Ruler, or King, would "wear out the saints of the Most High . . . and they shall be given into his hand until a time and times and the dividing of time" (Daniel 7:25).

Just as Djwhal Khul, the Tibetan Master, threatened, we find in the Word of God the prophecy that the last days shall bring destruction to the whole world as the Antichrist goes all-out in his attempt to overcome and dominate the people of God. Read of the vision given Daniel of this final world kingdom:

The fourth beast shall be the fourth kingdom upon the earth, which shall be diverse from all kingdoms, and shall devour the whole earth, and shall tread it down, and break it in pieces. (Dan. 7:23).

In the book of Daniel we also see that the Beast, the great last-days dictator or ruler, shall destroy the mighty and the holy people (8:24). But in the end, he "shall also stand up against the Prince of princes, but he shall be broken" (8:25).

Who is the "Prince of princes"? Jesus Christ! So we know that God's people shall suffer tremendous persecution from the Beast with the number 666, but Christ will have the final victory.

Again, I speak of the *real* Christ, Jesus, the Son of God, for the New Age has its own counterfeit "Christ." He is the one who will bring with him the mysterious number of the Beast and force it on the world.

The counterfeit "Christ" is evidently the one acknowledged by F. Homer and Harriette Curtiss. They claim that their Great Teacher of the New Age is, in fact, the New Age "Christ" who is to come.[14] And what is the *number* of their New Age "Christ," this Great Teacher? According to the Curtisses:

The number 6 is both the number of Christ and also of unrest. It symbolizes the mighty struggle of the Christ-force to penetrate . . . evil and manifest itself.[15]

The "Christ force" of the New Age will indeed manifest itself—in the person of the Antichrist. These people of Satan, the ungodly citizens of the planet who willingly receive the Mark, or his number, or his name, will *temporarily* be the victors *until* the return of the *real* Christ, Lord Jesus.

But this isn't the way the New Age sees it. Their "Christ," the man with the number 6, will lead the Christ-force (note the word "force") to victory:

The defeated army will be swallowed up and a new and purified land shall arise out of the waters. . . . The victors will remain as the seed of the New Race to people the New Land. . . . Out of the waters of affliction there shall arise a new and greater humanity with true Brotherhood, Love, Peace, and Harmony as its watchword.[16]

Here once again we see the lie of Satan designed to lure and seduce men's minds. Serve him instead of God and victory will be yours. You'll be the seed of a New Race of Man-Gods, and the world will enjoy brotherhood, love, peace, and harmony. But the Devil fails to explain that a *price* will be exacted for this. Everyone who has received the Mark will be told that to assure their salvation and to demonstrate their divine powers they must serve as warriors in the great battle against the Christian resistance forces. They must become accomplices of the New Age "Christ." As gods, it is their responsibility:

It is humanity itself that must save itself through the manifestation of God-powers . . . else humanity could never gain self mastery.[17]

666 = the Number of the Great Teacher

We can see, then, that, the "Christ-force" of the New Age is the combined forces of Satan, his Antichrist leader—the so-called "Great Teacher," and the hundreds of millions who will gladly receive the Mark, worship the image, and pay homage to the number of the Great Teacher.

In her explicitly detailed book outlining the Plan for a One World New Age religion and government, *When Humanity Comes of Age,* Britain's Vera Alder discusses the coming Great Teacher.[18] She says that as soon as he has consolidated world power, he will form and head a Spiritual Research Panel that will evaluate and combine all the world's religions and teachings, the occultic "ancient wisdom," and Mystery Teachings. This synthesis will then be given out to the world as a New Age Bible:

> The Research Panel would develop the new "Bible" of a World Religion which will be the basis of future education.[19]

Benjamin Creme's demon guide, Lord Maitreya, has also declared himself the "World Teacher." Creme has published a series of messages which he says were dictated to him telepathically by the Lord Maitreya in what he calls an "overshadowing" process.[20] In one of these messages, Maitreya is quoted as follows:

> Good evening, my dear friends. I am pleased indeed to have this opportunity to speak to you in this way.
> My aim is to make My Presence in the world at the earliest possible moment, and so begin my Work. . . .
> My Plan is to release into the world a certain Teaching, which will show men that there exists a new approach to Living, a new way forward into the future time.[21]

What is this "Teaching" which Creme's Lord Maitreya says he will release into the world? Undoubtedly it will be a teaching that denies the gospel of Jesus Christ, for Benjamin Creme has said that Maitreya, not Jesus, is the "Christ." Another significant element of this teaching will be the doctrine that the number 666, the image of the Beast, and his name are holy.

Why the Number 666?

To discover the secrets behind the mysterious number 666, we can go to two valuable sources of information. First, there is the ages-old practice of numerology. Second, we can profitably look at the very roots of the number 6, examining its dark spiritual origins.

Numerology: the Science of Numbers

God has his own system of numbers. For example, in the Bible 7 is the perfect number of completion, and the number 12 has great significance because Jesus chose twelve disciples. However, numerology was perverted into an occult science and an ungodly practice in ancient Babylon. The New Age Movement has revived this ancient, occult "science" of numerology.

New Age minister Geoffrey Hodson, a Bishop in the apostate Liberal Catholic Church, writes that "numbers can be used as symbols" and that "by the study of numbers one may learn the fundamental laws of the . . . universe and men."[22] According to Hodson:

> Every number has a certain power. . . . This power results in an occult connection.[23]

Hodson states that the number 6 is the symbol of man, balance, equilibrium, and harmony.[24] In the New Age understanding, this means the earth's purification and cleansing so that our planet's karma can be balanced and harmonized. Hodson also writes that 6 represents the age of psychic, godlike powers in man—psychology, divination, telepathy and so forth.[25]

In *A Dictionary of Symbols,* the author describes the number 6 as comprising the union of the two occult triangles (of fire and water). According to this authoritative source, the number 6 is also, as Hodson remarked, a symbol of balancing.[26]

6 = the Number of the Mother Goddess

In ancient Babylon, sexual intercourse was revered as a mystical rite in which a man and woman were *yoked* with the gods. From this religious practice and doctrine came the Hindu practice of Tantric *Yoga*, which also means to be yoked. Tantric Yoga, or ritualistic sex, is today a widly popular practice among some in the New Age.[27]

The religion of Babylon was primarily the worship of the Mother Goddess, who was later pictured in Revelation 17 as the great whore of Babylon, Satan's last-days world religion—a revived form of Babylonianism. In this religion six was considered the number symbolizing sacramental sexual ecstasy in which the participants achieved union with the divine universe and with the Mother Goddess. A triple 6—666—was the magic number of the Goddess Ishtar, also called the "Triple Aphrodite," because in her personage was the unholy trinity of Mother-Father-Son.[28]

6 = the Number of the Sacred Prostitute

Feminist New Age researcher Barbara Walker notes that the Egyptians, who worshiped the Mother Goddess, considered 3, 6, and 7 their most sacred numbers. Three stood for the Triple Goddess; six meant her union with the Father God; and seven stood for the seven planetary spheres. "The miraculous number 666," as Walker describes it, was very, very holy in the Egyptian religion of the Goddess.[29]

Walker describes Ishtar, the Great Mother Goddess of Babylon, as follows:

> Babylonian "Star," the Great Goddess who appears in the Bible as Ashtoreth, Anath, Asherah . . . the Queen of Heaven. She was also the Great Whore, described in Revelation 17:5 as Babylon the Great, the Mother of Harlots. . . . Men communed with her through the sexual rites of her harlot priestesses.[30]

It is a tragic fact that Solomon, a wise and great king, nevertheless failed God in his old age. The declining monarch disobeyed the Lord, taking for his brides younger women—possibly of great and alluring beauty—who were not of the tribes of Israel but of foreign peoples. Accordingly, these women worshiped the Mother Goddess and were able to turn Solomon away from the true God and persuade him to bring the perversions of the Goddess religion into the Temple.

Apparently, as part of this pagan worship, Solomon required the priests of the Temple to pay him 666 talents of gold per year (1 Kings 10:14). This was perhaps payment in recognition for his allowing these wicked priests to charge clients for the "sacred" services of Temple prostitutes.

It is significant to note that when Solomon had gone into sin through worship of the Goddess Ashtoreth (1 Kings 11:5), the Lord was angered and caused dissension and troubles to visit the land of Israel (1 Kings 11:9-14).

Virgo the Celestial Virgin

The Mother Goddess was at the head of the Mystery Religion (thus, "Mystery Babylon"). Hers was the religion in which temple prostitutes were employed as priestesses to initiate candidates into the "Mysteries." The religion was also marked by its beliefs in astrology, an occult science which originated in Babylon. The Goddess was the original Virgo of the Zodiac signs; ironically, the sign of Virgo represents the "Celestial Virgin."[31] To many in today's New Age Movement, the symbol of Virgo—and in fact the entire field of astrology—has profound religious significance. New Age occult astrology is not the fun and games of your daily horoscope in the newspaper. It is serious business—a field imbued with heavy theological and doctrinal overtones.

In one of Alice Bailey's many books published by the Lucis Trust, she mentions the astrological sign Virgo, informing her New Age readers that Virgo symbolizes the goddess principle and that:

> The symbology of Virgo concerns the whole goal of the evolutionary process, which is to shield, nurture, and finally reveal the hidden spiritual reality.[32]

The serious Bible student can easily gain a keen understanding of what Alice Bailey means by the "hidden spiritual reality" that will finally be revealed. All that's necessary is to pay close attention to other statements Bailey makes about the astrological Virgo, the Divine Woman.

> Another unique feature of Virgo is that it has a triple symbol.
> . . . This underlies the spiritual theory of Triangles. . . . It is through the fusing and blending of the three planetary

energies that our earth will be transformed into a sacred planet.[33]

In New Age astrology, Virgo thus represents the *triangle,* which, as I have explained, is an ancient satanic symbol much in vogue today among New Agers and occultists. As was said of the Mother Goddess of the Mystery Babylon Religion, Virgo, her astrological twin, has a triple aspect symbolized by the triangle. The New Age leadership preaches that the Force underlying the triangle symbol will soon transform earth into a magical and sacred New Age Kingdom.[34]

Is Virgo, according to New Age teachers, connected with the fateful number 666? Yes, indeed. *Virgo's is the sixth sign,* Bailey writes.[35] She readily acknowledges that this frightening number "is called the number of the Beast," but she assures us that this is okay and is nothing to be alarmed about:

> This idea seems to have a horrible fascination for many but what it really means is that Virgo is a symbol of the triplicity, 6 on the physical plane, 6 on the emotional plane, 6 on the mental plane. . . .[36]

So Virgo, the goddess, is acknowledged as represented numerologically by three 6s; 666 is her number—the number of the Beast.

The Beastly Son of the Goddess Comes Forth

We know from Revelation 13, however, that the Antichrist will be a *man,* a false man-god, and not a woman-goddess. But what we have been talking about is not the Antichrist, but the ungodly worldwide religious system he will head: Mystery, Babylon. This is what the New Age Goddess, astrology's Virgo, represents. From this perverse New Age Mystery Religion will spring forth a son. He will be Satan in the form of a man: a Man-Beast who leads a religious Beast system. He will be the Antichrist who rules and terrorizes a tribulation-plagued world.

Alice Bailey clearly understands Bible prophets, at least from the viewpoint of her master, Satan. Thus, Bailey abuses and twists prophetic references to reveal that Virgo, the symbol of the New Age spirituality, will indeed bring forth a son:

> Behold I will bring forth my servant, the branch (Zechariah 3:8). One symbol of Virgo is the woman with the . . . branch of fruit in her arms. Remember also the prophecy of Isaiah upon which our New Testament is based: "And a virgin shall conceive and bring forth a son."[37]

What son will Virgo, the goddess model for the New Age World Religion, bring forth? Certainly not Jesus Christ, the Messiah to whom the prophets Zechariah and Isaiah referred. He came forth 2,000 years ago. He is the Son of God and is Himself God. No, the New Age religion—the religion of the Goddess, 666, and of the Beast and his Mark—will bring forth the *Son of Perdition*. He will come, Paul told us in 2 Thessalonians 2:9, 10, "after the working of Satan with all power and signs and lying wonders, and with all deceivableness of unrighteousness."

Is Saturn the Antichrist?

Could the son of the Mother Goddess, the Son of Perdition who is the Antichrist, be a modern-day version of *Saturn*, the great Sun God of Rome? If we are to believe the astonishing teachings of prominent New Age religious teachers, Saturn is to come to life and is fated to become the Great World Ruler for the New Age Kingdom.

Saturn had his dark side, too. He was called the underworld's Lord of Death. The Hindus worshiped him under the name Shiva the Destroyer. Babylonian and Chaldean astrologers called him Aciel, the Sun of the Night.[38] Aciel is today the name of the spirit whom many witches and satanists frequently conjure up to do their bidding.[39]

Sri Aurobindo, a Hindu guru well-known in the New Age, affirms that Saturn is represented by the number 6. According to Aurobindo, this is because the planet Saturn is sixth of the nine planets in distance from the sun. Aurobindo also relates Saturn to the Mother Goddess and her trinity nature, commenting that "The 6 in the scale of the Trinity . . . is the point . . . wherein the Mother makes her appearance."[40]

Saturn was also recognized by Alice Bailey as an astrological symbol packed with deep meaning for the New Age future. She says that Saturn will rule the Age of Aquarius and that:

Saturn gives us discipline. Saturn opens for us the door of opportunity. Saturn, through spiritual exercises and trials, strengthens our spiritual muscles and enables us to emerge out of darkness into light.[41]

There's more, also, to reveal about the New Age's Saturn. Vera Alder provides us with the key to understanding as she discloses that in the chaos period to come on Planet Earth, it is "Saturn" who will bring all the pain and pressure: "Pain and pressure are borne upon this planet . . . from the planet Saturn."[42]

Alder also makes the astonishing disclosure that Saturn, the New Age code name for their false "Christ," is none other than Satan!

The Saturnian spirit, "Satan," let us not forget, ensouls the Third great major or Primary Ray of Deity and wields the great Laws of cause and effect, action and reaction—Karma!

Therefore, the world Initiation to which we are drawing near today is being brought to birth by a universal access of Pain and of pressure, to which humanity is responding with widespread action, leading, naturally, to . . . Initiation.[43]

666, Cosmic Fire, the Third Eye

Over and over we see references to the number 666 in New Age books, magazines, reports and speeches. We especially see this dreadful number being used in reference to the *third eye*, the point on the forehead between the eyes where energy forces and light are claimed to enter from the Universal Force Field (the impersonal "God" of the New Age). This is the third eye of the Hindus and Buddhists as well.

The New Agers and the Hindus call the site where the invisible third eye is located the *Agni*, or *Ajna Center*. I found some remarkable information when I researched the doctrinal and historical foundations of the Hindu religion in regard to this teaching about a third eye. It turns out that Agni was the Hindu male fire god who was the sexual partner of the Mother Goddess. Symbolically Agni was represented as fire from heaven: lightning. Ancient peoples later began to call him by his actual name, *Lucifer*. When you take Agni's Mark, you are in reality taking Lucifer's Mark.[44]

So when the New Age leadership teaches that the Agni Center is the third eye in which cosmic fire and light enter to bring inner transformtion to the initiate, what they are referring to is simply the flooding of Luciferic energy and thoughts into the person's mind.

It is ultra-important that we recall that Jesus described Lucifer in this manner: "I beheld Satan as lightning fall from heaven" (Luke 10:18). Could this give us an indication of the correct interpretation of Revelation 13:13? In that prophecy, the false prophet who serves the Beast is able to do "great wonders, so that he maketh fire come down from heaven on the earth in the sight of men."

Is the fire that comes down the cosmic fire of the New Age? Amazingly, this is exactly what Alice Bailey says is the case in her eye-opening *A Treatise on Cosmic Fire*.[45] Bailey, however, maintains this cosmic fire originates from Shamballa, the invisible New Age spirit world.

It is conceivable that at a future time, as a New Age disciple is being initiated, the celebrants will observe the wonder of a satanic stream of fire, or lightning, come down from above. It will enter the initiate's forehead *exactly where the Mark has been taken.* This event would instill awe and great reverence in those who see it, fulfilling completely the prophecy of Revelation 13:13.

In reading *The Keys of Enoch,* we begin to see just how important to New Age initiation is both the number 666 and the teaching of the third eye.

Its author tells us that "6-6-6" is the numerical sequence used by the "heavenly beings" to communicate with man, sending and receiving spiritual information. We are also told that this communication is done through use of "specific light and sound harmonics . . . by means of a pyramidal focus created . . . over the third eye."[46]

By using this heavenly sequence, 6-6-6 (666), it is explained that the individual's thoughts are elevated as if they were a "seed crystal" so that he can commune directly with the "Councils of Light in the Heavens."[47]

The Taming of New Age Man by the Beast

Beneath all the deceptive New Age phraseology in *The Keys of Enoch*, we discover the author's hidden occult message: the Mark on the forehead (the third eye) is the communication point, or symbol, between Satan and New Age man. Satan can communicate easily with New Age man because after he has received the Mark, he's *Satan's personal property*. He is marked for eternal damnation by his hellish father.

Of course, New Age man won't understand this until it's far too late. The natural man cannot understand the things of God; he cannot discern Truth. Fear of God is the beginning of all wisdom, and New Age man claims to fear no one. Therefore, the New Ager is easily convinced that the number 666 is not the number of a Beast but of a New Age savior and Great Teacher to come. And he can be persuaded that the cosmic fire that streams into the so-called chakra, or agni point on his forehead, is illumination from the Secret Hiding Place of the Ascended Masters. After all, he has already swallowed the twin teachings that there is no hell, and that there is no Satan and his demons who live there.

New Age man has been conditioned to believe the Lie. He has been tamed by the Beast. And through the propagation of New Age seed teachings in every realm of society and the proliferation of symbols that are now ceaselessly flooding our consciousness, the whole world is beginning to swallow the Lie.

PART TWO

In the Image of the New Age Beast

The Unholy Worship of the Symbols of Oppression

Thou shalt not make unto thee any graven image, or any likeness of anything that is in heaven above, or that is in the earth beneath, or that is in the water under the earth; thou shalt not bow down thyself to them, nor serve them. . . . (Exod. 20:4, 5)

Images are wonderful and mysterious things. . . .
Images are often associated with the creative process.
(Gay Hendricks and Russel Wills,
The Centering Book)

A flood of new and strange—yet ancient and archaic—symbols is overflowing America and the world. Watch the ads on television for just one night, especially on MTV, the rock music channel, or kids' Saturday cartoon shows, or read three or four popular magazines and look for the symbols. You'll be amazed. We are literally deluged with Satanic symbols—with pentagrams, triangles, rainbows, perverted crosses, pyramids, and more. The images are usually presented to us either in a subtle, indirect way or up front in a positive manner. Rarely are we given the impression that there is anything wrong with these images.

The Hidden Danger of Symbol Therapy

Modern psychiatry actually fosters and supports the New Age in its insidious campaign to spread far and wide the dangerously malignant symbols of Satan. Dick Sutphen, a hypnotist whose human potential seminars have probably been attended by tens of thousands, has even been successful in promoting what the New Age calls "Symbol Therapy." Sutphen's tape company, Valley of the Sun, has produced a series of six videotapes which bombard the viewer's mind with what is termed "thearpeutic symbols."

Sutphen says that Symbol Therapy will change your life, and he writes:

> Symbol Therapy uses powerful and effective superconscious visualizations, which can have positive, rejuvenative mental and physical effects. Symbol Therapy works by restructuring and redirecting certain unconscious energies. . . . (Symbol Therapy) relaxes your body, then directs you through the beautiful visualizations. . . .[1]

I believe that Sutphen, being a professional hypnotist, knows full well that the combination of intense visual imagery—"Symbol Therapy"—and the mesmerizing nature of New Age mood music will charm like a snake. It will turn the New Age victim into a pliant and submissive zombie whose mind is totally under bondage to Satan. Of course, this is just what Sutphen desires. It should be noted that he and his wife Tara (the same name as one of the Greek Mother Goddesses!) head a group called Reincarnationists, Inc. This group is dedicated to combatting Christian fundamentalists.[2]

Conditioning for the Image of the Beast

Man is being *desensitized and conditioned;* he is being *prepared* for the momentous day when the Image of the Beast will be erected in the churches and temples and man is forced to worship the image . . . or be killed (Rev. 13:15). He is also being taught to worship the Image of the Beast by inviting it into his own mind!

Which of the many satanic symbols we are being conditioned to accept and even appreciate and covet does Satan plan to use as his Image of the Beast? Which horrendous design will he require humanity to receive as his Mark? We cannot now say with surety and conviction that one or another is *the one* that the whole world will come to know as the dreaded Mark of the Beast. But there are at least three or four strong candidates we should consider. As we examine the many New Age symbols in common use, we will identify those with the greatest potential as the Mark and Image of the Beast.

Among the symbols we'll look at in the pages and the chapter that follow will be the:

* pentagram, the five-pointed star
* triangle
* circle
* Egyptian ankh
* rainbow
* Star of David and hexagram
* sun
* swastika
* all-seeing eye
* wheel
* lotus
* crystal
* diamond
* dragon or serpent
* yin/yang
* unicorn, pegasus, centaur
* mermaid

In examining New Age symbols, my goal is to aid you in Christian discernment: to help you as a Christian recognize the symbolic disguises of Satan. I am convinced that once we tear off the Mark of deception and expose the Devil's true appearance as revealed in his symbols, the Christian will be prepared to take action. No longer will Satan be able to indiscriminately display his symbols in open forums such as TV, magazines and other media. No longer will the Devil grasp and squeeze the minds of our youth by secretly transmitting his symbols through cartoons, movies, comic books, and toys.

We start our look at New Age symbols with an examination of the most pervasive of all: the unholy triangle.

The Triangle

The *triangle* is the supreme symbol of New Age satanism. Its use among New Age cults, churches, organizations—and businesses and corporations owned or led by New Agers—is widespread. We cannot truly understand New Age symbolism unless we comprehend the sinister, hidden meaning of the triangle.

The late Albert Churchward, a British researcher whose book, *The Signs and Symbols of Primordial Man* (1913) is today a classic, devotes considerable attention to the origins and significance of the triangle. He wrote that, to the ancients:

> The Triangle was a primary form of the Pyramid and a sacred symbol, because the Pyramid was typically the Pyramid of Heaven; therefore the triangle is typical of Heaven.
>
> In the Egyptian stellar mythology, (the god) Shu . . . first lifted up the heaven from the earth in the form of a triangle, and at each point was situated one of the gods, Sut, Shu, and Horus. . . . They are the trinity. . . .[3]

In other words, to the Goddess religion worshipers of Egypt the triangle represented the holy trinity of their three chief deities. This was Satan's mockery of the Holy Trinity of God, His Son Jesus, and the Holy Spirit.

Churchward's research also showed that the triangle with its apex, or point, facing downward represented Horus, the Sun God, while the triangle pointing upward characterized Sut, or Set, the Destroyer God. This is noteworthy today because in San Francisco we find the Temple of Set, led by Michael Aquino, the self-styled "High Priest of Satan."

Later in history, says Churchward, the Egyptians changed the names of the three principal (there were many others) gods of their unholy trinity. Osiris became the Father god, Isis the Mother Goddess, and Horus their Son. Greater and somewhat aloof was Ra, the unisex sun god/goddess.

For the Hindus, the triangle is also holy. This is because the Hindu religion of India emanated from the Babylonian Goddess religion. New Age encyclopedic researcher Barbara Walker states that the early Hindus and Egyptians, as well as Greeks, revered the Mother Goddess, whose divinity was represented by the all-important "female Triangle of Life":

> It was known as the Kali Yantra . . . or sign of the vulva. In Egypt the triangle was the hieroglyphic sign for "woman" and it carried the same meaning among the gypsies, who brought it from their original home in Hindustan (India). In the Greek sacred alphabet, the *delta* or triangle stood for the Holy Door, vulva of the All-Mother Demeter ("Mother Delta").[4]

According to Walker, the triangle is the universal sign or symbol of the Mother Goddess. "The triangle," she reports, "was worshipped in much the same way that modern Christians worship the cross." Once again we see the importance of the triangle in connection with "MYSTERY, BABYLON THE GREAT, THE MOTHER OF HARLOTS" (Rev. 17).

The Triangle Groups of the Lucis Trust

The Lucis Trust has as its logo the triangle with a representation of the unholy trinity inside it. Alice Bailey, the driving force behind the Lucis Trust, in 1938 organized an international network of Triangle groups, which today has thousands of participating units around the world. A Triangle group is made up of three likeminded New Agers who meet to visualize and meditate on an unholy trinity and to invoke "light and love."[5]

Alice Bailey told her followers that the Triangle groups must accept the grave responsibility for ushering in the New Age Kingdom:

> There is a desperate need for "bringing in the light." This process, when carried on with increasing intensity and frequency, will make possible the Externalization of the Hierarchy, the Return of the Christ, and the inauguration of the Aquarian Age.[6]

In the words of Sir John R. Sinclair, the official biographer of Alice Bailey, the Triangle groups operate "in love," which he defines as *setsun* or "keeping good company."[7] (The term *setsun* when broken down to its components, set and sun, unquestion-alby refers to *Set,* the Egyptian destroyer god who was linked with the unholy trinity of the *sun* god.)

The fact that the Lucis Trust concept of the triangle symbol is based on the ancient Egyptian sun god/goddess religion is confirmed by Sinclair. He quotes Bailey as saying that the point of the triangle represents Shamballa, the Spirit Kingdom of Lord Maitreya, the New Age "Christ":

> The point of the triangle is based in the Courts of Heaven (Shamballa) and from that point two streams of power pour forth into . . . the heart of the disciple. Thus is the Triad formed; then are the energies related unto the world of men; thus can the will of God appear, and thus can the Great Lord who guards the Council Chamber of this sphere of solar life carry his purpose to the holy groups (on earth) and thence into the minds of men.[8]

Benjamin Creme also links the symbol of the triangle with the coming World Ruler and "Christ," the Lord Maitreya: "In this coming time," Creme states, "the Christ will be known as the point within the Triangle."[9]

Helena P. Blavatsky, the nineteenth-century founder of Theosophy, from which the Lucis Trust, Benjamin Creme's Tara Center, and so many other New Age groups and cults sprang, discussed the religious meaning of triangles in *Isis Unveiled.* She noted that ancient Hindus engraved the mysterious and supernatural word *aum,* supposedly used by the gods to create the universe, in a golden triangle that was then placed in the sanctuary of the temple. The triangle and this word were also engraved in a ring that was worn by the high priest of the temple as a sign of his exalted position. It was also framed in a golden sun on the altar, where every morning the priests offered sacrifices to the forces of nature.[10]

The Occult Flag of Nicaragua's Sandinistas

It is no accident that Theosophy, the Lucis Trust, and Benjamin Creme's Tara Center have so warmly embraced the triangle. Nor is it a coincidence that the Marxist-Communist dictators of

Nicaragua—the "Sandinistas"—have adopted the triangle, the horn, and the sun for their national flag. John Barela, Christian evangelist and author of the outstanding book *Antichrist Associates and Cosmic Christianity,* has exposed the occultic nature of the Nicaraguan flag:

> Central America's biggest troublemaker is the terror-exporting military state of Nicaragua. Look in your encyclopedia for a picture of the Nicaraguan flag. Examine this vicious government's national banner.
>
> In the middle of it for all to see is a pyramid—with rays shooting out of the occultic triangle. Notice, too, the little horn.
>
> Familiar? Did it get there by chance? By coincidence? Hardly!

The New Age triangle can be found in a multitude of shapes, forms, and sizes and is often combined with other symbols such as the circle, the sun, the crescent moon, the square, and the Star of David.

These are the same symbols you'll find in all of the worldwide, esoteric groups that we've discussed.

This is the official flag of the Republic of Nicaragua. it's not the flag of the old government—the old Somoza regime that had its faults, but was friendly to the United States. This is the new flag of the Sandinistas, the so-called Communist revolutionaries now ruling Nicaragua. . . . The symbols on this new flag are unquestionably religious—but darkly and occultly so.[11]

The triangle is very popular among witches and satanists as the above symbols amply demonstrate.

New Age Worship of the Triangle

The modern-day veneration of the triangle by New Agers is phenomenal. Satan has assigned top priority to seeding and conditioning all of society with this ungodly religious symbol. In *The Rainbow Bridge,* the New Age authors—who mysteriously identify themselves only with the cryptic term "the Two Disciples"—describe the triangle as the connecting point between man and the spirit world "Hierarchy." The Hierarchy is located at the apex of the triangle pointed upward, while humanity is at the base of the triangle.[12]

Man connects with the unseen Hierarchy, claim the Two Disciples, by creating an *image* in his mind. Once achieving an altered state of consciousness, the individual builds a triangular channel which "consists of building, mentally and imaginatively, a series of small triangles . . . which, when aligned, forms the verticle channel" upward to the spirit-world known as the Hierarchy.[13]

The authors of *The Rainbow Bridge* also propose that the atmosphere of the whole planet is permeated by an invisible, triangle-shaped energy force field. To achieve higher conscious-

These are just a few of the many ways New Agers are today using the triangle.

ness and divinity, men are told to mediate and link their minds with this *higher power:*

> The Planetary Etheric Network is developed in triangles based on this triangle of power which is linked with humanity . . . through Hierarchy. All meditating groups should link with the nearest point of this triangle to contribute and receive hierarchical energies. . . . This is the planetary . . . Rainbow Bridge.[14]

The authors also describe Planet Earth as a Network of Light composed of interlinking triangle energy force fields. Link up with these universal forces, they maintain, and you will be one with "God." When enough people on earth do link up to this network, they claim, the New Age "Christ" and all his hierarchy of spirits will appear to establish their New Age Kingdom. Then the "sons of men" will be One.[15]

Djwhal Khul, the demonic Tibetan Master, reveals that the triangle, through the GREAT INVOCATION, represents the combined energies of the Solar Father, the Christ, the Hierarchy, and humanity. In Christian terms, this means the triangle represents the combined energies of Satan, his false New Age "Christ," the demonic angels of hell, and mankind:

Institute of the Healing Arts

CLASSES:
Yoga - Acupressure - Healing
Tai Chi - Meditation - & MORE

PRIVATE APPOINTMENTS:
Acupressure - Reflexology
Hands-On-Healing

WEDNESDAY EVENINGS:
Healing treatments (donation only)

Institute of Spiritual Awareness

*May the Light of Spiritual Awareness brighten your path.
May Its presence be your guide at every turning point.
May Its beauty be the life that you share with others.*

CLASSES AND SEMINARS IN SPIRITUAL UNFOLDMENT
SUNDAY HEALING SERVICE 10:30 AM
SUNDAY CELEBRATION 11 AM

The triangle is often used as a sign or logo for New Age churches and groups that present seminars and other training programs such as the above. (Addresses deleted.)

THE GREAT INVOCATION relates the will of the Father of of Shamballa, the love of the Hierarchy, and the service of Humanity, into one great *Triangle of Energies;* this triangle will have two major results: the sealing of the door where evil dwells, and the working of the Power of God, let loose on earth through . . . the Plan of Love and Light.[16]

The "door where evil dwells" that is to be sealed is clearly the door that leads people to Jesus Christ. Keep in mind that to Satan, Jesus is the enemy. He is the evil one, and Satan desires that the pathway to God through Jesus be sealed forever.

Khul further explains that, as the *Point within the Triangle,* the New Age "Christ" becomes the "awakener of the hearts of men":

This he accomplishes by transmitting the energies from the three points of the surrounding triangle to humanity. This blended, impersonal energy, triple in nature, will be spread abroad universally . . . automatically causing . . . unity.[17]

The illustration on the left depicts the triangle combined with the heart, while in the one on the right we see pictured the symbol of the Order of the Golden Dawn, a New Age occultic organization.

Whitley Strieber, whose harrowing UFO abduction experience I shared earlier, is convinced that the two small triangles cut into his skin were given as a Mark during a mysteriously weird initiation rite. He believes this triangular Mark has overriding religious significance:

> The (triangle) symbol is very ancient . . . and throughout much of history was tremendously important. I have had a lifelong interest in it—really, an obsession. . . . Buckminister Fuller, in his autobiography, called it the "fundamental building block of the universe." It is the central symbol of growth in many ancient (religious) traditions. An understanding of it is the key to the riddle of the Sphinx and the Pyramid as the Mark of eternal life. G. I. Gurdjieff relates it to the "three holy forces" of creation and it is the main sense of the Holy Trinity.[18]

The Triangle as Trinity

Buckminster Fuller, the famed inventor mentioned by Strieber, was a bona fide, ardent New Ager. Gurdjieff's Universal Mind-Energy Force teachings are at the core of many New Age doctrines. It is understandable, therefore, that they, like Strieber, would ascribe such fundamental importance to the triangle symbol. It does represent *their* trinity—the unholy trinity that excludes Jesus Christ and blasphemously mocks God.

The popularity of the triangle design in the New Age Movement reflects a carefully orchestrated attempt by Satan's demons.

Its use is at epidemic levels. In the book *Focus on Crystals,* the New Age author uses this symbol to represent the "Kundalini fire"—the transformation of a person's mind so that he is changed into a New Age disciple.[19] M. Scott Peck, the New Age psychologist whose book *The Road Less Traveled* was a "Christian" as well as a secular best-seller, has used this symbol to demonstrate man's progress on an evolutionary chart from being a lowly virus and bacteria to his current exalted form as a man.[20]

Peck also uses the triangle to picture man progressing from "undeveloped spirituality" (the base of the triangle) to "spiritual competence." In Peck's theology, spiritual competence is achieved only when a man realizes there is no personal God, that "God" is instead only our unconscious minds. Man, to Peck, is himself evolving and growing to become God.[21]

The Return of the Enneagram

A currently popular variation of the triangle is the *enneagram,* a symbol that has several triangles arranged so that nine points touch an outer circle. Sir John Sinclair, in his commentary on the legacy of Alice Bailey, founder of Lucis Trust, remarks that the enneagram originated in ancient Egypt. He suggests that the nine points on the enneagram represent nine different groups of New Age workers: financiers and economists, psychologists, telepathic communicators, workers in the field of religion, educators of the New Age, trained observers, scientific servers, political organizers, and magnetic healers.[22]

Djwhal Khul, the spirit guide who revealed this diagram and its meaning to Alice Bailey, confided to her that once these nine groups come together, a "tenth group"—which he failed to identify—will come forth to bring in a One World Order.[23]

The enneagram also is a Hindu symbol. Sri Aurobindo, an Indian Hindu guru whose writings and teachings hold a strange fascination for American and European New Agers, connects the enneagram not only to the Mother Goddess of the Hindus but also to the goddess myths of Greece and Rome.[24]

Spouting a mishmash of astrological nonsense, Aurobindo maintains that the secrets of the enneagram hold the key to the energies of the planet Pluto. He who unravels these secrets and discovers the mystery of the "Sacred Triangle," as he terms the enneagram, will enjoy riches and wealth and be sexually fertile.[25]

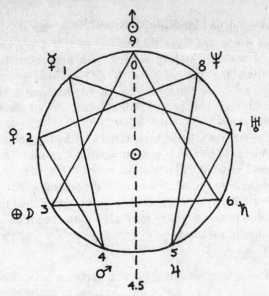

The enneagram currently is an item of fascination in the New Age.

Now a new use for the enneagram has been devised. A Catholic priest, Reverend Jim Cook, is giving special seminars. He calls the enneagram "a system of spiritual self-discovery." Cook teaches that the enneagram identifies nine basic personality types, the compulsions of each, their causes and how to spiritually overcome these compulsions. Somehow this New Age cleric even ties in the personality traits of Jesus.[26]

The use of the enneagram is the rage among some Catholic charismatics—Roman Catholics who speak in tongues. Its popularity is spurred by a 1984 book: *The Enneagram: A Journey of Self-discovery,* by two priests, Rev. Robert Nogosek and Rev. Patrick O'Leary, and a nun, Sister Maria Beesing.[27]

The enneagram is simply a device Satan is using to introduce thousands to his symbol, the triangle, and to acquaint these people to the use of symbols as a panacea for their life problems.

Here Comes the Sun

Pagan and primitive peoples worshiped the sun as a god. But that was millennia ago, right? Surely, twentieth-century, educated man could never be fooled into revering a huge, burning, molten rock in the sky as divine, could he? The answer is yes, he could, if he is a New Ager. As preposterous as it may seem, the New Age has revived the ages-old belief in the Sun God—and millions are falling for this lie. Hitler once said if you're going to tell a lie, make it a big one and people will swallow it. A little lie they won't buy!

The sun symbol is greatly respected and commonly displayed by New Agers. "The sun is a great magnet," so said *The Secret Doctrine* of Theosophy's Helena Blavatsky.[28] *The Beacon*, a magazine published by today's Theosophical Society, recently editorialized that once a person becomes "born again" into the New Age and becomes an aspirant for higher initiation, the sun takes on new spiritual meaning:

> As consciousness awakens, the sun becomes recognized. . . . Then gradually the inner spiritual nature of the sun—"the Heart of the Sun"—becomes known to the aspirant as he begins to respond to its . . . pull: to the great "magnet" of the sun. . . . Occultly, it is said that . . . the "spiritual eye"—the ajna centre—develops in response to the dawning spiritual sun.[29]

Geoffrey Hodson, author of *Hidden Wisdom* and other New Age-oriented books, contends that the sun is the spiritual guide for spiritually advanced persons who meditate and seek higher consciousness:

> The physical sun is used as a symbol for both the all-pervading, omni-present spiritual sun and its consequent presence in man . . . When successful, meditation on the (sun) leads the aspirant into its heart . . . giving place to all-pervading sun-power, sun-life, and sun-fire. In ecstasy he knows himself as one with the sun . . . the sun is everything.[30]

Barry McWaters professes a belief that both the earth, which he calls GAIA the Earth Goddess, and the sun are living, divine beings. McWaters is affiliated with a group that calls itself

The sun symbol has been revived by the New Age. Pictured on the left we see the face in ths sun, an ancient symbol, while on the right is a scene from an Egyptian pyramid demonstrating worship of the sun deity.

the Institute for the Study of Conscious Evolution. He has written that once we recognize the planets as divine, "we begin consciously to acknowledge an endearing love for the sun that we have always known yet never been quite able to explain."[31]

Again and again, we find New Age teachers and leaders espousing the divine sun doctrine. "God lives in the middle of the Sun," says popular New Age lecturer Ken Carey. Can this be some kind of New Age joke? No, Carey is sternly serious; he even teaches his many eager students that *angels* live inside the center of the sun.

> From a center in the Sun, resting in a sea of eternal peace, the angels await . . . focus of Universal Truth. The stage has

been thoroughly prepared. . . . Soon, very soon, a Holy and Integrated Child of Eternity will take charge of its destiny.[32]

Who is this "Holy and Integrated Child of Eternity" coming to take charge of our destiny? Evidently Carey refers to the false "Messiah"—the New Age "Christ," for he and other New Age leaders believe that the great Central Sun God will soon send to earth the Great Teacher to reign over humanity and usher in the One World Order.

"The Christ . . . might be called the Solar Archangel," writes Edouard Schure in *From Sphinx to Christ.*[33] Edgar Cayce, the late psychic, seer, and New Age pioneer whose books are in great demand today, insisted that the sun is simply "an angel in another dimension."[34]

John Randolph Price printed in his *Quartus Report* the text of a message said to be received from an entity calling himself "Helios" and sounding uncannily like a Roman centurion:

Hail co-servers now manifest in . . . the earth. "I AM" Helios, known to you as the Solar Logos for the system of worlds in which your blessed Planet Earth reverberates. . . .
    Children of Light . . . please hear my words. . . . The Cosmic Moment has arrived when this Planet Earth must move forward in the light. . . . Precious Souls, be the cup, the Holy Grail that you have volunteered to be. The entire company of Heaven is awaiting your invitation to assist you. "Ask and you shall receive. Knock and the door will be opened."[35]

Elizabeth Clare Prophet likewise is a sun-worshiper. Her demon spirit guide, Kuthumi, has told the members of Prophet's Church Universal and Triumphant to "meditate on the Great Sun Disc."[36] Prophet teaches that the sun is the "sacred fire of God" and that man must be "always obedient to the cosmic intelligence of the Mighty I AM Presence in the Great Central Sun."[37]

Our kids are also getting a poisonous dose of this New Age teaching. In Arthur Clarke's movie *2010,* a new sun suddenly appears radiantly in the sky, bringing peace to earth just as the two hostile superpowers, the U.S.A. and the Soviet Union, are about to wage all-out nuclear war. Clarke reveals in his book of the same title just who this mysterious and peaceful force appearing as the "sun" is: Its name is *Lucifer*.[38]

The New Age is quite innovative in its use of sun symbols, as seen in the above examples.

The Sun: The Babylonian Connection

The reason New Age Leaders have latched onto this nonsensical doctrine is clear: It is perfectly consistent with the *pantheistic* notion that a personal God who loves man does not exist. It is also a throwback to the doctrinal system of ancient Babylon, where Satan's early church flourished in its iniquities. In Babylon's astrology, the Sun God was the ruler and chief God of the Zodiac. Also, in worshiping the sun and the earth as planetary deities, today's devoted New Age believer is, in effect, paying divine homage to and honoring Ra and Horus, the ancient Egyptian sun gods, Marduk, the ancient fire god, and Set, the god of fire, lightning, and thunder.

The Babylonian monarch and lawgiver Hammurabi was said to have received his laws from the god Shamash, known as the "Lord of the Sun."[39] Baal worship, infamously portrayed throughout the Old Testament, was also the worship of the sun god. "The Sun," wrote Hislop, "as the great source of light and heat, was worshipped under the name of Baal."[40] Hislop also noted that the symbol of the Greek gods Apollo and Helios was the sun.

The Hindu faith is also consistent with the New Age emphasis on the sun symbol. Corinne Heline, whose *New Age Bible Interpretation* is a horrendous commentary that poisonously distorts and twists the Scriptures, favorably observed that the sacred books of India contained this stanza indicating the Hindu worship of the sun god:

> May that Sun who contemplates and looks into all our worlds be our protection. Let us meditate on the adorable ruler; may it guide our intellects. Desirous of food, we solicit the gift of the splendid Sun, who should be worshipped. Venerable men, guided by understanding, salute the divine Sun with oblations and praise.[41]

The Bible expressly forbids worship of the sun (see Deuteronomy 17:2-7). The prophet Isaiah prophesied the fall of the Sun God at the last day when the Lord returns (Isa. 24:20-23). in addition, Job displayed great wisdom by uttering these words setting forth God's thoughts concerning worship of the sun and the heavens:

> If I beheld the sun when it shined, or the moon walking in brightness; and my heart hath been secretly enticed . . . this also was an iniquity to be punished by the judge; for I should have denied the God who is above. (Job 31:26-28)

New Age Idolatry and the Beast

In this chapter we've examined two very important New Age symbols: the triangle and the sun. Each one reveals that the New Age World Religion is definitely an *old religion* with occultic roots that weave deeply underground into times and ages gone by. The Beast of Mystery Babylon is about to be unleashed, and his symbols go before him to soften up the world for his astonishing appearance. In the following chapter we will discover yet more signs of New Age idolatry that point to his imminent arrival.

SIX

Beauty and the Beast

Because, when they knew God, they glorified him not as God, neither were thankful, but became vain in their imaginations, and their foolish heart was darkened. Professing themselves to be wise, they became fools, and changed the glory of the incorruptible God into an image made like corruptible man, and birds, and four-footed beasts, and creeping things. (Romans 1:21-23)

One form of the Circle is a serpent with a tail in its mouth. . . . It is the return to Unity . . . The Serpent Circle is, therefore, ever the symbol of the destructive.
(A. S. Raleigh,
Occult Geometry)

The Bible makes clear that we are to worship the Creator and *not* His creation. Yet, the New Age is bent on idolatry. In *Initiation, Human and Solar,* a Lucis Trust book, New Age disciples are told that the following idols, or symbols, are very important for spiritual initiation into the New Age religion: the lotus, the triangle, the cube, the circle and the point, the line, certain signs of the Zodiac, and the cup, or the holy grail. Also mentioned are the following animal forms: the goat, the bull, the elephant, the man, the dragon, the lion, the dog, and the bear.[1]

These symbols are mind-pictures or images that become idols to the New Ager. Indeed, New Agers frequently buy and display idols of stone, wood, steel, plastic, and crystal representing these forms. Yet, in using these images the New Age believer is practicing idolatry in violation of God's commandment: "Thou

93

shall not make unto three any graven image, or any likeness of anything that is in heaven above, or that is in the earth beneath, or that is in the water under the earth . . ." (Exod. 20:4, 5).

The New Age practices idolatry on a grand scale. Some of the idols of the New Age are beautiful, even magnificent. For example, take the rainbow. What a marvelous work of God! The rainbow is an immensely popular New Age symbol. And there's the diamond, the crystal, the rose, and the lotus blossom: all things of beauty. All the handiwork of our God. But tragically the New Age lie attempts to turn these fantastic creations into things of horror.

It is like the Devil to try to soil and putrify God's brilliant creation. The Devil's greatest and fondest tool is to change the loveliest creations of God into symbols of deception. In a real sense, the battle in the last days is the struggle between Beauty and the Beast!

In this chapter, we'll take a look at some things of beauty that the Devil is working to convert into symbols of ugliness: stars and crystals and diamonds and the rainbow. We'll also examine some diabolical symbols that you will immediately recognize as evil, such as the pentagram, the dragon, the horns, and the swastika. Also, we'll peer into the mystery of the all-seeing eye and investigate the dark satanic underpinnings of what on the surface appears to be an ordinary everyday symbol: the circle. And we'll delve into the evil meanings hidden in the unicorn, the flying pegasus horse, and the mermaid.

The Pentagram: Sign of the Devil

The most familiar and perhaps most blatantly occult symbol of the New Age is the *pentagram,* the five-pointed star. The pentagram is known universally as the sign of the Devil among Satan-worshipers and witches; yet the New Age leadership has sought to present it as "good": as a holy symbol of "white magic" imbued with supernatural power. Thus, we find the pentagram—also called the *pentacle*—being displayed in some unexpected places. Papa Smurf of TV's lovable blue Smurf Family resorts to its use to enchant and charm and cast spells, enticing millions of our young to respect and perhaps become demonized by the Devil's magical symbol. Meanwhile, pentagram necklaces and jewelry are sold in department stores and gift shops and this horrible symbol is a mainstay on satanic rock music videos shown on MTV.

The pentagram, with its unmistakable occult meaning, has for centuries been a preferred favorite among secret societies and mystery groups. Today you will still find it on display in the lodges of Freemasons and the ladies of The Order of the Eastern Star. As evangelist John Barela's research proves, the pentagram has "a place of honor and prominence at the Mormon Temple in Salt Lake City."[2] This is not surprising considering the Luciferian and Masonic roots of the Mormon Church and its founders. Another New Age group with an occult orientation, the Order of the Golden Dawn, which reportedly has an official membership of some 40,000, conducts two rituals using the pentagram.

As we'll discover in Chapter 14, the New Age has definite plans to include the pentagram star in its initiation ceremonies during which all of mankind is to be demonized and obey the Image of the Beast in receiving the Mark on the forehead or right hand.

The satanic pentagram is a welcome symbol in the New Age Movement. This five-pointed star of Satan can have two points up so that the horns can be viewed.

The Infamous Roots of the Pentagram

The wicked occultic pentagram has a long, infamous history. Celtic priests called it the witch's foot. In the Middle Ages it became known in Britain and elsewhere in Europe as the goblin's cross, devil's sign, and the wizard's star. Among the druids of Great Britain, it was the blasphemous sign of the Godhead.[3] "In ancient times," symbolism expert Rudolf Koch has written, "it was a magical charm amongst the people of Babylon."[4] The pentagram was also used by the Babylonians as a healing device and as a medium for bringing good fortune.

So again we come upon another case of Satan reviving the symbolism, ritual and practice of the evil religious system he so successfully established in the days of Nimrod and Semiramis in Babylon. MYSTERY BABYLON is alive and well in the symbols

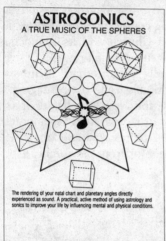

ASTROSONICS
A TRUE MUSIC OF THE SPHERES

The rendering of your natal chart and planetary angles directly experienced as sound. A practical, active method of using astrology and sonics to improve your life by influencing mental and physical conditions.

POWER of the PENTAGRAM

Actual Size

Dealer Inquiries Invited

The **PENTAGRAM** is an ancient symbol of extreme power that for centuries has been used to ward off evil and bring good fortune to its bearer.

This authentic symbol has a deep rooted history among believers who used its power for influencing people and events. It is said that its power is in its ability to magnify and channel the psychic force of its wearer.

Historically correct in design and individually created by hand, it includes a genuine 5pt. cubic zirconia crystal in its center, and is finished with a layer of 22Kt. gold to preserve its beauty.

Complete with a 20" triple rope 22Kt. gold layered chain it is a distinctive, attractive pendant that cannot be found in stores anywhere.

Mail $15.00 for each Pentagram to:

Name .... LP

Address ....

City .... State ...... Zip ......

SATISFACTION GUARANTEED OR MONEY REFUNDED

Findhorn Celtic cards and jewelry from the British Isles.

Catalog available $1.00
Dealers inquiries welcome

Above we see actual ads from New Age magazines advertising the sale of pentagram-related products (addresses deleted).

and idolatry of the New Age World Religion. Some Christian authorities today believe that the pentagram may well turn out to be the Mark of the Beast of Revelation 13.

The pentagram of the New Age comes in a variety of shapes and configurations. These are roughly described by Manly P. Hall in his classic book on the magical arts and satanism, *The Secret Teachings of All Ages:*

> The pentagram is used extensively in black magic, but when so used its form always differs in one of three ways: The star may be broken at one point by not permitting the converging lines to touch; it may be inverted by having one point down and two up; or it may be distorted by having the points of varying length.
>
> When used in black magic, the pentagram is called "the sign of the cloven hoof," or the footprint of the devil. The star with two points upward is also called the "Goat of Mendes," because the inverted star is the same shape as a goat's head. When the upright star turns and the upper point falls to the bottom, it signifies the fall of the Morning Star.[5]

The Ravaging of God's Wonderful, Multicolored Rainbow

Ever since God created the beautiful and colorful rainbow in the sky as a covenant of His love for mankind, pagans led by Satan have worked to pervert its true meaning. The Irish legend of the leprachaun with his pot of gold at the end of the rainbow sought to instill in man a covetous desire for treasures and prosperity on earth. In the practice of voodoo black magic in Haiti and Africa today, the rainbow is depicted as an event celebrating the marriage of a "rainbow god" to the "serpent god."[6]

In the ancient Jewish Kabbala—now being revived by New Age teachers of today—mystical rabbis taught that the rainbow symbolized a sexual rite. The bow of the rainbow was supposedly the phallus of the male god which descended into the kingdom of the womb, the queen or goddess. The union was said to create immense divine powers.[7]

The New Age undoubtedly has grasped onto the rainbow because of its connection with the teachings of Tibetan Buddhism, from which many of the New Age doctrines have risen. The Tibetans believe that the rainbow symbolizes man's ultimate perfect state—divinity, when he has achieved an inner unity of good and evil, shadow and light, and becomes one with the Great One.

In other words, the New Age teaches that man's path to godhood is symbolized by the "Rainbow Bridge," which man crosses over by achieving higher consciousness. The reward at the other end of the rainbow: self-empowerment, immortality, divinity.[8]

Djwhal Khul has remarked: "personalities have learned how to build the Antahkarana [Rainbow Bridge]. . . . The processes given in the RAINBOW BRIDGE have brought thousands to the point of purification and cleansing."[9] Another New Age authority has passed on this message from the demonic "Hierarchy":

There is a desperate need at this time for disciples to make this first link of building the bridge to the . . . Hierarchy, for it enables disciples to become channels for the transmission of energies so urgently needed by the Christ and His Masters for the Coming Externalization of the Planetary Hierarchy.[10]

Initiation into the New Age, say the authors of the best-selling book *The Rainbow Bridge,* will infuse a person's soul with energy forces so he can "take part in this final period of the changeover from the Piscean to the Aquarian Age."[11]

Benjamin Creme has also seized on the powerfully moving symbolic image of the rainbow to promote his false "Christ," Lord Maitreya. Creme has boasted that Maitreya has become active behind the scenes around the world because he embodies certain "rainbow energies":

The World Teacher is the stimulus behind a whole range of activities; not only religion. He is as much the stimulus behind the scientific discoveries and the educational concepts which are today engaging men's minds as He is with religious matters.

He will inaugurate the new world religion which will

engage a large part of His energy, but he is the recipient and transmitter of a great *rainbow of energies* from various sources which stimulate many different aspects of our life.[12]

New Age Color Therapy

Colors have a peculiar fascination for New Agers. Evidently, as part of the initiation rites, aspirants for the Mark will have their visual senses overwhelmed by a colorful, vibrating explosion of lights. The use of the rainbow bridge analogy is a step toward conditioning and hypnotizing people in advance. Elizabeth Clare Prophet and other New Age leaders preach about the Seven Rays of the Initiations, referring to the colors of the rainbow prism. The seven colors of the rainbow spectrum are said to be "qualities of the Godhead" to which a person should aspire.[13]

Through visualization, meditation and other means of achieving Kundalini or transformation, the individual focuses on the seven colors of the rainbow. In so doing, he unknowingly imbeds satanic images in his mind. Swirling in a sea of mesmerizing images, the colors become *mandalas*—hypnotic picture-scapes of kaleidoscope images that reprogram a person's mind to accept the lies of "The Presence," who is the Devil. Here's how Elizabeth Clare Prophet describes this process:

The light from the Presence is released through various centers or *chakras* focused in the body of man. As you decree, the power of the Word flows forth . . . animated by the threefold flame: the point at the center of the forehead which is the focus of the All-Seeing Eye of God (the third eye). . . .

This process, known as visualization, is based on man's ability to "image forth" or to imagine.

Each day of the week there is released to the earth from the Heart of Alpha and Omega a special concentration of one of the seven rainbow rays of God. As you use the decrees daily, you will be working with the seven rays—the rainbow of light which flows into your world through the prism of the Christ Consciousness. The flame colors are (1) blue, (2) yellow, (3) pink, (4) white, (5) green, (6) purple and gold, and (7) violet. Visualize these flame colors as tangible, living fire enveloping your mind and body, saturating your world with the God-qualities desired, while cleansing your being of all that is less than His perfection.[14]

It is important we understand the full implications of what influential New Age cult leader Elizabeth Clare Prophet is telling us in the above passage. First, she reveals that each person has an energy point *on his forehead* which is sent light messages, or images, from the Presence (the New Age "God"—Satan). Man himself, she adds, *invites* this Presence and his image into the mind through *visualization* or imaging. Finally, she recommends a sinister form of daily *color therapy* so that your mind may constantly be saturated with *flame* colors.

Prophet confidently assures her thousands of devoted followers that "the miniature sun of illumination within is the golden pot at the end of the rainbow of light's extension into your world."[15] But in truth, New Age disciples who follow Prophet's prescription for spiritual success will not find a pot of gold at the end of the rainbow. Instead, someday, unsuspectingly, they will visualize and be seized by a grinning pack of vicious demon beings staring at them through the fiery flames of hell.

The Rainbow Haze of LSD

On and on, I could add further proof of how the New Age has attempted to destroy the Biblical Truth about God's rainbow covenant with man. Take the famed writer and philosopher Aldous Huxley, for instance. Huxley, along with Alcoholics Anonymous founder Bill Wilson and other anti-Jesus activists of the 1930s, was a pioneer in LSD experimentation.[16] This dangerous illegal drug introduced an entire generation to mind-destroying color-imagery because it so often induced in the mind strange, bizarre swirling images laden with colors and esoteric meanings.

Aldous Huxley proposed that LSD and other ways of achieving altered states of consciousness could open one's mind to a greater reality, which he called "Mind-at-Large." (Jung used the term Collective Unconscious for the same concept; others use the idea of a World Mind.) Once our mind links up with and allows the images to flow in unimpeded from this Mind-at-Large, rainbow colors bombard our senses:

Everything seen . . . is brilliantly illuminated and seems to shine from within. All colors are intensified to a pitch far beyond anything seen in the normal state.[17]

Colorful Angels of Light

Satan and his angels, the Bible warns us, often come as "angels of light." They also come as *colorful* angels of light. Marilyn Ferguson, who uses the term "The Aquarian Conspiracy" to describe the New Age Movement, gives eleven accounts of New Agers experiencing colors and lights. She uses such adjectives as "golden light," "intense white light," "sparkling lights," and "ultra unearthly colors" to characterize these experiences.[18] This all takes on great significance once we realize that a dazzling profusion of light and colors has for centuries been used to hypnotize and charm. We also recall that, at his creation, the name Lucifer meant "the light bearer" or "the shining one."

Thus it is Lucifer whom Vera Alder, the noted British New Age author, refers to when she states:

The life of the Deity before he began to build his form was expressed as white spiritual light. He had to divide this great Ray of Light . . . splitting it up into [three Major Rays] . . . the Red Ray (Will), the Blue Ray (Love-Wisdom), and the Yellow Ray (Intelligent Activity).

This great Cosmic manifestation is repeated for us by our little earthly rainbow, when the white light of the sun is subdivded into these seven colours before our eyes.[19]

So in New Age doctrines we find an occult explanation of how the rainbow originated from "the sun"—the Sun God, or Lucifer. Next we find in New Age doctrine the lure used to seduce mankind into linking his mind with that of the Sun God, Lucifer, and his many subordinate "gods." The rainbow symbolizes man's evolutionary path, the goal of which is to exalt man as god:

Mind was a gift of the gods to man and was to be used as a rainbow bridge whereby he might pass from earth to heaven.[20]

Penetrating the Mystery of the All-Seeing Eye

What do the following institutions have in common:

> The United Nations Meditation Room
> The Great Seal of the United States
> Egyptian Pyramids
> The Prayer Room in the United States Capital
> The Temple of Understanding

Answer: The *all-seeing* eye prominently on display.

Perhaps the best way to comprehend what the all-seeing eye represents is to examine the architecture of the Meditation Room of the United States Building in New York City.[21] The Meditation Room is only thirty feet long, eighteen wide at the entrance and nine at the other end; so it is shaped as a pyramid without the capstone. Inside, the room is dimly lit, but coming from the ceiling is a narrow but concentrated pinpoint beam of light which radiates down to a bleak stone altar.

On the wall straight ahead is a breathtaking, modernistic mural that is dynamically endowed with occult symbolism, containing twenty-seven triangles in various configurations, a mixture of black and white and colored background, and a snakelike vertical line. At the center is the *all-seeing eye,* which grips the millions of annual U.N. visitors with its stark, beckoning image of suspicion and omnipresence.

At the time of its construction in 1957, the U.N. Meditation Room was said by then-United Nations Secretary Dag Hammarskjold to represent the unity of all world religions. Notably, this same Dag Hammarskjold worshiped a "God" that excluded Jesus Christ as Lord, and yet his book of that era, *Markings,* won raves from many Christian leaders.[22]

Back to Egypt with the All-Seeing Eye.

The all-seeing eye does, indeed, represent unity—a unity that is inclusive of witchcraft, satanism, Hinduism, Shintoism, Buddhism, and every weird and strange cult that has ever existed, but a unity that *excludes* Jesus Christ. The origins of this symbol are in the Egyptian Mother Goddess religion. Hathor, the Sun-Eye Goddess, was thought to come out of the dark night with her piercing eye that emanated from the very interior of the sun. Hathor was the Mistress of the Vulva, the goddess of drunkenness and partying, dance, music and song, and sexuality and fertility. In *The Egyptian Book of the Dead,* the dead are pictured as sitting with Hathor under a tree, to keep her company and seek renewal for themselves. She was the Cow Goddess (mistress of the Bull God) and as the sun's eye, she, it was taught, uncovered the rebellious and punished them.[23]

This same Cow Goddess later was worshiped as a golden idol by Aaron and the children of Israel in the Sinai desert during Moses' absence, a treachery which kindled God's anger and led to divine punishment. The Sun God with his all-seeing eye later became known as Horus, and it is he who is mysteriously shown on our U.S.A. dollar bills in the capstone of the pyramid (the reverse side of the Great Seal). The U.S. Treasury Department has verified to me in a letter that this symbol did, in fact, have its origins in Egypt and that the committee formed in the eighteenth century to design the seal—which included Benjamin Franklin—intended to present the new nation of the United States of America as a successor of the ancient government and culture of Egypt!

Why does an ancient Egyptian sun god, Horus, have such macabre fascination for so many in the New Age today? Simply because Bible prophecy reveals that Satan's end-time church will be a revival of his earlier religious system first established in Babylon, and later in Egypt, centuries before Jesus Christ was born to Mary. Murry Hope, a New Age historian of the ancient Egyptian era, explains the modern connection this way: he approvingly states that the god Horus, as the son of Isis, Mother Goddess of Egypt, is not just a divinity from the past but a deity for today as well. In fact, Hope insists that Horus could become tomorrow's New Age, Aquarian *Savior:*

> The aeon of Horus is the Aquarian Age, say the mystical sages, a time when the Son of Isis will return . . . and bring peace, light, and love to all mankind. We love it! . . . It all sounds tremendously promising. . . .[24]

There are many versions of the all-seeing eye.

The all-seeing eye is the capstone of the pyramid pictured on the reverse side of the Great Seal of the United States of America. Few people realize that this symbol honors the ancient Egyptian Sun God.

The Divine Third Eye

New Age "bibles" and leaders also teach that the all-seeing eye of Horus is the same as the *eye of Shiva*. Shiva is the Hindu equivalent of Horus the Egyptian Sun God.[25]

This same eye of Shiva is also said to be the third eye—the

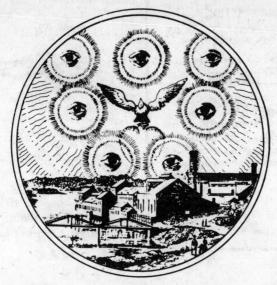

The all-seeing eye is a pervasive symbol in the New Age World Religion.

Ajna Chakra point or center—in the forehead of New Age believers. With their third eye, the eye of Shiva, the New Ager is told to meditate and visualize until an image or thought-form takes shape. This image is often either the image of the person's "all-knowing spirit guide," perhaps an ascended Master or an angel who directs his daily life, or else a god or goddess from the past who comes as an ancient archetype (thought-form from the Collective Unconsciousness—the Universal Mind).[26]

In effect, in the New Age World Religion, believers are taught that through certain kinds of spiritual techniques, they may activate the all-seeing, all-knowing divine eye in their forehead. They will then become Christlike or godlike in power. They become one with Shiva and Horus.

With his all-seeing eye, the New Ager imagines he can connect with the great universal intelligence—the Force of angelic beings and discarnate ascended Masters. It is in this realm where Count Saint Germain, Lord Maitreya, Djwhal Khul and all the other New Age "Christs" and "wise persons" live.

Here are two examples of how New Agers are conditioning society with the all-seeing eye symbol. (Address deleted.)

Special Delivery: From Lucifer's Mind's-Eye to Your Mind's-Eye

The Keys of Enoch is one principal New Age bible that informs New Agers that their third eye magically connects with these other-worldly entities. It states that from the heavens, these wise entities "oversee creation through the Father's eye of creation and the Eye of Horus."[27]

Who is the "Father"? In truth, the "Father" of the New Age is Lucifer. He is the one, says *The Keys of Enoch,* who has established the "Brotherhood of Light."[28] In the New Age the "Brotherhood of Light" is simply a synonym for the demon organization of Satan that is in fact pulling the strings of the New Age leadership.

The Keys of Enoch teaches that this "Brotherhood of Light" communicates through its all-seeing eyes to the all-seeing eyes of New Age believers on earth:

They align their eyes with the eye network patterns of the individual species, for the eye is the opening. . . .[29]

This demonic textbook also instructs New Age readers that this communication is threefold: It is a link established between the "Divine Eye of the Father," the all-seeing eye of the spirit entities (the "Brotherhood"), and that of the New Age believer. The "divine images" that are produced by the "Father" are sent by light waves into "the Eye of Horus placed upon the face of the elect":

> The Eye of Horus is the "eye of the Lords" serving the Living Father of Creation which is placed upon the third eye region of the elect. Therefore this alignment of the "divine eyes" . . . permits you to acquire . . . wisdom . . . and to work within the complete network of a divine hierarchy.[30]

Christians with the discernment of the Holy Spirit can easily decipher and see through this absurd gibberish. Clearly, the New Age populace is being prepared by Satan to receive his Mark. They are being seduced into believing that with this Mark, their all-seeing eye will be activated and they will have acquired a direct link with their "Divine Father"—the Universal Mind—and his wise, all-knowing Hierarchy. They will be One with the Force. But in truth, they will have come under a spirit of deception and be under total bondage to Satan.

The Vicious Circle

The satanic *circle* is well-known among witches and Satan-worshipers. This symbol also has ancient significance. It represented the Sun Gods and Goddesses of Egypt and Rome. *Circe* (thus Circle) was the pagan Roman Sun Goddess, and her symbol was the circle.[31]

To New Agers, the circle represents the never-ending *eternal recycling* of man's spirit through reincarnation. Since it is an unbroken line formed as a ring, it represents world religious and political *unity*, or *oneness*. To many in the New Age, it represents the Earth Mother, the Mother Goddess:

> The circle is truly the most beautiful of symbols, the most perfected of forms. It contains all the knowledge and from it

we can understand everything in creation, because as a symbol it represents . . . the Divine Mother, the Complete Manifestation . . . therefore it is the symbol of Unity . . . Consciousness . . . Love.[32]

The Serpent Biting Its Tail

In many New Age publications, we also discover the bizarre shape of a serpent biting its own tail and thus forming a circle. Vera Alder uses this symbolic picture message on the front cover of her book *The Initiation of the World*. What does it mean? A. S. Raleigh reveals this symbol as destructive in his book *Occult Geometry.*

> One form of the Circle is a serpent with a tail in its mouth. . . . It is the return to Unity; it is (creation and man) swallowing itself; this reuniting is Unity. The true Circle symbolizes evolution, the Serpent Circle involution . . . the power brings Unity out of diversity. . . . *The Serpent Circle is, therefore, ever the symbol of the destructive.*[33]

The Point Within the Circle

Another variation is the point, or dot, within the circle, resembling a simple bull's-eye. Increasingly, this is being used by New Agers. New Age teachers say that the point refers to the Supreme One, the god behind all gods. Christians would know this entity as the liar, Satan, who blasphemously portrays himself as the one true God.

The point within the circle is the sign of Lucifer.

In fact, the point within the circle had its origins in Babylon and Egypt. In 1913 Egyptologist and symbols expert Albert Churchward wrote:

> The point within a circle is one of the hieroglyphic signs of the Sun-God, Ra. . . . It is held to be the One Supreme Power, whatever that power may be. . . .[34]

In one New Age children's book I have in my research collection, the author tells youngsters that the point within the circle is the symbol of Mother God. The author also deceptively manages to bring to the child's attention the image of the sun:

> We often think of our Creator as being our Father, but forget that our Creator must be a Mother too, for we all need a mother, not just a father. Think of Father God as being like the sun, giving life and strength, and Mother God as being like the earth, the place where new life grows and is looked after.
>
> The Sun, symbol of Father God, shines down on Mother Earth. The light and warmth go right into the earth and new life starts to grow. Mother God gives the new life form, and cares for it, with the aid of angels and fairies.
>
> Mother God is often called Divine Mother and we can picture her also as a beautiful woman. She is close to all women, especially mothers, and helps them to be wise and loving with their children. She is close to all children too, and will help and comfort you if you feel unhappy.[35]

And More Circular Paths to Satan

Other variations of the circle include Hindu-like mandalas and sun wheels. An especially powerful occult symbol is formed whenever the circle is used to contain another occultic symbol within. For example, the *pentagram* is formed by enclosing the five-pointed star within the circle, and the satanic trinity symbolized by the *triangle* takes on added sinister meaning when the triangle is inside a circle.

The so-called peace symbol is formed by inverting a twisted cross and enclosing it within a circle. This was the symbol used as the backdrop for the altar of Anton LaVey's Church of Satan that gained such notoriety in the sixties and seventies.

Perhaps the most diabolical and heinous of all symbols is the cross within a circle. *This indicates to the New Age occultist that Jesus Christ is contained, or restrained, within the Circle of*

Examples of New Age mandalas, wheels, and other circular symbols common to the New Age.

The peace symbol is really the perverted upside-down cross inside a circle.

Satan. Its bold but evil suggestion is that a sovereign Satan holds authority over God. Sometimes the cross is constrained by three outer circles. This is symbolic of the desecration by Satan of the Holy Trinity of God.

The cross within three circles was the Mark of the Beast of infamous British satanist Aleister Crowley. Crowley literally branded this Mark between the breasts of women who worshiped him as the High Priest of Satan. Crowley called himself the Beast and the Antichrist with the number 666. Although he is now deceased, his horrible works live on.[36] Reportedly one of his disciples was L. Ron Hubbard, founder of the Church of Scientology.[37]

The New Age and the occult have found many ways to desecrate the cross.

Elizabeth Clare Prophet claims that her spirit guide, Count Saint Germain, appeared wearing a garment adorned with the symbol of the cross within a circle. This false New Age "Messiah" was quoted as saying:

> I have entered this room wearing a white robe. A gold cross in a circle is upon this garment. Beloved, it is the garment of those saints robed in white who march in the armies of heaven with the Faithful and True. I have added to this garment my purple cape of the Knight Commander. . . . And my sword is a flaming sword, like unto Excalibur. . . .[38]

Thus, Prophet's lying demon spirit portrays himself as Christ, coming again at the end of time with the saints of heaven, as prophesied in Revelation 19 through 22. But Saint Germain's true identity is exposed as he goes on to encourage the reader to believe in the divinity of man and to trust "God" as a Guru:

Beloved ones, cast out fear and doubt. Cast out whatever is the prevention of thy Godhood. Let God be your Guru.[39]

Desecrating the Cross: The Unholy Ankh

The *ankh* is an ancient Egyptian religious symbol which means eternal life or immortality. It has over the centuries been used as a good-luck charm by occultists and superstitious folk alike. Today the ankh is very popular among New Agers. You see it everywhere on items of jewelry—prominently shaped into necklaces, rings, belt buckles, etc.

The New Age claims that the wearer of ankh jewelry will be the beneficiary of wisdom, peace, prosperity, and a long and healthy life. The circle or oval atop the cross is a sign of fertility.

In truth, the ankh is a sacrilegious example of a satanic circle surmounting the cross. Ungodly in the extreme, it attempts to depict Satan as supreme over the sacrifice of Jesus.

Three versions of the Egyptian Ankh.

The New Age Swastika

Were Hitler and his Nazi henchmen the inventors of the swastika? Popular misconception holds this to be the case. But careful research proves conclusively that the swastika is a venerable and ancient symbol of ancient Babylon, and also India where the early Hindus emblazoned it on their temples. Even today we find the swastika painted on the walls of some Hindu temples in India.[40]

In 1913, some two decades before Hitler's ascent to power in Berlin, Germany, Albert Churchward documented the worship of the swastika among the Aztecs of Mexico, the primitve Indian tribes of North America, and the witchcraft-styled Druids of Britain from 3000 B.C. until A.D. 300. *Astonishingly, the Druids displayed the swastika inside the satanic triangle.*[41] This reveals the satanic origins of both symbols.

The swastika is an ancient pagan symbol, as proven in this drawing taken from the swastika totem of a native American tribe (from the 1913 book by Albert Churchward). Also, observe the circular, Hindu-like mandala.

It is undeniable, then, that from the beginning of civilization Satan has inspired pagans around the world to paint and erect symbols and idols of the swastika.

To the Hindus, the swastika was the primary symbol of divinity. In his *Occult Geometry*, published in 1932—a full year before Hitler assumed his post as Chancellor and Führer of Germany—A. S. Raleigh remarked:

> The SWASTIKA is the cross of India. It is the form employed by the Hindus. . . .[42]

Raleigh, an occult British researcher, described the swastika as the "wheel of fire," as the "weapon" of the Hindu "Christs," as a "destructive force of creation," and as the "symbol of unity."[43]

Raleigh observed that there are two forms of the swastika. "One represents the wheel of fire revolving to the right, thus the arms bent backward to the left; the other represents the swastika revolving to the left, and thus the arms bent back to the right."[44]

"The left hand swastika," Raleigh noted, symbolizes "the destructive principle."[45]

Quite obviously, Hitler's Aryan race theories and his swastika were both of satanic origins. Today the New Age finds merit both in Hitler's poisonous racial theories and in his sign of the swastika. I recently discovered that a Presbyterian church in suburban Houston, Texas, has a huge swastika draped on the wall behind the main altar. Below it is a much smaller cross. When a shocked visitor inquired about this, he was told by the ushers at the church that the swastika was a holy symbol of "ancient Christianity."

And More Symbols of the New Age

The New Age also has other symbols to offer in its attempt to program minds and fill up men's consciousness with perverse satanic images. Among the most popular of these additional symbols are the lotus, the diamond, the dragon or serpent, the horns, the mermaid, the pegasus, the unicorn, and the ever-popular pyramid and crystal.

Each of these symbols has a connection with the ancient religions of Babylon and Egypt. For example, the *lotus* symbolizes the female vulva of the Mother Goddess, the *diamond* the male organ of the ancient Father God of paganism. Thus, when a New Ager speaks mysteriously of the "diamond entering the lotus" during religious initiation ceremonies, he literally is referring to sexual intercourse as a New Age holy ritual.[46]

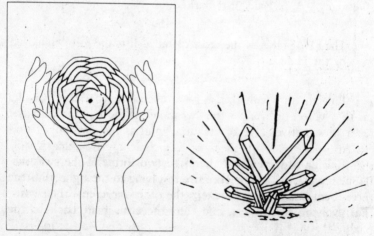

The crystal and the lotus blossom are beautiful creations of God that Satan's New Age followers seek to corrupt.

The *dragon,* or serpent, was the symbol painted on the great Gate of Ishtar that travelers passed through as they entered ancient Babylon.[47] The Bible describes Satan as the dragon and as the *serpent* (Rev. 12:9). The New Age must take particular delight in its portrayal of the dragon as a creature to be loved and taken to heart by New Age disciples. One finds the dragon gracing everything from newsletters to jewelry. There are also crystal dragons as ornaments and idols.

The dragon gets its share of attention in the New Age as shown by these symbols from New Age publications. (Address deleted.)

Also painted on the Gate of Ishtar was the *bull,* the sign of the King of Babylon who was the supreme man-god of the Babylonian religion. The *horns* of the bull later were attributed to the form of Satan. Leo Buscaglia, best-selling New Age author and psychologist, recently attempted to make the ancient bull god a contemporary symbol. His book *The Way of the Bull* was advertised as "a journey toward fulfillment" and as "a quest for awareness and peace."[48]

The *mermaid* was popularized recently in the hit movie *Splash*. New Agers were thrilled because, to them, the mermaid—half-female, half-fish—represented the goddess from the sea, the "fish-tailed Aphrodite." Ancient Canaanite peoples in Bible days knew this deity as Dagon the Fish God.[49]

Again we have the Babylonian connection, and we also have Bible prophecy, for we find in Revelation 13:1 that the Antichrist of the last days is described as a Beast which rises up out of the sea.

The *pegasus*, or winged horse, originated in Greek mythology as the symbol of the Pegae, a water-priestess. The pegasus was said to be the son of the Moon Goddess Medusa. His hoof was shaped like a *crescent moon*, which today is yet another New Age and occult symbol.[50] The pegasus is depicted today in the kids' cartoon series "She-Ra," and crystal pegasus horses are common as amulets and decorative pieces in the homes of New Agers.

The *unicorn* is today pictured as a friendly and loving, gentle creature with great appeal to kids. But his origins are occultic. Nimrod, the "Great Hunter" and man-god of Babylon, wore a headdress with a single horn protruding from the front. According to *The Lore of the Unicorn,* the unicorn goat was worshiped as sacred in pre-Christian Persepolis, Greece. In ancient China, statues of human heads with a horn were thought to keep demons away from homes.[51]

Odell Shepard, author of *The Lore of the Unicorn,* also wrote that the unicorn was a common idol in ancient Babylon and Nineveh where it was used as a charm and a talisman.

The Pegasus flying horse and the horned unicorn are ancient mythological creatures given newfound life as New Age symbols.

The *pyramid* has a close relationship in symbolic significance to the triangle. Indeed, the pyramid is shaped in triangular form. A number of New Age communities and groups, such as the Institute of Healing Sciences in New York, have erected pyramid-shaped structures. Some New Age churches display small pyramid replicas on their altars.

New Agers believe in pyramid-power. Some wear miniature pyramids on chains to bring positive energy forces into their bodies; others make cardboard pyramids and place them into close proximity with foodstuffs, believing in the curative and preservative powers of pyramids.

It was while she and her husband were making pyramids out of paper for preserving food that the demon Ramtha appeared as an apparition to Seattle housewife J. Z. Knight. Ramtha announced he was a 35,000-year-old reincarnated warrior spirit who had come to guide Knight on her journey to divinity. Subsequently, Ramtha (note: *Ram* is the *goat,* a long-established symbol of the Devil) is now an international superstar in the New Age movement.[52]

Speaking from the lips of Knight, whom he indwells, Ramtha announced to one crowd of worshipful New Agers: "In the seed of Lucifer lies God and demons."[53]

The *crystal* is a beauteous work of God that has become perverted by the New Age. The crystal is thought to have the power to heal, to provide prosperity and happiness, to effect all manner of miracles. New Age admirers meditate on crystals, use them for occult divination and fortune-telling, wear them around their neck as a way to attract positive energy into the body, and display such hand- and machine-crafted crystal objects as stars, pyramids, triangles, dragons, and unicorns.

The *yin/yang* is an ancient Chinese symbol that stands for the unity of opposites: for example, the unity of good and evil, negative and positive, and the feminine and masculine sexes. The New Age cherishes this symbol for obvious reasons. Satan wishes to erase distinctions so that moral values become confused, so that the separate but equal roles of man and woman are fused together, and so that bisexuality and homosexuality become acceptable lifestyles.

Considering the fact that the New Age holds little of Judeo-Christian values sacred, it should come as no surprise that the six-pointed Jewish *Star of David* is changed by some in the New

The yin-yang symbol is prevalent in the New Age as evidenced by the several illustrations shown here.

Age into a thing of evil. The Star of David is constructed by merging two triangles, one with the point up and the other with the point facing downward. Some New Age teachers contend that the Star of David symbolizes sexual union between the Mother Goddess (the triangle pointing down) and the Father God (the triangle pointing up).

Inside a circle, the Star of David becomes the *hexagram*, perhaps the most evil sign in the occult world. From use of the hexagram, we have the word "hex." The hexagram is used to put a curse on someone and to call up a demon during a ceremonial rite.

SEVEN

Satan's Design to Seduce the Mind

No man, when he hath lighted a candle, covereth it with a vessel, or putteth it under a bed, but setteth it on a candlestick, that they who enter in may see the light. For nothing is secret, that shall not be made manifest; neither any thing hidden, that shall not be known and come abroad. (Luke 8:16, 17)

A symbol veils or hides a secret, and is that which veils certain mysterious forces: These energies when released can have a potent effect. . . . (Foster Bailey, *The Spirit of Free Masonry*)

The New Age symbols now proliferating throughout society are evidence that Satan is *conditioning* man's mind for the days of horror and unparalleled chaos that lie just ahead. He is conditioning man's mind to accept the *Lie* (2 Thess. 2) and be seduced by the Antichrist into gladly receiving his Mark, his number, and his name.

I have asked a number of New Agers why they chose a certain symbol for their organization's logo. Not surprisingly, the genuine response is that they didn't know *why* they chose a triangle inside a circle, an inverted cross with bent branches, a pyramid, or a pentagram star. "This image just popped into my head," they usually say. "I just couldn't get it out of my head; it kept vividly returning."

I have no reason to doubt most of these deluded victims.

119

Satan is a master at manipulating the minds of people who have given sway to him in their lives by first rejecting Jesus Christ. To those who have no heavenly protection, Satan's thoughts increasingly become *their* thoughts. So when a symbol "pops into their heads," they automatically think it to be their own creative idea.

However, I want to make it clear that *the top echelon of New Age leaders know exactly what these symbols mean and the purpose behind their use today.* Once a person is fully initiated into the New Age, he is made aware of the satanic nature of symbols and of his own role in Satan's Plan to control and dominate the world.

Today's witches and Satan-worshipers active in the New Age are also well aware of the use of symbols. They use symbols in ritual and incantation to invoke demon spirits. They also create sinister symbols in the form of talismans, charms, amulets, prayer-sticks, and masks to accomplish the casting of spells and other evil objectives.

It is also clear that most New Agers, even if they first come by their symbols without evil intent, soon begin to realize the dark nature of these symbols. Yet, their minds are so clouded with satanic evil and deception that they often delight in retaining these vile symbols. In fact, I find that New Agers recognize one another through their common use of symbols.

Someday in the not-too-distant future, Satan will pop ghastly new thoughts into the heads of his earthly disciples: thoughts that make the Mark attractive and desirable and that cause the disciple to find Christian believers repulsive and a dangerous threat to society. Eventually the compelling thought will come to a New Age society that if Christians are eradicated and removed, the planet and mankind will be healed and transformed into God. In that moment, the top leaders of the New Age, who have known all along that this day would come, will give the command to their subordinates to see that this is done . . . and it will be.

The Secret Nature of New Age Symbols

The hell-invented symbols to which the seduced minds of New Agers are irresistibly drawn inevitably become *living objects* of consuming fascination. New Agers are taught to meditate while visualizing or fixedly centering their *spiritual* eyes on a symbol. Often the symbol is hung on the wall or imbedded into an idol, and it literally becomes an object of worship.

New Agers are also taught that symbolic images lift one into a desirable altered state of higher consciousness. By concentrating with intensity on either a single symbol or a number of sometimes rotating and moving satanic images and geometric patterns, the individual becomes hypnotized—he is mesmerized into a trancelike state in which his mind becomes a playground. Satan's demons then have the power to stir and manipulate his mind as if it were putty.

It is undeniable that New Age symbols possess dynamic yet diabolical and sinister power to shape man's mind. Thus it is easy to understand why Satan is giving such great emphasis to the widespread proliferation and use of symbols.

New Age symbols are the keys which Satan uses to unlock the mind and reprogram it with evil. I have discovered, too, that after a time New Agers actually *get hooked on symbols*. They become symbol-addicts and come to believe that they can't live without their symbols. Visualizing symbols provides a satanic high, a euphoric lift, without which they fear they will slip into the abyss of despair and utterly lose control of their senses.

Symbols, then, are tools by which Satan seduces and controls man's mind. New Age authority Alice Bailey showed a keen understanding of this when she wrote that "a symbol is an outer and visible sign of an inner and spiritual reality."[1] Through symbols, she states, the soul progresses and a magical work is done in the minds of New Age disciples. The Plan thus penetrates "into the consciousness":

This is beginning to happen with increasing frequency and from day to day more and more intelligent men and women are coming (or are being brought) into touch with the emerging ideas of the Hierarchy. . . . The thoughts of men are being turned to the Plan, to the use of the will in direction and guidance, and to the nature of dynamic force.[2]

Bailey also give us insight into the demonic intentions regarding the use of symbols and images. We discover that symbols spontaneously call into our minds and bring to our lips the *name of the Beast.* The advanced New Age disciple will be able to envision—to summon from his subconscious mind—the image of a certain symbol and, automatically, that will conjure up the image and name of Lucifer, his lord and master.

The Secret Nature of Symbols

Symbols are used to stir a person's consciousness and move him emotionally to feel or act in a certain way. In a real sense, symbols have *secret powers.* A symbol can unleash dark forces deep inside the soul. Therefore, the New Ager who immerses himself in the symbols of Satan will soon find himself captive to hidden forces far beyond his capability to cope. Foster Bailey, prominent New Age leader, alluded to this when he wrote:

> A symbol veils or hides a secret, and is that which veils certain mysterious forces. . . . These energies when released can have a potent effect.[3]

Foster Bailey goes on to say that "through the right understanding of symbolic work, certain creative energies can be brought into play."[4] However, Bailey fails to define these "creative energies" that, "when released can have a potent effect." This is indicative of Satan's Mystery New Age Religion, which recruits its victims by promising them certain, undefined *powers* if they will blindly enter into the initiation path required for New Age citizenship.

Satan deludes his New Age victims, offering up to their vain imaginations the idle promise of profound spiritual enlightenment. "Trust me," he says with all the aplomb and confidence of a super con artist, "and I will reveal to you through my symbols and images the mysteries of the ages—the hidden secret of how you can become a god!"

The True Mystery Revealed

How different is the message of God in the hearts of His people. The Bible reveals once and for all the Mystery of the Ages. It is Jesus Christ who is:

. . . even the mystery which hath been hid from ages and
from generations, but now is made manifest to his saints.
(Col. 1:26)

Reading the Bible is a breath of fresh air. Its openness is
available to all who seek Jesus Christ, repent of their sins, and
commit themselves to Him.

For in him dwelleth all the fullness of the Godhead bodily.
And ye are complete in him, who is the head of all
principality and power. (Col. 2:9, 10)

The cross is a symbol which openly reminds us of the sacrifice of Jesus Christ. That is the image that we should cherish—
of God's deep love for us through His Son. His life and sacrifice
for us is described by four different writers—Matthew, Mark,
Luke, and John—in the Gospels. *The Secret of Secrets has been
revealed.* Jesus Christ, who was with the Father from the beginning and who created the worlds (John 1), is Lord, and He calls
us out to serve Him and Him alone:

Set your affection on things above, not on things on the
earth. . . . When Christ, who is our life, shall appear, then
shall ye also appear with Him in glory. (Col. 3:2, 4)

The symbols of evil, though, come veiled as secrets. Buy
them now and discover later the awful truth. You will find but
fleeting powers in these symbols because they are based on man-
made philosophies inspired by Satan and are intended not to
bring you to know God, but to imagine vain deceits that *you* can
become God:

Beware lest any man spoil you through philosophy and vain
deceit, after the tradition of men, after the rudiments of the
world, and not after Christ. (Col. 2:8)

The worship of symbols is New Age idolatry. Christians
must not worship or use symbols in any way to create or

enhance spiritual experiences. Even the cross with all its symbolic importance does not suffice as a picture or image of Christ, nor should its display be the focal point of our praise and worship of God. Neither is the cross a substitute for faith: "Faith," the Bible teaches, "is the substance of things hoped for, the evidence of things not seen" (Heb. 11:1).

Though symbols may represent Satan and inspire his earthbound followers to evil beliefs and acts, the unseen God is our fortress, and in the invisible yet majestic God is our hope.

> Jesus saith unto him, Thomas, because thou hast seen me, thou hast believed; blessed are they that have not seen, and yet have believed. (John 20:29)

Our task as Christians is to battle against the demonic images that Satan attempts to instill in our minds. We do this not through our own power but by calling on divine intervention:

> For the weapons of our warfare are not carnal, but mighty through God to the pulling down of strongholds, casting down imaginations, and every high thing that exalteth itself against the knowledge of God, and bringing into captivity every thought to the obedience of Christ. (2 Cor. 10:4, 5)

The Origins of New Age Symbols

As we have observed, the many New Age symbols being used today to condition mankind for the New Age World Religion of the Beast of Revelation first had their origins in Babylon and Egypt. From here the Mystery Religion of the Goddess spread throughout the world, to China and Japan in the Far East and to India, throughout the Middle East and on into Greece, Rome, and Europe. The prevailing World Religion at the time of Jesus and his Apostles was the religion of the Goddess, in its many localized forms. Only Judaism and, later, Christianity departed from and were opposed to the Great Mother Goddess Religion.[5]

This seductive but thoroughly wicked religion was centered around the worship of idols. Its vast system of gods and goddesses were all linked to and subordinate to the unholy trinity of the Great Goddess, her husband, and their son. Along with its debauchery and its man-god evolution doctrine, the Babylon Mystery Religion of the Goddess had its symbols (the Image and Mark of the Beast), as well as its magical names and words of power (the Name of the Beast). In addition, its doctrine included the magical science of numerology (the Number of the Beast).

My research proves conclusively that every known New Age and occult symbol in use today in the latter part of the twentieth century had its origins in the ancient Babylon Mystery Religion.

This brings us directly and without detour to Revelation 17, where the Lord revealed that Satan's last-day religious system would be a revival or reawakening of *Mystery Babylon*! Satan has been held back for centuries from his long-cherished goal of completely dominating and brutalizing the world. He can do nothing until God's timetable permits.

But now Satan and his demons are finally being unleashed. They have evidently been empowered to come forth energetically to prepare the world for "great tribulation, such as was not since the beginning of the world to this time, no, nor ever shall be" (Matt. 24:21).

In Chapter 14, entitled "Passport to Hell: The Great Luciferic Initiation of All Mankind," I will describe just how the visualization and imaging process is to be used in the Initiation of mankind into the Mystery of Iniquity. Satan has truly demonstrated in his development of ingenious symbols and techniques for their manifestation a mad genius of monstrous proportions. He has, moreover, had thousands of years to prepare for this day. The symbols the New Age so eagerly displays today were designed in the Devil's psychological workshop of architectural design and first put to effective use in Babylon and Egypt. As historian S. Angus has noted, "A Mystery Religion was a religion of symbolism" in which men were moved to ecstatic religious experiences.[6]

However, only the initiate was given a peek into the true nature of the symbols of the Mystery Religions. To all others, the symbols and image remained hidden and concealed.

The Power of Symbols

Symbols have a unique power to transform man's mind, shape his thinking, and stir him to action. This is why every corporation and organization—government and private—uses logos, emblems, and symbols. Think for a moment about some recognizable symbols: the cross, the Statue of Liberty, the Stars and Stripes. Each of these symbols instantly brings certain pictures and thoughts flowing into our minds and sometimes almost overpowers our emotions and feelings.

Singing "God Bless America" while Old Glory gently ripples in the breeze can bring tears to our eyes as a feeling of patriotic fervor grips us. Certainly as a Christian, the sight of the cross must have at one time or another moved you to tears and also to feelings of gratitude and amazement that God loved you so much He died and shed His precious blood for *you.*

On the other hand, pornographers and purveyors of filth and smut bank on the fact that once a person has watched an X-rated movie or examined a pornographic bank of pictures, he has allowed his mind to be captivated by images that cannot easily be dismissed. Such images become symbols of lust that etch, scar and disfigure the mind. Invariably only God can heal that person's mind and forever dissolve these perverse images.

A symbol becomes, then, a dynamic reality imbued with either good or evil value. If we wish to truly learn what makes a person tick—to understand his deepest longings and desires—we need only discover what symbols he most cherishes. He who is possessed by Satan is also possessed by the symbols that represent Satan.

The Perversion and Misuse of the Christian Cross

In our study of New Age idolatry—what we can rightly call the unholy worship of the symbols of oppression—we have found that Satan has taken delight in taking legitimate symbols, some of the Christian faith, and blackening them with dark meaning. A favorite of the Devil is to symbolically warp and degrade the cross. Thus, we discover that the New Age leadership has designed a number of symbols that misuse the cross in one way or another. For example, the cross may be pictured:

*   *Inside a triangle, pyramid, or circle—all satanic symbols.* The twisted message of this is the fabrication that Satan has God under control. A specially devious and heavily occult method of denigrating God and showing disrespect for the Almighty is to project the cross against a field of black, encompassed by the triangle, the circle, or another satanic symbol.

* *Mixed with or affixed to a satanic symbol—for example, with a loop or circle or atop a triangle.* This physical placement of the cross—connecting it to a satanic representation—is thought to be degrading to the purity of the True God.

* *Inverted, or lying sideways or at an angle.* The upside-down cross is popular with satanists because it defiles God and mocks Jesus' sacrifice. A cross that lies at an angle also is derogatory and is again a slur on God's purity.

* *With broken, misshapen, bent, or disfigured horizontal crossbars.* This symbolizes to occultists a broken and defeated Jesus. The "peace symbol" is one example. It is an especially wicked symbol that has in the past few decades acquired favored status among many New Agers, liberals, and radicals in the peace movement.

* *As a swastika, with all four bars or branches bent.* As I revealed in the previous chapter, the swastika is an ancient occult symbol.

Ravaging the Rainbow

Recently, when I told a group of Christians how the New Age had perverted the symbol of the *rainbow*, many listeners were startled, with good reason. After all, the rainbow symbolizes God's covenant with man and the creation to never again destroy the earth by flood (Gen. 9:11-17). This, then, is a holy symbol, worthy of remembrance by God's people today. Yet, New Age leaders have defiled this divine sign and given the rainbow symbol horrendous meaning. They *have* ravaged the rainbow.

A great number of Christians continue to use the rainbow as a positive symbol. Some even place it on their Bibles and books or display the rainbow in poster or decor form in their home or office. Personally I see nothing wrong with this. *Why should we yield to the enemy a sign given us by our God?* Yet, we must keep in mind that the New Age abuses this beautiful sign of God's love, and avoid their propagandistic efforts to promote New Age error.

Stars of the New Age

Another precious symbol of God that the New Age and the occult misuse is the *star*. We know from the Bible that Jesus is the "bright and the morning star" and that God frequently used the symbol of the star in the Book of Revelation. But Satan, being aware of man's carnal fascination with stars, has over the centuries used the "star" for his own unholy, symbolic purposes. The worst example, of course, is the pentagram, the five-pointed star. Generally, however, we need not be concerned that the star is an occult New Age symbol unless it is enclosed within a circle or triangle, or is used along with the crescent moon.

For Good or Evil?

We have seen that New Agers have adopted for evil purposes triangles, stars of various geometric configurations, and the triple (trinity) circular design. We must be very cautious about categorizing every single use of these symbols as evil. What we *can* do, however, is determine *who* is displaying the symbol and *for what purpose*.

For example, the Lucis Trust, an openly anti-Christian New Age organization, has as its logo the triangle. We can make the reasonable determination that its use is for repugnant reasons. If, however, a fundamentalist Christian church whose pastor has impeccable credentials as a solid man of God were to adopt the triangle logo, it might be an innocent situation. If we ask the pastor why, he might even tell us that the triangle was selected because it symbolizes the Holy Trinity. It would, of course, be better for him to avoid the use of the triangle because of its New Age occult connotation, but we cannot fault his good intentions.

In addition, we should be aware that the triangle, the star, the rainbow, and others are commonly used by organizations whose originators, quite possibly, have no foul thoughts in mind. The triangle is unquestionably an architectural model and a mathematical symbol, for instance, and the star and rainbow are in vogue among artists. (I note that the U.S. flag innocently uses the star, as does the Lone Star flag of the State of Texas.)

Nevertheless, used in a spiritual or religious context the triangle and other New Age symbols we have discussed and illustrate in this book *are almost always chosen for their occult value and significance.* For example, the triangle is the most popular of all occult symbols and I find no justification for its use by Christians. Even if we claim our use is benign, we must contend with the fact that, overwhelmingly, the New Age and much of the public view the triangle as a mystical and anti-Christian symbol at best. Why should we stubbornly insist on making the triangle into a sign of positive value if its use can be misconstrued and is subject to so much detriment?

So the key I believe is to use good judgment in evaluating whether the use of a questionable symbol is for evil purposes. And always, Christians should rely on the Holy Spirit for discernment.

Of course, if a group or church uses a symbol that is *clearly occult* in nature, there is no reason to take this lightly. The pentagram, the horns, the Egyptian ankh, the crescent moon with an accompanying star, the swastika, the triangle within a circle, the circle within a triangle, and the pyramid are *virtually always* a sign of satanic influence. Yes, we should apply common sense and good judgment before we accuse someone who uses these symbols of wicked interest; but we don't have to play into the hands of the Devil, foolishly excusing, explaining away, or too quickly dismissing such use.

The Image and Symbols of God

Can an image be made of God, a representation of his appearance, form or shape? The Bible tells us that is not possible. Jesus told us that God is a spirit and that he must be worshiped "in spirit and in truth" (John 4:24). "No man hath seen God," says the Bible (1 John 4:12). It is true, of course, that the magnificent light from the Throne of God has been observed by man, and we know that God appeared as a burning bush to Moses, But the majesty and aura of God is evidently so strong, so astonishingly powerful and overwhelming, that for a man to "see" God would be for him to be consumed by an unquenchable fire.

When I hear a television evangelist, preacher, or other person claim to have had an intimate and chummy talk with a "Jesus" or "God" who appeared to him in normal street clothes, in ordinary human form, or even as the historical Jesus, I immediately discount it. The fact is, God is so holy and His countenance so unparalleled and breathtaking that any man who encounters God face-to-face would never describe him in terms of the ordinary.

We find in Revelation that the Apostle John, who was there with Jesus as one of the twelve disciples during the Lord's earthly ministry, decades later encountered quite a different form of Jesus on the Isle of Patmos. Hearing a mighty voice, John turned to see who spoke to him. Here's what he saw:

> I saw seven golden candlesticks, and in the midst of the seven candlesticks one like the Son of man, clothed with a garment down to the foot, and girded about the paps with a golden girdle. His head and his hair were white like wool, as white as snow; and his eyes were as a flame of fire; and his feet like unto fine brass, as if they burned in a furnace; and his voice like the sound of many waters. And he had in his right hand seven stars; and out of his mouth went a sharp two-edged sword; and his countenance was as the sun shineth in its strength. (Rev. 1:12-16)

Obviously this is not the same Jesus we often see in the pictures in our children's Bibles, the one some of us buy pictures of to hang on our living room wall. Nor is the Jesus described in Revelation the suffering Jesus hanging on the crucifix in our Episcopal and Catholic churches. This was not an image of Jesus devised by man's mind. *This was the living, victorious Jesus! This was God.* And his appearance was so incredibly awesome that, awestruck at what he saw, John literally collapsed in a heap:

> And when I saw him, I fell at his feet as dead. And he laid his right hand upon me, saying unto me, Fear not; I am the first and the last; I am he that liveth, and was dead; and, behold, I am alive forevermore, Amen, and have the keys of hell and of death. (Rev. 1:17, 18)

No image, no symbol can properly represent God. The cross is an admirable attempt by Christianity not to envision the person of God, but rather to keep in remembrance the *gift* of God made possible through the death and resurrection of His only begotten Son, Jesus. Still, the cross is a powerful symbol. It is an image that is stirring and inspirational to Christians, but detestable and loathsome to those in the New Age who despise Christ Jesus and who have no regard for His sacrifice nor belief in Him as Savior and Lord.

The Ugly Symbols of the Adversary

Satan also has his symbols: images, shapes and forms that represent the evil he stands for. His people of the New Age gravitate to these symbols. Their minds absorb them, are engrossed and spiritually consumed by them.

Satan is a hideously ugly creature. Because of his rebellion against the heavenly host, Satan and his demons were evidently cursed by God and their beautiful natures transformed into horribly frightening shapes and forms. Though he and his dark angels often come to man disguised as angels of light, this is an illusion. This image is but an illusory thought-form the Devil transmits to man's mind. Lurking behind this facade of light and beauty is the *true* Satan—the bloodthirsty and power-hungry Beast of Perdition!

The Christian who loves God and is given the spirit of discernment is not fooled by Satan's outwardly beautiful appearance. He sees the Devil for who he is, for God exposes the Lie. Likewise, the person of God recognizes the symbols of Satan as things of revulsion. They are repugnant to the Holy Spirit who resides inside the hearts of Christian men and women. Indeed, satanic symbols are, for the Spirit-filled Christian, chilling reminders that Satan is the master of deceit, the fount of perversity, and the father of death.

EIGHT

The Image that Lives . . . and Speaks!

And the smoke of their torment ascendeth up forever and ever; and they have no rest day nor night, who worship the beast and his image, and whosoever receiveth the mark of his name. (Revelation 14:11)

It is valuable to learn how . . . we can finally create and manifest . . . THE MASTER IMAGE . . . so that you can at last be ONE WITH ALL OF LIFE. (William Wolff, *Psychic Self-improvement for the Millions*)

Once the whole world falls under the iron rule of the Antichrist, all of humanity must undergo the Initiation that leads to the Mark being permanently received on the forehead or right hand. It is conceivable that this Mark will be the mind-absorbing Image of the Beast—the symbol that perfectly represents him. In worshiping the Mark, the symbol that has been visibly placed on their physical body, men will know that it is Lucifer whom they worship. They will know it is his name that grips their senses and his number that pervades their lives. His Image will be alive in their minds! The secret will have been revealed:

And he hath power to give life unto the image of the beast, that the image of the beast should both speak, and cause that as many as would not worship the image of the beast should be killed. (Rev. 13:15)

Spiritual Exercises

This ability of an image, or symbol, to spring to life, to move and speak within the receptacles of men's minds comes about through certain "spiritual exercises" that New Agers are learning today. *Visualization and guided imagery,* for example, are satanic methods of conjuring up and manipulating images. The use of visualization has long been a powerful vehicle of occultists; but today psychology—whose founders were almost without exception satanists and perverts—has brought occult visualization to the masses. Sadly, millions of Christians today have been introduced to visualization by men like Episcopal priest Morton Kelsey, and mystical Catholic priest Thomas Merton.[1]

Images That Come Alive

Such un-Biblical techniques as Zen Buddhist forms of meditation and certain kinds of *inner healing* actively employ occult visualization and meditation (not to be confused with reading, studying and actively meditating on God's Word). All are useful to the Devil in training and conditioning men's minds, and preparing mankind for the Image and Mark of the Antichrist.

The late occult Swiss psychiatrist Carl Jung, friend and colleague of Sigmund Freud, is the modern-day father of symbology and also of visualization and inner healing. Jung admitted to possession by various spirits (demons), and one of his books was written through his hands by a demonic author. Jung believed that man could create reality with his thoughts. *Therefore, man can use thought-power to give life to symbols.*[2]

Jung based his beliefs on his study of the ancient Eastern religions such as Hinduism and on gnosticism. New Agers practically worship Carl Jung, and they devour his writings. Particularly popular are his works on symbols and images. I have yet to meet a top New Age leader who does not know of and embrace Jung's theories. Given their dependence on Jung's demonically inspired writings, New Agers are convinced that through visualization and meditation they can make symbols come alive and that these symbols will ever after have life, living on in the Collective Unconscious of the universe.

The Myths and Images of Morton Kelsey

Carl Jung's imagery and visualization techniques and his symbolism have recently been the subject of many books that have flooded both the secular and the Christian marketplace. Episcopal priest and theologian Morton Kelsey is a big fan of Jung's psychology. Kelsey believes the Bible must take a secondary role to mythical images and visualized thought-forms we can create in our own minds. We can "know" God through experiencing myths and helping them come to life in the spirit world:

> We know God and we know a world beyond by experiencing it, and then we express our experiences in images, in myths. Conversely as we come to understand and experience the myth, we are brought into contact with the realm of the spirit. . . . I can only repeat that I have experienced them and I know the reality of these things of which Jung speaks, of which my theology speaks.[3]

Drugs, fantasy, dreams, imagination—these are all acceptable avenues to get images to surface in one's mind, Kelsey insists. Such images become real and are just "Pure Gold," he exclaims in one of his many books, *Prophetic Ministry.*[4]

Jungian and paganistic imagery and myths cannot effectively be used as a first step on the path to discovering God. Regrettably, this is simply a lie of the Devil. We cannot find God through Jungian archetypes and paganistic myths, nor by constructing mythological gods and goddesses and heroes and heroines in our vain and flimsy imaginations. *This is the pathway away from God.* We find God only through obedience to His Holy Word, the Bible, which counsels us to go direct to Jesus Christ as the only intercessor between man and God. What a dangerous deception to believe that, somehow, un-Biblical fantasy, myth, and make-believe can lead one to God.

Sacred Sex with the Goddess

Scores of Catholic priests would agree with Kelsey and Jung. They read the mystical writings of Saint Ignatius Loyola, a long-deceased Catholic monk. Loyola taught a form of silent meditation in which you induce divine images to appear in your mind. Recently on an airplane trip, I happened to sit next to a Benedictine Catholic monk who confided to me that the many brothers who lived in his isolated monastery in the Midwest practiced Loyola's meditation techniques. He related that during his own meditation period, "the Goddess" (he believed in a feminine deity) came to him and that he and she engaged in sacred and holy sex.

This obviously very dedicated monk genuinely believed that this was a holy and acceptable religious experience, and he seemed surprised that I would find it so disgusting and unnatural.

The Hindus, of course, have for centuries practiced a similar form of meditation, *bhakti yoga*. New Age researcher Robert Anton Wilson has described the imagery of bhakti yoga this way:

> In bhakti yoga, you form a love-bond with a particular divinity, dedicate every waking moment to Him (or Her) and invoke that Divine Being by every method possible especially *vivid visual imagination*.[5]

Images of a New Age Camelot

New Age leaders *want you* to study mythology and exercise your imagination to create divine living images. Elizabeth Clare Prophet and others promote the Camelot experience, encouraging followers to create and obey images of King Arthur, his royal knights, and other medieval personages. Alice Bailey and the Lucis Trust lead followers into a study of Hercules and the Greek mythologies. Still other New Age authorities invite students to conjure up images of Egyptian and "Atlantean" pharaohs, priestesses, gods, and goddesses, as well as centaurs, unicorns, and other mythological beasts.

New Age medical doctor Robert Leichtman and writer Carl Japiske, active in a group calling itself Light, contend that out there in the Collective Unconscious of the universe are all these mythological divinities, heroes, and heroines that man has in ages past created with his own mind. Men supposedly have the psychic ability to actually create images and thought-forms that come alive. We tap into these *archetypes*—call them up—

through meditation and visualization, as well as by "using systems of divination such as the Tarot, I Ching, numerology, the Runes, and astrology."[6]

As "divine archetypes," these images are said to be "spiritual lights of heaven":

> By learning to work with the archetypes, we can interact creatively with the divine Plan. We can learn to be inspired. We can enrich our lives. We can start to play our part on earth with greater effectiveness.[7]

Leichtman and Japiske believe that archetypes are divine beings who act as creative forces with great powers to transform us. But we must, they add, be willing and able to serve as the inspired agent of the archetype on earth. "If we tap the real archetype, it will sweep through the whole of our life and change it."[8]

Recommended: Use of Occult Symbols

It evidently helps if you also use occult symbols while visualizing and imaging up these divine archetypes, these man-created gods from the past. Benjamin Creme, in one issue of his *Transmission-Meditation* newsletter, gave his readers specific instructions on how they should meditate and visualize "the Buddha, the Embodiment of Light and Wisdom on the Planet."[9] Creme instructed the New Age disciple to visualize white light, the sun, and the Buddha sitting in a Lotus posture. The disciple should also create an image of brilliant golden white light emanating from the ajna center between the eyebrows on the forehead of the Buddha. He should visualize this light entering the minds of men everywhere.

Creme's specific formula even has the visualizer see in his mind the "Buddha" standing at the head of an inverted Y-shaped table. As we discussed earlier, the inverted Y is an ancient occultic symbol of an upside-down, twisted cross. Encircled, it become the infamous "peace symbol" of the hippies, also used in Anton LaVey's Church of Satan.

Bible Prophecy and the Image

Bible prophecy tells us that the Image of the Beast will actually live and speak. It is possible today, through laser holography technology, to create an image of light that can move and speak as if alive. Indeed, this has been demonstrated. I have written about this amazing new high-tech development previously, and I have written several books on robots. With advanced computer brains and artificial intelligence software, a robot can "come alive:" it can walk, talk, see, hear, even smell!

It is conceivable that the Image of the Beast could be a laser holographic image or perhaps a robot that New Age priests and ministers someday will set up in churches and temples throughout the world. All would be forced to worship this image, since it would *represent* the Beast himself.

Note that the image need not be a statue or other perfect facsimile or lifelike representation of the Beast. Revelation 13:14 states that the people of earth will "make an image *to* the beast," and that this man-created image will then be given life by the false prophet who is empowered by the Beast to oversee the One World Religion. Thus, the Image could be of any shape or form that Satan wishes to use to induce blind obedience in the minds of men—whatever symbol or image that inspires them to follow the Beast.

I personally believe that the Image will be a supernatural one rather than a laser holographic image or a robot. Satan has amply demonstrated the power to send vivid, realistic visions, thoughts, and images to his New Age followers on earth. New Age literature is filled with reports of such images. They range from pictures of occult symbols to images of spirits from an unseen world masquerading as angels, as mythological heroes, or as ancient gods.

Satan also has the power to delude his victims into thinking that *they* can control and manipulate these images and spirit entities. Indeed, many New Agers have been fooled into believing that *they* are the god and that the images that appear are *their* obedient servants! Someday, though, the Bible informs us that the Devil will stop all this charade. New Agers will then discover the frightening and unpleasant truth, and they will have to suffer the consequences of their rebellion against God.

Psychology: The Imagery Toolbox of the Devil

Psychology is therefore leading droves of men and women into the New Age camp. These victims often begin by innocently using the techniques recommended by psychiatrists and counselors, many of whom are labeled "Christian." One such individual teaches yoga relaxation and breathing techniques and exercises. Although this teacher may not realize the end result, such methods will put the patient or meditator into a trancelike state in which the mind will become susceptible to invasion by demons. Here's part of what this teacher tells his students to do, all under the guise of creating an image of "God" in the mind:

> Repeat this breathing exercise several times. Next, try to imagine God; keep searching in your mind (for however long it takes) to form an image of God. When the image is there, you will know it.
> Do not worry if this first exercise takes a long time.
> After the image is clear, focus on it for as long as you can.
> You may have to fine-tune it by focusing on each part of the image and visualizing yourself with that image.
> Eventually it will speak to you. . . .[10]

"Eventually it will speak to you," says this Christian meditation expert. What a chilling statement in light of Revelation 13:15, which prophesies that the Image of the Beast shall be made to speak!

This teacher advises that however long it takes, unfailingly the image of "God" will appear and speak. What will "God" look like when He finally does appear? We are told simply that we will know Him when He arrives as an image in our mind. Since, to the satanists, God is the horned devil and since the witches worship the Goddess, we assume that this "God" can come in any shape or form it wishes—sort of a "God" for all imaginations.

The New Age teaches that any time we desire, we can reach into the universal force-field and call up living images. All that's necessary is to use the right technique and they'll magically appear, speak, and act. To the New Ager, the image is real, and if it is perceived as the Master, the superior "God"—even the Beast in disguise—he will obey the Image of his Master:

We get what we *image* . . . if you can hold one image—to the exclusion of all other thoughts—for thirty-three and a third seconds, it will succeed in "sinking into your subconscious" and in due time it will manifest in your life.

It is valuable to learn how we can make our wishes come true, not for selfish, mundane reasons, but so that we can finally create and manifest . . . the MASTER IMAGE . . . so that you can at last be ONE WITH ALL OF LIFE . . . (part of) a mighty international organization. . . .[11]

Satanists today believe that they can, through imaging and visualization, energize or command demons to do their bidding. Likewise, New Age worshipers stress that through visualization, breathing exercises, positive imaging, and other techniques, they can summon their deities to come forth to serve them. New Agers believe that one's thought-power puts the energy force to work for them so that an image can come alive and act and speak. Foster Bailey puts it this way:

Through the right understanding of symbolic work certain creative energies can be brought into play. . . . A symbol is a precipitation or appearance on earth of that which is rooted in an inner cause. It is an outer effect of inner livingness.[12]

Norman Vincent Peale, the "father of positive thinking," and today an ardent and dedicated New Ager who believes in communication with the dead and occult visualization, has said:

Who is God? Some theological being? He is much greater than theology. . . . God is energy. As you breathe God in, as you visualize his energy, you will be reenergized.[13]

Contrary to this un-Biblical statement by Peale, God is not simply an energy force. He is a supremely powerful and sovereign being who lives independently from us. We cannot breathe Him in, nor "visualize his energy." That is far beyond our relatively puny human capabilities. These are just satanic concepts designed to deceive us into thinking we can use the powers of our own minds to create God in any image we choose. What New

Age man does not know is that once we begin to visualize and attempt to create a divine image to guide our lives, Satan steps in and conveniently provides us with the image *he* wants us to worship and obey. You are fooled into thinking *you* are in control while the Devil delightedly conforms your thought-patterns to his.

Man is designed by God to be a creature whose thinking is molded by successive images and symbols. We are counseled by God to continually think pure thoughts and ward off even the appearance of evil. Satan is well aware of the vulnerability of man's mind. This is why he and his agents work furiously to invade every facet of our lives with symbols that reflect his twisted thinking and with mind-warping images that mirror his own grotesque shape and form.

Allowing their minds to sink into the abyss of an altered state of consciousness through meditation, visualization, hypnotism, drugs, chanting, or other means, the New Ager turns over control of his brain to the Devil. Satan then sends the "Image of the Beast" into the opened-up, submissive mind. New Age leaders see this as a favorable event. It is called the opening of the chakra point—the ajna center—in the forehead. Christians know it as demon possession and bondage to the Devil.

How Satan Reprograms the Mind

With an elaborately orchestrated array of differing satanic images, Satan is able to completely *reprogram* a New Ager's mind. This reprogramming is variously termed Kundalini (serpent power), transformation, rebirth, cosmic consciousness, Christ-consciousness, shaktipat, attunement, or paradigm shift. Whatever it's called, it is a process by which Satan enters the mind and takes complete control. Afterwards, the person thinks like Satan and is eager to do his bidding. He is an indentured servant of a greater lord who keeps him captive through images used to control and direct his mind.

Joseph Chilton Pearce, psychologist and best-selling author of *Magical Child Matures,* a book prescribing how children and adults can reprogram themselves into the New Age, reports that the images that come to him as he meditates are vivid and profound in their effects.[14] He says that the Goddess of creation

(Shakti, a Hindu representative of the Babylonian Harlot) even comes to him, dancing in a delightful sensuality:

> Often in meditation, displays of imagery unfold in waves of interchanging patterns, three-dimensional, full of color, and breathtaking. The Shakti of creation dances before me, delighted to have a witness of her expertise. Geometric patterns and tapestries of exquisite movement occur.[15]

Satan clearly has the ability to paint exquisite and powerful images in the minds of his New Age followers. Often these images have a sexual connotation, which involves a goddess figure. Sometimes, the individual imagines he has sexual intercourse with the Goddess. (Women are also seduced by images which purport to be heroes or gods, or a soulmate from a past life.)

The Mother Goddess of Babylon was the image that pervaded Israel during the days of Ezekiel, Jeremiah, and the other prophets. Her image, physically through idolatry in the temples and mentally in the minds of her followers, was the "image of jealousy" that so angered God. His wrath fell upon the people of Israel (see Ezek. 8). Today the Goddess has returned; she lives as an unholy image in the minds of many New Agers.

Communion with the Mother Goddess

Whitley Strieber, author of Communion, was visited by the Babylonian goddess Ishtar in images given him by demonic entities. Not only did he have sexual relations with her, but, Strieber claimed, Ishtar and her demon companions were able to touch his head with a magic wand of some kind so that images began to swirl about in his mind. In effect, Strieber's mind was being programmed by these images.

> It's like there are huge, swirling . . . she's got something, she points it at me, it makes tremendous swirling pictures in my mind, of . . . I don't know what it's of. It's very . . . they're pictures of abstractions. Things fitted together. (Pause) I feel much calmer, much better. They're abstractions, like triangles

and circles and things. And they're fitted together in order. The triangle with the circle in it and the square comes around it and it moves all very smoothly, and it makes me feel better.

I recalled seeing a landscape floating in air . . . which on closer inspection proved to be a triangle. Then there followed a glut of symbolic material, so intense that even as I write I can feel how it hurt my whole brain and body to take it all in . . . triangles, rushing pyramids, animals leaping through the air.[16]

In Whitley Strieber's vision are all the classic signs of initiation with the Image and Mark of the Beast. His mind is radically changed as the swirling images make him "feel better." He views powerful symbols of evil—the triangle with a circle in it, combined with the square. The triangle is especially significant in its occult nature. The fact is, Strieber gave himself over to the Devil, as he himself implies in this key passage in which he describes his emotional upheaval and his loss of autonomy in the presence of the goddess:

Her gaze seemed capable of entering me deeply, and it was when I had looked directly into her eyes that I felt my first taste of profound unease. It was as if every vulnerable detail of my self were known to this being. Nobody in the world could know another human soul so well. . . . I could actually feel the presence of that other person within me—which was as disturbing as it was sensual. . . .

The realization that something was actually occurring within me because this person was looking at me—that she could apparently look into me—filled me with the deepest longing I can ever remember feeling . . . and with the deepest suspicion.

There was in her gaze an element that was so absolutely implacable that I had other feelings about her, too. In her presence I had no personal feelings at all. I could not speak, could not move as I wished. . . . If I could give up my autonomy to another, I might experience not only fear but *a deep sense of rest*. It would be a little like dying to really give oneself up in that way, and being with her was also a little like dying.[17]

Why was Whitley Strieber chosen to be victimized by Satan and fed these images that so totally engrossed and warped his mind? The answer is simple: Strieber himself *chose* to serve the Devil. He did so by rejecting Jesus Christ, and then dabbling in the occult. His fascination with satanic symbols was just one facet of his occult involvement. For example, Strieber remarked of his intense interest in the triangle:

> The (triangle) symbol is very ancient . . . and throughout much of human history was tremendously important. I have had a lifelong interest in it—really, an obsession. . . .[18]

Strieber's #1 bestseller, *Communion,* was said to be an account of his experiences of being abducted by UFO aliens, led by a goddess-like creature. However, Strieber himself has stated that he really doesn't understand just exactly what happened to him. He expresses a puzzling bewilderment.

I greatly pity this man, for if he had read and studied the Bible instead of the ancient occult literature he professes to have studied, he would know why *he* was chosen. Perhaps with God's grace and protection he would never have been chosen in the first place to have the images of Satan and the goddess religion implanted in his brain.

Certainly if he had the knowledge of Satan's devices and techniques, and had accepted Jesus as Lord, Strieber would have known that the voice of the goddess Ishtar that came to his wife in her sleep one night was not that of a goddess but a demon:

> One night in April (my wife) talked in her sleep. . . .
> Suddenly she said in a strange basso profundo voice: "the book must not frighten people. You should call it *Communion,* because that's what it's about."[19]

Unfortunately, the New Ager who has a mystical spiritual experience in which he sees in his mind satanic symbols and images does not believe these are of the Devil. It is not uncommon to hear a New Ager describe a vision of satanic imagery as being from "God." New Age doctrine teaches that Satan is nonexistent and is a creation of malicious Christian fundamentalists. Therefore, the New Age believer assumes that the images in his head come from energy forces—what Jung called the Collective Unconscious and others term the Universal Mind. To the New Ager, these energy forces outside him and within him are "God." His is a *God of Forces*.

The Complete Guide to Receiving the Mark

One of the most complete and comprehensive guides to the coming initiation of mankind and worship of the Image of the Beast is *The Keys of Enoch*. We must give Satan begrudging respect for the creation and publication of this advanced New Age action manual. Its exhaustive text gives us a detailed, step-by-step account and explanation of what the Image of the Beast is, how it will be made to speak and "live," and how it will be used to reprogram man's mind so he will love, worship, and obey the Antichrist who is the Beast. An examination of some of its key passages will demonstrate how thoroughly evil, yet revealing, is this New Age guide for the last days.

A *New Language of Light*

Demonic beings, called "Luminaries" and "intelligences" in *The Keys of Enoch*, are to assist Satan in bringing to mankind a "Language of Light." This language of light will be in the form of energy codes, or "keys," that create a picture or image directly in the minds of men and women in the New Age.

> Man is participating in the "great leap forward" with a host of other intelligences. . . .
>
> The keys . . . are the codes of the luminaries. . . . The creative mind of the Universe . . . speaks through luminaries.
>
> The keys . . . are given in the transmission of Living Energy Codes within the people of God. They are sent to reveal the codes of light . . . to code spiritual mankind into the fifth dimension . . . with a mutual programming.[20]

The Image Speaks

The Bible tells us that the Image of the Beast will actually speak as if alive. *The Keys of Enoch* states that as man listens to demonic beings who send him coded energy messages or light—through the "hook-up" of his mind to theirs—the image of light (the vehicle) that is created shall be able "to speak."

> A hook-up will take place between the spiritual forces. . . . Through this hook-up (the image) has the ability To Speak.
>
> How does a vehicle speak to us? Through light consciousness forms by means of polarized energy . . . the message it brings speaks of the Great Infinite Way and our role.[21]

The Image Is Sent by the Masters

The Keys of Enoch repeatedly emphasizes that the image (the code of energy knowledge) that materializes inside the New Age believer's mind, comes into focus and speaks to him, is sent by a Higher Intelligence and his helpers, who are described as "a small family of Masters":

> The codes of light extend through telethought communications. . . . You as a "believer" can receive . . . from a Higher Evolutionary Master Intelligence of Light . . . this transmission of knowledge.
>
> This energy was first brought into focus and dispatched to this planet by a small family of Masters who set up a domain in order to restore the fallen planetary consciousness to be in harmony with the Father's universe.[22]

Regrettably, the author(s) of The Keys of Enoch fail to confess that the "Father" whom this New Age Bible refers to is Satan, and his small family of Masters are all demons from hell. According to The Keys of Enoch, once you begin to receive and obey the "image" that is broadcast to you by the Father (Satan) and his Masters (demons), it will act as:

> A still "small voice" within the body which advises you on real day-to-day decisions in the world so that our consciousness will not err in executing the Father's will.[23]

This we can believe: that men and women who tune in to Satan's Image will be led by a demonic voice within that guides their daily activities with exquisite detail.

In the Beginning Was the Image

Twisting the words of Genesis, the writers of this demonic textbook instruct readers that the Word of God is a "light pictograph" (i.e., a picture made of light particles) that takes form and shape as real living things that become permanently etched in one's mind. Again and again we are told this—that the image is a thought picture or pattern of light that becomes real and is fixed in the New Age believer's mind:

> In the Beginning was the Word, but the beginning of the Word proceeded as a light pictograph and became form. . . . The light pictographs are thought-forms from the Higher Intelligence . . . patterns that can be retained by the spiritual mind.[24]

The Image Is Composed of Ideas and Knowledge in Graphic Form

"Enoch," the demon spirit who imitated the Enoch mentioned in the Bible and gave the New Age *The Keys of Enoch* through a human disciple, also used the terms *ideographic and cybernetic* to describe the Image of the Beast.[25] Ideographic means an *idea* displayed in *graphic* form or shape, and cybernetic indicates that the image conveys *knowledge* to the person who receives it in his mind. Furthermore, he explains that the pictures, or pictographs, come through a system of pulsating light waves sent directly from the Higher Intelligence (Satan) on the throne into the mind through the agni center, or chakra point, between and above the eyes on a person's forehead:

> Enoch told me the Language of the Throne works as instant communication . . . using ideographic and pictographic cybernetics. This is a language of symbols.
>
> Therefore the brain must be trained to handle complex ideographs and pictographs through a unique Light process which coordinates all the Chakra Centers.[26]

Again we see the consistency of doctrine among the many New Age leaders and their bibles. All speak of the agni or ajna center on the forehead as the transmitting and receiving point for images from beyond.

The Image Will Permanently Change You

We are told that the image is like a language—a language of symbols. The image that you receive into your mind will totally *change you*. Your thinking will go through a paradigm shift once you have the image firmly implanted in your mind. Satan's fire will be like a flaming torch that irreversibly burns an image into your brain.

> The fire letter calligraphy of the Language of Light alters the memory . . . affecting the psychological, neurological, biochemical and cosmological levels of thought-attunement. The knowledge of this language comes from a core memory of information being shared by the Higher Evolution.
>
> At this time you will use and communicate through your mind's eye in the flaming pictographs of life. No longer will the former things of human speech . . . be called to mind.[27]

After this radical, fiery transformation it will subsequently become easy to activate and reactivate in your mind the image the Higher Intelligence (Satan) has permanently placed there. With the pathways to your mind now wide open, anytime he wants he can send you new images:

> When the mind is activated, the brain can receive new ideographic [i.e. "living" holographic forms] and cybernetic geometrics of Light . . . which are made fully comprehensible . . . and . . . seeded into the mind of man.[28]

The Image Will Seal You

The fact that your mind is taken over and is being used by demonic forces means it has been *sealed*. Thereafter, you will continually receive messages from the Higher Intelligence (Satan) on how to carry out your role in the Plan. *The Keys of Enoch* tells us you will have become an anointed disciple carrying out divine instructions received from the Image in your head that lives and speaks:

> I was told by Enoch that "the Light pictographs" will seal the bodies that will be resurrected.
>
> Therefore I was told that those anointed through divine pictographs would receive their knowledge through pictographs of light. . . .[29]

The Image Is from Lucifer

Who is this Higher Intelligence that shall seal the minds of New Age disciples by sending them a "divine" Image? *The Keys of Enoch* names him "Metatron," which in ancient occult literature stands for none other than Lucifer, the Devil. Metatron is called the "Left Hand of the Father," a position in obvious opposition to Jesus who sits at the right hand of God.[30]

"Metatron" is simply a synonym for an evil entity who was known among the priests and priestesses of the wicked, ancient, pre-Christian Babylonian Mystery Religion. This is admitted to by indirect reference in *The Keys of Enoch:*

> Creation is thus united and brought together, having been "finally solemnized for eternity by Metatron." [Who is] The "Left Hand" of the Father.
>
> The sacred texts that are now being recovered will show a profound scientific meaning connected with the name "Metatron" in the pre-Syriac and pre-Coptic civilizations of the ancient Near East which understood Metacreation.[31]

Pre-Syriac and pre-Coptic refers to Babylon and its surrounding environs—Chaldea, Assyria, Sumeria, etc.

The Image Will Make You a "Christed" Soul

Thus, Lucifer will reward the "anointed" with his personal *seal.* As *The Keys of Enoch* explains it, when you are sealed you become a full-fledged citizen of the New Age Kingdom—you are received "into the image" of the new god species. Lucifer, as

"Metatron," remolds and renews your mind and soul so that you become a "super-species creation," a divine personality. You are, the book says, grafted into the "Tree of Life."[32] Thus you earn the high position of being your own Christ—you are a "Christ-ed" person, thanks to Lucifer:

> The souls are "Christed" and given the Metatronic seal so that they might be quickly purified and raised on high . . . like the Light Body of Enoch.[33]

As a "Christed" soul, you are thus given the name of your Master (the "name of the Beast") which is the "final seal":

> Metatron's name is used because He is the "final seal" for all the bodies of Light.[34]

All the World Shall Worship the Image

You will, of course, not be alone in receiving the seal of your new Master, and his name and image. Every person on the planet will be reprogrammed by the new image. Indeed, human language itself will become obsolete, replaced by the new images of light which will become the universal language. All men will thus be united in purpose. The Tower of Babel will have been rebuilt through the conquest and reshaping of men's minds by the images that proceed from the Beast:

> Human language will "eventually" be replaced by the language of light pictures.
>   . . . there will be a "conscious reprogramming" of mankind on this planet. . . .[35]

According to The Keys of Enoch, all this will take place in stages over the next fifteen years, culminating in the year 2004. The images in people's minds will revolutionize the globe. Men will be new creatures whose minds are filled with thoughts of love, peace, and unity. The New Jerusalem will have arrived. America will be the central site of world unity, the place where, sometime after the year 2004, a Higher Evolutionary Council of specially anointed supermen will meet and put the final touches on organizing the New Age World Religion and Government that shall prevail.[36]

The Higher Evolutionary Council will undoubtedly have as its head the New Age "Christ" who, in reality, will be the Beast or Antichrist prophesied in Revelation. This "Council" is the same group of evil men who are variously called the Council of Wise Men, the Spiritual Cabinet, and the Hierarchy by other New Age writers and leaders.

This elite circle of New Age dictators, under the personal direction of the New Age "Christ," will be led by the Image as their head to serve Satan's purposes. They will thus embark on a "divine" mission to destroy Christianity and to rid the world of Christian believers. Their inner "god"—the Image of the Beast who resides in their minds and who guides their every step—will easily persuade the New Age disciple that this is a holy thing he must do. The New Age Kingdom must be built. It's all part of the Plan.

PART THREE

Night Cometh

Marked for Extinction: A Death Sentence for Christians

Yea, the time cometh, that whosoever killeth you will think that he doeth God service. (John 16:2)

Death is not a disaster to be feared; the work of the Destroyer is not really cruel or undesirable. . . .
Therefore there is much destruction permitted by the Custodians of the Plan and much evil turned into good.
(Djwhal Khul,
The Tibetan Master)

Death, pain, bloodletting, chaos. Is this what lies just ahead for humanity? Is chaos and mass suffering inevitable to bring in a New Age of love, peace, and joy? The answer, according to the leaders of the New Age, is yes, this is what it will take for mankind to become godkind.

Dr. Christopher Hyatt predicts that the New Age will come to pass only after bloodletting and pain on a mass scale.[1] Djwhal Khul, Alice Bailey's "Tibetan Master," says that one-third of all humanity must die by the year 2000.[2] John Randolph Price was told by his spirit guide that up to two and one-half billion might perish in the coming chaos![3] Ruth Montgomery's books predict that turmoil and destruction will be visited on millions who will pass on into spirit.[4] Meanwhile, Maharishi Mahesh Yogi warns that "the unfit and ignorant won't survive."[5]

Now the Devil knows that as a Christian you are sealed by God and reserved by Him for eternity. Satan can't take this away from you. But, he sickly reasons, he *can* destroy your flesh. Once every Christian is removed from the earth, the Evil One can then have free rein to pillage, plunder, and rape the remaining inhabitants of this planet. That is his goal, his lustful objective. It is what drives him, motivates him, dooms him.

Given this inflamatory and menacing rhetoric by New Age leaders and demagogues, only a fool would deny that Satan has some terrible things in store for those who refuse to allow the Mark, the number, or name of the Beast to be indelibly etched on their hand or forehead.

His hunger and craving for total power and his sinister objective of establishing a One World Government and a One World Religion under his absolute leadership incites Lucifer to command his human disciples in the New Age to plot the destruction of every Christian man, woman, and child alive today. Make no mistake: Satan counts you and I as but lambs fit for slaughter. His eye rapturously feasts itself on the Throne. We are in the way. We are obstacles to his coronation as Planetary Monarch. We have to die.

The Bloodshed to Come

At this point you may be asking yourself, can Texe Marrs *really* mean what I have just read? Does Satan actually plan to physically destroy Christians and others who refuse his coming initiation into the New Age World Religion? Can this be so?

Does the New Age have specific plans for a coming era of purification, or cleansing, of the earth in which all Christians will be persecuted and murdered? The horrible truth staggers the imagination. New Age leaders, inspired by the denizens of hell, are preparing and steeling their followers for the arduous task that lies just ahead: the massive taking of human life believed necessary if a New Kingdom is to dawn on this planet.

In a recent issue of *Magical Blend,* a slick and popular New Age magazine financed by the Silva Mind Control System organization, Dr. Christopher Hyatt addressed what many New Agers call "the Christian Fundamentalist Problem." Labeling fundamentalists as "The Shadow emerging in society," he complained that the fundamentalists were "digging their heels into the ground" and attempting to "enforce its dogma." He predicted, however, that the fundamentalist forces will be overcome. There will be a "changing of the guards."[6]

Hyatt went on to reveal just how this "changing of the guards" will take place. "I see," he stressed, "that the Earth still requires some blood before it is ready to move into new and different areas."[7]

> The Guards of the Ancient era . . . the one dying right now . . . are not willing to give up their authority so easily. I foresee, on a mass scale, that the New Age is not going to come into being as so many people believe and wish to believe. I see it as requiring a heck of a lot of blood, disruption, chaos, and pain for a mass change to occur.[8]

Hyatt, author of the aptly named book *Undoing Yourself,* is head of the Golden Dawn Society and Temple, an occultic group that had its origins in 1887 in England. Initially called the Order of the Golden Dawn, this elitist society has over the years included in its membership some of the most renowned men in the world—for example, the Irish poet W. B. Yeats—as well as some very curious characters, such as Arthur Madras, the creator of *Dracula,* and occult author Dr. Israel Regardie.[9]

Bloodshed as a Cleansing Laxative

According to New Age religious doctrine, bloodshed will produce a purgative effect: a healing and cleansing of Mother Earth, much as a laxative cleans out and purges the human biosystem or a soothing rain heals a parched desert. Such a cleansing is said to be absolutely necessary for survival of both mankind and the planet:

> Your earth's immune system is now critically dysfunctional and it is not inaccurate to describe the consciousness of your earth as that of victim. Therefore, toward its own survival, the earth seeks a cleansing, a transformation into balance and health.[10]

In the New Age view, the cleansing and healing of Mother Earth involves the removal of all those who have a *negative consciousness*. Unity of all religious—even satanism and witchcraft—is *positive,* but to insist that Jesus is the *only way* to salvation is not only undesirable, it is dangerously *negative*. Christians are at a lower and inferior level of consciousness. They are an *inferior spiritual race.*

Spiritually inferior people, such as Christians, are said to send out negative thoughts unto the ethers of space which damage the earth's sensitive ecological system. The current planetary crisis can only be healed and transformed when negativity is finally vanquished and dissolved. "Crises," remarks one New Age teacher, are "the result of accumulated negative thought forms."[11]

Just how many "negative" Christians and other New Age unbelievers and skeptics will have to be removed from this life before a healing and cleansing—a purification—has taken place and a proper level of race consciousness has been achieved? Best-selling author Ruth Montgomery, considered the Herald of the New Age by many, says that her all-knowing spirit guides have given her this shocking revelation:

> Millions will survive and millions won't. Those who won't will go into the spirit state.[12]

Those who perish and pass on into spirit, according to Montgomery, are those of lower consciousness who cannot fit into the New Age Kingdom that is to arrive as we boldly move into the twenty-first century. The Age of Aquarius "will bring joy and happiness unexcelled since the days of the Atlantean era," she trumpets, but only those whose minds are "open to the reality of one world" will be around to enjoy it.[13]

She believes that one requirement will be that all who are to become citizens of the coming era of happiness and plenty must be willing to communicate with the dead. Only by cooperating with these wise and loving spirits from another dimension will man have instilled in him such values as "courage, compassion, love, and cooperation."[14]

True Christians will certainly never meet Montgomery's chief prerequisite for New Age citizenship. The Bible plainly brands communication with spirits, or necromancy, an abomination before the Lord (Deut. 18).

Another prerequisite for entrance into the supposedly glorious and imminent New Age Kingdom is to blasphemously claim that we, mere men and women, are divine gods. Indeed, John Randolph Price and many other New Age teachers insist that anyone who denies human divinity is not only unfit for New Age citizenship, but is *The Antichrist*. Price's definition of the Antichrist is simple:

Any individual or group who denies the divinity of man.[15]

Price, head of both the prestigious Planetary Commission and the Quartus Foundation, headquartered in Austin, Texas, on December 31 each year leads thousands of New Age churches, cults, groups, and organizations in the celebration of a World Healing Day (also called the World Instant of Cooperation and World Meditation Day). On this day, at 12:00 noon Greenwich mean time, hundreds of millions of New Agers and occultists from around the globe meditate simultaneously visualizing world peace and invoking their spirit guides, the Universal Force, or some other false deity to usher in the New Age Kingdom. The Planetary Commission reported that up to 500 million participated in this event in 1986, a mind-boggling 875 million in 1987.[16]

Will Two and One-half Billion People Be Slaughtered?

John Randolph Price says that his own spirit guide, whose name is Asher, has warned that if these annual world events do not magically succeed in "healing," "purifying," and "cleansing" the world, a great calamity will befall mankind. There will be rage and violent action, Asher confides, and the people who reject the New Age "will experience the greatest emotion of fear and panic." The horrible end result of all the casualties: *two and one-half billion men, women, and children will be killed.*[17]

This is how John Randolph Price recalls, in part, the remarkable meeting and conversation he had with the demon Asher, whom Price glowingly describes as an "Awakened One":

John: "In my imagination, I found myself on a high cliff standing about twenty yards from the precipice— talking to an Awakened One who called himself Asher. And I said, "You have the gift of prophecy. What do you see for our world? What is your vision of the future?"

Asher: "The mass consciousness must be stopped, or shall we say 'changed,' otherwise the cataclysm will occur. . . ."

John: "We can do it. I refuse to accept any idea that we can't clean up our mess. The race mind can be penetrated and its vibration changed through sufficient prayer and meditation. I know this with all my heart. Otherwise, the whole concept of the Planetary Commission is meaningless."

Asher: "Listen closely. Many changes will soon take place in the world. I am not referring to a climax resulting from man's inhumanity to man, at least not specifically. While this cruelty will seem to accelerate for a time, the major changes will take place through the force of nature as she seeks, by law, to reclaim her planet. . . . Is not order the first law of the universe? Order means balance, and nature is out of balance. She must regain her equilibrium. To do this she must eliminate the force of negative energy emanating from the race consciousness of man that is causing the imbalance—to relieve the pressure. In a way, you could say that nature will become a part of the Planetary Commission to heal the planet. . . ."

John: "You make it sound a little ominous. And I think you're forgetting about the effect that the World Healing Meditation will have on conditions. . . . I like to think that the building process will be done in peace and harmony, and that the activities of the Commission will result in a dramatic change for the good of all mankind."

Asher: "I will tell you what I see. Through the spiritual work of millions of people . . . there will be a uniting of spiritually minded people on the planet through a particular vibration in the ethers. The fusing of energies . . . will not eliminate all local hostilities. It will . . . revamp the concept of established 'religion and church,' and serve as a ring of protection for more than three billion people. That number represents those already on the spiritual path, in addition to those in the ascendancy toward a spiritual consciousness. . . ."

John: "But you've only covered slightly more than half of the world's population. What about the others?"

Asher: "Nature will soon enter her cleansing cycle. Those who reject the earth changes with an attitude of 'it can't happen here' will experience the greatest emotion of fear and panic, followed by rage and violent action. These individuals, with their lower vibratory rates, will be removed during the next two decades. Those who expect change and face it calmly with faith will move through it virtually untouched and will be the builders of the future. . . ."

John: "What I am hearing is both horrible and hopeful. I know that one of the most serious problems we have today is overpopulation, but wiping out more than 2-billion people off the face of the earth is a little drastic, don't you think? . . ."

Asher: "I can only tell you what I see at the present time. I might add . . . who are we to say that those people did not volunteer to be a part of the destruction . . . and regeneration—for the purpose of soul growth? Never forget that each individual has free will and free choice."[18]

Alice Bailey's spirit guide, Djwhal Khul, concurs with Asher, his demonic associate, in sounding the dark threat that billions who refuse to bow to the New Age gods will be massacred in the near future. Khul puts forth the doctrine that due to their racial inferiority—their spiritual deficiencies—a full one-third of mankind will be removed from the earth by the year 2000. As the majority vault into an entire new dimension, a glittering, radiant, and terrific world of divine man, this one-third will simply vanish.[19] This would mean about *two and one-half billion* to be slain, given global population estimates of 7.5 billion for the year A.D. 2000.

Where will the missing two and one-half billion people have gone? They'll be physically dead. But New Age leaders and demons protest that this isn't so bad. Physical death isn't final, not if you believe in reincarnation and rebirth. Djwhal Khul maintains that the dead will be held back in another world or dimension where, after they are chastened and reeducated, they will be reincarnated and thus continue to work out their karma and their own evolutionary destiny. Meanwhile, here on earth the World Teacher, the New Age "Christ," his Hierarchy, and the New Age masses will go about the business of setting up the Kingdom:

> The objective of the new social order, of the new politics, and the new religion is . . . to bring in the rule of the Kingdom. . . .[20]

Djwhal Khul reveals that this task, the Great Work as he calls it, is in fact already under way, being the duty of two important groups of New Agers: *thinkers* and *servers*. The average New Age believer is among *the thinkers of the world,* while the more exalted, elite clique of men are known as the *New Group of World Servers.*[21] Khul tells us that the latter group are sort of the royalty, the rulers of tomorrow's New Age global empire. Even today these chosen leaders are working diligently, often behind the scenes, to usher in the New Era:

> These are the people who are beginning to form a New Social Order in the world. . . . They are occupied with the task of inaugurating the New World Order, by forming throughout the world—in every nation, city and town—a grouping of people who . . . stand upon the essential divinity of Man.[22]

David Spangler, often praised as the architect of the modern phase of the New Age revolution, concurs with Djwah Khul's desire to have Christians disappear off the face of the earth. He proposes: "These ones could be withdrawn into an inner realm that would be their home," while the higher consciousness New Agers would be active on Planet Earth "building the new world."[23] Then, twisting Scripture unmercifully, he adds:

> There is a suggestion of this in the Bible when it speaks of Satan and his minions . . . being bound for a thousand years.[24]

What the diabolic Spangler is doing is threatening Christians with the same fate that God has prepared for Satan and his ungodly followers. If nothing else should awaken sleeping Christians to the dangers of the New Age, *this should!*

Some New Age leaders threaten Christians in an indirect, yet more sinister and deceitful manner. Matthew Fox, a heretical Catholic priest, nature worshiper, and witchcraft advocate whose influence continues to grow among New Age intellectuals, has announced that once the earth has been transformed into a New Age paradise, its *four billion* inhabitants will become "individualized prophets," blossoming from the divine seed they are to total godhood.[25] The only problem with this is that the world's population is already now at the *five and one-half billion* mark!

A man as shrewd as his name, Matthew Fox silently and slyly erases one and one-half billion people from existence! We can only conclude that this is a prime example of New Age-type positive thinking. To *mention* the horrors that might be perpetrated to reduce the world's population by hundreds of millions would be—in the New Age view—unwholesome; it would be negative thinking. This type of positive thinking and positive confession fits in well with the Devil's message of "think no evil, see no evil, hear no evil." Tragically, it reminds us of the Germans who blithely and uncaringly went about their daily lives in such towns as Buchenwald while the cattle trains brought in human cargo and the smell of human flesh wafted in the air from the ovens of the Nazi concentration camp nearby. After the war, most of the townspeople insisted they hadn't a clue to what was happening right in their midst.

The New Age Race Theory

It is inevitable that New Age leaders and disciples demonstrate hostility and a finely tuned animosity toward Christians. Satan's agents have put forth the poisonous doctrine that all of mankind is divided into six different spiritual races. The highest two in consciousness—the superior races—are the Aryan and the Aquarian. Every New Ager seeks through a spiritual quest, or initiation, to be elevated—transformed—in consciousness to the superior Aquarian Root Race. At this exalted level, the initiate supposedly becomes a god, able to exercise divine mental powers. All the powers of the universe are made accessible to the superhuman who has achieved racial superiority as a proud collective member of a unique human species: *homo noeticus* (new man), or *homo universalis* (planetary being).[26]

What prevents a New Age man or woman from ascending to this highly coveted, godlike state? Christians, with their negative thinking, their sin of separativeness, are the stumbling-blocks. Christians are pictured as the culprits whose negative mind powers prevent others from assuming divine powers greater than those even the Greek mythological gods possessed.

New Age teachers have also proclaimed that it is the *bad karma* of Christian fundamentalists that is holding the whole world back from a glorious *Planetary Initiation*. All of humanity would instantly be transformed into "christed" beings (gods) if only all Christian "thought forms" were eliminated and their karmic debt paid through their death and suffering. Bodily and spiritually remove all the Christians from the planet and—presto!—universal godhood![27]

Christians as Cancer Cells on the Body of Humanity

New Age leaders have described those of us who reject New Age teachings as something akin to cancer cells, as poisonous substances, even as waste materials. We are racial rejects and bad apples that ruin the whole barrel of humanity.

New Age "prophets" F. Homer Curtiss and Harriette Curtiss, founders of the Order of Christian Mystics and authors of a multitude of New Age, occult, and Mystery Religion books, some years ago contended that mankind is "standing before the mighty portals, waiting for the curtain of time to rise on the

New Age wherein wonders . . . will seem commonplace."[28] All that's necessary for man to begin to manifest such wonders, they emphasized, is for an "elimination" of certain "unhealthy" (e.g., Christian) elements:

> The fetus of the New Humanity is already stirring in the Womb of Time and, like the human mother, humanity must learn to eliminate its waste materials and poisons and give the fetus proper nourishment or the life of both the child and the mother will be endangered. . . . This is the work of the present transitory conditions.[29]

Djwhal Khul, the demon chieftain who has through his human protegé Alice Bailey of the Lucis Trust in New York City given the New Age a collection of over a dozen unholy "bibles," also sees Christians as a dangerously unhealthy blot on humanity:

> A violent streptococcic germ and infection . . . makes its presence felt in infected areas in the body of humanity. Another surgical operation may be necessary . . . to dissipate the infection and get rid of the fever. . . . Let us never forget . . . that when a (life) form proves inadequate, or too diseased, or too crippled . . . it is—from the point of view of the Hierarchy—no disaster when that form has to go.[30]

What does Djwhal Khul mean when he says that those human germs and infections who are inadequate, too diseased, or too crippled have "to go"? Simply that they must die. The Hierarchy (Satan and his demons) are of the "point of view" that such people must be killed. But, astonishing as it may seem to the logical mind, Khul goes on to assert that the massacre of such lowly human "germs" will be a "good," even holy, act perfectly in keeping with The Plan. After all, he reasons that:

> Death is not a disaster to be feared; the Work of the Destroyer is not really cruel or undesirable. . . . Therefore there is much destruction permitted by the Custodians of the Plan and much evil turned into good.[31]

According to New Age theology, which is nothing more than the lie of Satan, a violent death can be cleansing and purging for the soul. It can mercifully wash out the karmic debt built up by a person from this and previous lives or incarnations. Following the necessary suffering and death, the individual can then be instructed of his spiritual failings and shortcomings by the Masters in the spirit world beyond. Properly instructed and trained, the person can then be reincarnated into a new body and assume a much more happy and joyous existence as a New Age member of society.

In this distorted view, to kill a Christian is to provide him or her a valuable service. Such a deed is also useful to humanity since it hastens the coming of the New Age Kingdom when men will be gods. New Age authorities teach that it is also a necessary and justifiable act that "God," the universal force, would smile upon.

In fact, the God of Forces (Satan) *will* be pleased, for he passionately hates men and women who love the real God of this universe.

The Prophecy of Jesus Christ

This frightening and belligerent yet self-righteous New Age doctrine that would justify the mass murder of Christians will bring to fulfillment the momentous prophecy of Jesus. Christ soberly warned His disciples:

> If the world hate you, ye know that it hated me before it hated you. If ye were of the world, the world would love its own; but because ye are not of the world, but I have chosen you out of the world, therefore the world hateth you. (John 15:18, 19)

> Remember the word that I said unto you, The servant is not greater than his lord. If they have persecuted me, they will also persecute you. (John 15:20)

> But this cometh to pass, that the word might be fulfilled that is written in their law, They hated me without a cause. (John 15:25)

> . . . yea, the time cometh, that whosoever killeth you will think that he doeth God service. (John 16:2)

Read that last verse again and again until the horrible gravity of its meaning seeps in: "Yea, the time cometh, that whosoever killeth you will think that he doeth God service." The awful truth is that Lucifer has so possessed and manipulated the minds of many New Age leaders and followers that they eagerly desire to do their "God" a service. The false love that is today a cardinal teaching of the New Age will ultimately be its prime justification for this supreme act of obedience to the dark controlling powers: They will kill the Christian for his own good and for the good of humanity, but *most of all because they "love"* *him so much*. They will kill him to do a service.

Killing Christians a Holy Act

The New Age teaches that the removal and physical destruction of all Christians will be a *holy act*. This is carefully and elaborately explained in a key New Age bible called *The Keys of Enoch*. First published in 1978 by a group calling itself the Academy of Future Science, this incredibly revealing text—618 pages in length—describes the wrath that will befall those who, in the last days, refuse to embrace the New Age religion and its gods. It speaks of a "great cleansing" to take place as the earth is advanced to the New Age, an era in which our planet will enjoy "a higher orbital frequency."[32]

The death and passing from the scenes of the unbelievers in the New Age will open the earth up for a higher "spiritual frequency." This higher frequency will, in turn, allow a "New Communion" to occur as the higher angelic beings (Christians call them "demons") join and merge with the holier race of humans, who have become gods.[33] All this is supposedly to transpire around the year 2005, following a series of wars between the forces of good (New Age) and evil (Christians).

> And it will occur after the wars between the Sons of Light versus the Sons of Darkness that a "New Age" will occur for all mankind surviving the great changes among all the vicissitudes of this planet.[34]

Who are the "Sons of Darkness?" This can only mean the Christian believers, whom many in the New Age profess to be the Antichrist.

Not surprisingly, *The Keys of Enoch* teaches that the Antichrist is not a man (Revelation 13 says he *is* to be a man). Instead, he is said to be the collective spirit of all those who stick to the "contaminated" man-made doctrines of Christianity and who teach against the "Living Word" given by New Age religious leaders. This "Living Word" is said to consist of new "mystery texts" to be revealed later, as well as the Dead Sea Scrolls. These new mystery texts, or "Sacred Scriptures," shall be brought to man by interplanetary messengers who will reveal them only to the New Age "Sons of Light."[35]

If we are to believe *The Keys of Enoch,* the Holy Bible of the Christians, the true Word of God, is in fact the "abomination that maketh desolate" (Matt. 24:15; Mark 13:14; Dan. 11:31). It must be abolished and replaced by the new mystery texts and other New Age scriptures. But this can only be accomplished once the Christian and his Bible are absent from the earth.

What, then, will become of the slaughtered Christians? According to *The Keys of Enoch,* they will not really die. As the righteous, New Age race moves upward to a higher evolutionary plane—a new, more advanced world of peace and joy where they will receive glorified bodies of light—the lower beings who refused the New Age doctrines and who as a result suffered death will simply return to the primeval earth and begin the reincarnation process all over again.[36]

Only the "Elect" are fit for the new world of higher evolution, say the New Age occultic authors of *The Keys of Enoch.* And *who are* the Elect? "The Elect are 'the people of the Plan.' "[37] This is the same Plan exposed in my book *Dark Secrets of the New Age*—the repugnant, thirteen-point Plan of Satan to bring in a One World Order in which he and his legions of demonic beings, aided by human disciples, rule Planet Earth with iron fists and supernatural terror.

Soldiers of Darkness

Peace I leave with you, my peace I give unto you.
(John 14:27)

*Yes, the call is out for World Warriors. . . . Similar to
the blue bereted U.N. peacekeeping soldiers . . . their
perimeters are the globe.* (Donald Keys,
Earth at Omega)

*This special group, in training now, is the spiritual
shock troop of the coming Aquarian Age.* (Foster Bailey,
Things to Come)

Revelation 13 prophesies that the Antichrist will exercise total power over all who dwell upon the earth. He will have authority to require all to take his Mark and to order the arrest and death of any who will not worship his Image. Absolute dictatorial powers will require him to have an army of fanatical supporters willing to carry out his orders. Even willing to kill in his name. He will need to organize a massive Army of Evil.

New Agers are already eagerly and enthusiastically enlisting in this Army of Evil. The signs of this are everywhere. Lord Maitreya, the shadowy figure known by many New Agers as their "Christ" or Messiah, has repeatedly sounded the trumpet for his followers to become more militant and belligerent. Through his human voice, Benjamin Creme, Lord Maitreya has arrogantly crowed:

The time of My Emergence has arrived; and soon now, in full vision and fact, My Face and Words will become known.

167

May you be among those who quickly find and recognize Me, for, if you do, you may become My Warriors.

My Army is now on the move and soon the clash of battle will be heard. The outcome of this battle is assured, for at my side are True Sons of God.

Take your places in the ranks of My Army, My friends, and create the New Time, the Time of God.[1]

This false Messiah of the New Age has also declared:

My Army of Light is assembled, is ready. Banners flying, eyes uplifted, they march forward into the future, into the Light which beckons, and in that Light shall they see Light.

My Army is on the move, is marching bravely into the future.

Join those who already fight on the side of Light, on the side of Truth, of Freedom and Justice. Join my Vanguard and show the way for your brothers.[2]

The sad truth is that these are drumbeats of discord that will inspire his New Age followers to march with Lord Maitreya to oblivion. Like lemmings marching bravely into the sea, in the days ahead many New Agers will prove obedient to their commander-in-chief, the lying demon whose alias is Lord Maitreya. Read carefully the pronouncements of this cunning creature from hell, and note how this Lord Maitreya cleverly conceals his hidden intent. He speaks of the Plan of his demonic associates, the Masters of Wisdom, whom he says are godlike entities inhabiting the unseen spirit world of "Shamballa":

My Army of Light is on the march and soon the Great Battle will have begun. My People are preparing My Way and will show you My Plan. My Masters of Wisdom are now assembling Their various groups and soon the world will know that I am here. My Army has laid its plans and soon will follow results. Already the signs of change are appearing, the clouds are lifting, and a new hope seizes mankind.[3]

Benjamin Creme, articulate head of the Tara Center, the group headquartered in North Hollywood, California, and London, England, that is promoting this false "Christ," says that *Jesus Himself worships and serves the Lord Maitreya.*[4] He further declares that very soon every man and woman will serve this New Age "Messiah." For now only his New Age disciples hear his voice and join his Army and fight for his cause. Soon you and I must do likewise.[5]

Killing as an Act of Patriotism

But in *whose* service do these New Agers eagerly march and fight? Is theirs a heavenly call? Or is it Satan, the Lord of This World, whom they serve? Lord Maitreya reveals the answers:

> Will you take part in this great work and fulfill the world's need? There is no higher call than that to serve the world.[6]

The "Great Battle" that Lord Maitreya refers to has indeed commenced. But it is a conflict in which New Age soldiers serve *the world* and not God. Their cause is worldly. Their field general and his officer corps, Lord Maitreya and the Masters of Wisdom, are worldly. Jesus, who told Pilate, "My Kingdom is not of this world," also declared that His people, His followers, hear *His* call and obey. His call is heard as a soft but insistent voice straight to the heart, delivered special delivery from heaven above. Only those born again in Jesus Christ can hear it.

The militaristic spirit being stirred inside the breasts of New Agers will some day explode into cascading torrents of anger and acts of cruelty. The Army of Evil, whipped into a spiritual frenzy by the inflammatory lies of the New Age Beast, will strike out at Christians who stand with Jesus Christ to oppose the One World Order and Religion of the New Age. The New Age warriors of the rainbow will serve under the Lord of This World (John 14:30). In killing Christian resisters, they will think they are doing their god a service, just as the Nazi guards of Germany's concentration camps thought they were doing their master a service.

Someday it will be viewed as a patriotic act of the global citizen to shed the blood of Christian believers. This view is already being shaped. Listen to this message of a demon spirit who came under the mysterious names "The Old Man of the

Hills" and "Orion," which was delivered as a patriotic address to the followers of Elizabeth Clare Prophet's Church Universal and Triumphant:

> I am a devotee of freedom and I am proud to be called a patriot of life! Patriots, I summon you in the service of the light. . . . In my house, my house of light, you will find mementos of patriots of freedom who in every nation have won for the cause of the Great White Brotherhood some noble gain for the Aquarian cycle, for the master of freedom, and for the soul of humanity.[7]

Orion's "Great White Brotherhood" is none other than Lord Maitreya's "Hierarchy": demons whose residence is hell and who wander hungrily throughout the earth seeking whom they might devour. Their cause is Satan's cause; whatever gain their "patriotic" human counterparts achieve is Satan's gain. Throughout the centuries, from the days of the early Christian church of the apostles, such worldly "patriots" have spilled the blood of Jesus' martyrs.

Orion admits that his master is the "Lord of the World," whom he further identifies as "Sanat Kumara," the code name New Agers use for their lord and master, Lucifer.[8]

The Cosmic Secret Service

It is common for New Age leaders and the spirits they call up to speak in riddles, to use secretive code names, undecipherable acronyms, and cryptic phrases. Theirs is a Mystery Religion, and they relish things occultic and hidden. Their underworld master has taught them that they can best accomplish their and his goals by veiling and masking his intentions. Amazingly, one of Satan's demons, quoted extensively in Elizabeth Clare Prophet's book *The Great White Brotherhood*, even claims he is a member of a shadowy spirit-world group called the *Cosmic Secret Service*.[9] Could there really be such a demonic group working behind-the-scenes? Before we too quickly dismiss the claims of this demonic spirit, we should first consider these unassailable facts:

(1) The Bible tells us that Satan *does* have a well-defined, hierarchical organization (see Ephesians 6:12 and Daniel 10:12, 13) and operates through deception and fraud (see 2 Timothy 3:13 and 2 Corinthians 11:14, 15).

(2) New Agers readily believe such claims. Elizabeth Clare Prophet has built an international organization that reportedly has over 300,000 devoted but deluded followers. She annually takes in millions of dollars, operates a national TV "ministry," and publishes books that sell in the hundreds of thousands of copies each.

(3) The successful "ministry" of Elizabeth Clare Prophet is a classic example of how the coming Antichrist will be able to easily manipulate and control men's minds. Mesmerizing and entrancing her large audience with chants, affirmations and sermons given with a hypnotic cadence, she has demonstrated the ability to induce fanatical loyalty and obedience. She readily admits and boasts of constant contact with such dead luminaries as a mysterious medieval mystic dubbed Count Saint Germain, a character titled Lanello, supposedly of King Arthur's mythical court, an oriental mystic named Koothumi, the Virgin Mother Mary, and countless other Ascended-Master, spirit-god entities. Yet, her many supporters are convinced that her accounts are genuine.

The self-proclaimed "Ascended Master" whom Prophet claims serves in the Cosmic Secret Service has assumed the code name "K-17." His true identity as a demon from hell is only thinly disguised as he announces the reason for his coming. Note his remark that he comes with "legions" of others like him:

> I come as a representative of the Cosmic Secret Service. . . .
> With me also I bring legions of the Cosmic Secret Service,
> those who have walked the earth among mankind as you do
> now . . . and who have the fervor of sacred fire and of the
> cosmic honor flame, who carry scepters of authority—for
> they have won their battles of light . . . behind the scenes in
> the governments of the nations.[10]

If Satan's secret agent K-17 is to be believed, his demonic coworkers—transformed into angels of light—keep tabs on the enemy. Which enemy? Obviously Christians who oppose their master:

> Also with me are angels of light, angels who guard the secret destiny of every nation, the destiny of America and the destiny of a soul! These angels carry with them notations in their notebooks of all those forces and forcefields that are . . . against the raising of the feminine ray in this age.[11]

In speaking of the raising of the "feminine ray in this age," K-17 refers to MYSTERY, BABYLON THE GREAT, THE MOTHER OF HARLOTS AND ABOMINATIONS OF THE EARTH. This is the last-days, worldwide Church of Satan prophesied in Revelation 17. Thus K-17 stresses that America's destiny is to exalt the "Divine Woman," the Mother Goddess, and thus bring in a "golden age of God-government."[12]

This lying demon attempts to turn black into white by proclaiming that he and his ilk fight the opposing tide of darkness. He predicts the "victory of the seed" of the "Divine Woman" so that her people can live in liberty, free of those who oppose *her* religion. Ominously he forecasts the imminent arrival of "the one who comes riding upon the white horse."[13] This is undoubtedly a reference to the first horseman of the Apocalypse (Rev. 6) who comes disguised as a man of peace but is quickly followed by death and hell. The rider of this white horse will be the Antichrist come to deceive by bringing an illusory peace.

K-17 also asserts that he and his legions come carrying the weapon of the "all-seeing eye of God," a term describing the all-seeing eye of Horus the Sun God, the Son of the Harlot, the Mother Goddess of Babylon and Egypt.[14]

Like so many other demons who have come to rouse and inspire the millions of New Age disciples to bloodshed and violence, K-17 calls on New Agers to join his "spiritual army" and to sacrifice their very lives for the joint cause. With demonic and deceitful patriotic fervor, he cries out:

> There is a shadow across America this day . . . the call goes forth. Who will give the answer? Who will say: "I am here to defend liberty no matter what the price! I will pay with . . . the blood of my life!" Sons and daughters of liberty, we are

so close and so One—our legions with your own. We mingle with you; we walk beside you.[15]

What an incredible statement! A cry by a Satanic underling directly to tens of thousands of hopelessly deluded New Agers. The signs are all there. For example, the statement that K-17 and his legions are "One" with their human followers clearly alludes to demonic possession and guidance of New Agers. Any Christian man or woman with a true spirit of discernment can only shudder to think of so many who read and yet do not understand when this demon utters the frightening words, "We mingle with you; we walk beside you."

Answering the Call

Hundreds of New Age leaders have answered the clarion call of their demon overlords. Don Keyes, a United Nations lobbyist, top official with Planetary Citizens, and a coauthor of the New Age manifesto for the future entitled "Planetary Initiative for the World We Choose," is just one of the many who is eagerly and boldly pushing his followers to activism. In his best-selling *Earth at Omega*, he encourages readers to help "planetize the earth," declaring:

> We are already in the midst of the final planetary revolution—the final stages of human organization on Planet Earth. . . . To cross over the threshold and enter a world of new and exciting promise requires us to fulfill the tasks immediately before us. . . .
> You can . . . become a Steward of Earth, a Midwife of the New Era, a Warrior for Peace and humane change, or a White Water River Rafter Guide, taking us through the rapids of global transition.[16]

But what does a Steward of Earth, a Midwife of the New Era, a Warrior for Peace *do* to help bring in a New Age Kingdom on Planet Earth? Keyes is convinced that transformed New Age disciples must become militant "change agents"—warriors who, like martial arts warriors of old, will protect New Age society against chaos and marauders:

Yes, the call is out for World Warriors. . . . Our World
Warriors will have no foes except separatism, selfishness and
ignorance. Similar to the blue bereted U.N. peacekeeping
soldiers . . . their perimeters are the globe.[17]

Don Keyes teaches his followers that as World Warriors they
must acquire "the right use of power as a higher calling."[18] But a
higher calling from whom? Keyes provides the answer: New Age
warriors must keep in mind "that the first aspect of the Deity
(Lord Shiva) or the first person of the Holy Trinity (the Father) is
the Lord of *power,* will and purpose."[19] So we find Keyes, one of
the New Age's most highly respected political statesmen, blasphemously promoting a false god—the Hindu deity Shiva—and
an unholy trinity. (The Hindu trinity is composed of a Mother
Goddess—who originated from the Babylonian deity described
in Revelation 17, a Father God, and their God-Son.)

"The power" that Keyes wants New Agers to wield on a
global basis is in reality the *power of darkness.* The Hindu deity
Lord Shiva is literally known in India as "the Destroyer," the
"God of Destruction," and the "God of Chaos."[20]

This same God of Destruction is worshiped by the leaders of
New York's prominent New Age occult group, the Lucis Trust
(formerly Lucifer Publishing). To the leaders of the Lucis Trust,
he comes under the code name Sanat Kumara. Djwhal Khul, the
Tibetan Master and spirit guide who has dictated so many books
to the Lucis Trust's Alice A. Bailey, says that he is a servant of
Sanat. Understandably, then, Khul is scornful of Christianity and
of Jesus Christ. His Plan is for a new type of "Christ," the
coming World Teacher, who will organize the New Age World
Religion based not on God but on the human spirit. His "Christ"
is Lord Maitreya, the same one Benjamin Creme and the Tara
Center worship.[21]

Both Djwhal Khul and Benjamin Creme believe that Lord
Maitreya is a powerful, reincarnated god-man who represents
Sanat Kumara. Lord Maitreya is the "Christ" of the Aquarian
Age, who will reign over the earth while a greater god whom he
serves, Sanat Kumara, pulls the strings behind the scenes. Maitreya's assignment is to marshal the forces of destruction, to
direct the World Warriors of Don Keyes, to field a combined

human and demon Army. The mission of this Army will be, first, to attack and conquer God's people on earth, the born-again Christians, and second, to go up directly against God.

We Want Your Bodies

So we see that already the New Age's drum and bugle corps is sounding the call for disciples to get in formation and line up behind the New Age "Christ" and his field commanders. They are urged to join the "team" and fight for the Plan:

> We are a Team, a United Team working together. . . .
> Organize groups and come together . . . for personal and
> planetary awakening. Realize there is a larger "Plan."[22]

New Age author Neil Cohen's spirit guide tells him that this Plan emanates from a "Beloved and Radiant One," otherwise unidentified. Evidently this "Beloved and Radiant One" needs the expendable flesh-and-blood bodies of human beings to carry out his Plan.[23] "Helios," a demon who in *The Quartus Report* blasphemously claimed to be the "Solar Logos" (Word), waxed chummy when he confided: "What you must understand, Dear Hearts, is that God needs a body. . . . He must be channeled through a physical body."[24]

Since the Bible records that the true God is so powerful and majestic He merely *spoke* the entire universe into existence, we can safely conclude that Helios and the other false deities now communicating with the physical world are of the Devil. God certainly does not need the bodies of mortal beings to bring in His millennial Kingdom. Instead, he instructs Christians to go forth and *preach His gospel to all the earth.* Revelation 19 tells us that Jesus Christ, the one true God, will someday personally descend from the clouds with a Heavenly Army to defeat the Evil One and restore sanity and righteousness to the planet.

The New Age Army of God's adversary, the Devil, will be smashed into oblivion upon Jesus' return. It is this New Age Army whose membership is now being carefully cultivated and recruited by Satan. The Devil, through his earthly human re-cruiters, has even composed an Oath of Office to which many of his new recruits swear upon enlistment. This Oath of Office takes either of two forms, THE GREAT INVOCATION or the WORLD HEALING MEDITATION.

The Great Invocation

The Lucis Trust has been pushing THE GREAT INVOCATION for decades. Many other New Age groups and churches have adopted it. Possibly millions around the globe now recite and meditate daily on its three lengthy stanzas. Worse, pastors of a number of mainline Protestant churches have recommended it to their congregations. This is a sure sign that the great apostasy is in progress because this occult meditation is nothing less than an invitation to Lucifer to come forth from his hiding place, savage the world, and set up his unholy kingdom. Consider just these few shadowy lines from THE GREAT INVOCATION:

> Let the Forces of Light bring illumination to mankind. . . .
> Let power attend the efforts of the Great Ones.
> So let it be, and help us to do our part.
>
> Let the Lord of Liberation issue forth. . . .
> Let the Rider from the Secret Place come forth, and coming, save.
> Come forth, O mighty One. . . .
>
> Let Light and Love and Power and Death
> Fulfill the purpose of the Coming One. . . .
>
> Let purpose guide the little wills of men—
> The purpose which the Masters know and serve. . . .
>
> From the centre which we call the race of men
> Let the Plan of Love and Light work out
> And may it seal the door where evil dwells.
>
> Let Light and Love and Power restore the Plan on Earth.[25]

The demon Djwahl Khul told Alice Bailey that he gave this meditation out to the world *under instruction from the New Age "Christ" who resides on Shamballa with his spirit helpers, the*

Hierarchy. In reciting and visualizing its content, the individual meditating is, Khul notes, invoking this "Christ" other than Jesus to appear.[26]

Knowing their source and their true meaning, how grotesque then are the words of this evil meditation—words such as "Forces" and "Power," "Coming One," "Rider from the Secret Place," "Masters," and the "Plan."

World Healing Meditation

Equally revolting to Christian senses are the blasphemous phrases we find in the WORLD HEALING MEDITATION. Sponsored by the Planetary Commission, this meditation is a combination invocation and affirmation. First the user calls upon the "One Presence and Power of the Universe," invoking that oneness be restored to the world and decreeing that mankind be returned to "Godkind." Affirmations include the following selfish and un-Scriptural assertions of human divinity:

I begin with me.

I am a living soul and the spirit of God dwells in me, *as me.*

I and the Father are one, and all that the Father has is mine.

In Truth, *I am the Christ of God.*[27]

The last line of this rather lengthy meditation is a command similar to that used to conclude spells in witchcraft: a magical "It is done. And it is so."

Each year on December 31, tens of millions pray and meditate in unison using the WORLD HEALING MEDITATION. The Planetary Commission reported that a staggering total of 875 million people participated in 1987 alone!

John Randolph Price says he has been told by Asher, his powerful spirit guide, that if enough people participate in the WORLD HEALING DAY events and use the WORLD HEALING MEDITATION, the world can be healed. But if enough people do not participate, the planet will be plunged into a severe period of destruction and chaos. The earth will be healed and cleansed through this destructive process, but up to two and one-half billion people—all New Age unbelievers—will have been removed.[28]

Asher's threat reminds us of Hitler's "final solution" to the "Jewish problem." Hitler first came up with an early plan to deport all Jews to the Island of Madagascar in the Indian Ocean. When that plan ran aground, Hitler was asked what to do next: "I have other thoughts now, less friendly," replied the German Führer.[29]

Asher's warning to Price that The Planetary Commission must succeed in its ambitious quest to convert humanity . . . or else should set off an alarm in the minds of men. They should now realize that they must make a choice to serve under one or the other: either the Great Commission of Jesus Christ *or* the Planetary Commission of the Devil. There is no room for indecision. Every person must choose whom they will serve.

The New Age Subversion of the U.S. Armed Forces

At first glance it may seem facetious to compare the stanzas of THE GREAT INVOCATION and THE WORLD HEALING MEDITATION with the Oath of Office administered to the young men and women who embark on military duty in the U.S. Armed Forces. But look again. The New Age has infiltrated the U.S. Army, Navy, and Air Force in a big, big way.

Officials at the Pentagon have used that facility to conduct meditation services and even to participate in the Planetary Commission's WORLD HEALING MEDITATION.

On November 5, 1987, the International Affairs Division, Office of the Vice Chief of Staff of the Department of the Air Force reserved Room 5B1062 in the Pentagon for the "World-wide Healing Meditation service to be held on 31 December 1987." The Pentagon Meditation Club then issued the following bulletin: "At noon Greenwich time, December 31, 1987 (7:00 a.m. EST), military and civilians at the Pentagon will join with people in more than 100 countries praying and meditating for world peace in the second annual World Healing Day. This activity at the Pentagon is part of the Pentagon Meditation Club's Spiritual Defense Initiative (SDI).

"Every day in the Pentagon military and civilians meditate to produce the 'Peace Shield Effect.' Edward Winchester, Club President, explains that meditation produces a transformation in the energy field radiating from the human body, often referred to as the 'aura' or 'halo.' With a small biofeedback device, the Cameron aurameter, he demonstrates for Pentagon personnel the size of their personal Peace Shield before and after meditation.

"Winchester says that the activities on World Healing Day will be an important step in building a national and global Peace Shield, which has significant implications for dealing with problems such as hunger, disease, and crime, as well as problems of national security."[30]

The Creation of a "New Age Army"

Recently I met in New York with Kevin Garvey, an eminent Catholic scholar and researcher who shared with me some of the information he has acquired regarding the New Age influence within our military service. That influence has especially made itself felt, said Kevin, in the upper echelons, among the high-ranking brass. But it impacts lower ranks as well. Military personnel are often ordered to attend such New Age mind control and spiritual training programs as est and Lifespring.

Kevin's research also turned up the alarming fact that in the early 1980s, officers at the prestigious Army War College at Carlisle, Pennsylvania, prepared a study aimed at creating a "New Age Army." These officers, some of whom were graduates of Werner Erhardt's est or former members of the radical university group Students for a Democratic Society, recommended the Army adopt meditation, psychic powers, magic, and neurolinguistic (mind-talk hypnosis) training.

My own investigation has uncovered a small cadre of officers who reportedly are training a select clique of radical "Christian" women in how to use guerrilla war methods, terrorist tactics, and psychological warfare techniques to accomplish conservative goals in American society.

It is important to remember that the New Age can be either conservative or liberal in its politics. Satan doesn't care what political persuasion his servants are. New Agers are active in *liberal* social causes and world peace movements, but some push for *conservative* causes that even fundamentalist Christians would support. For example, we find Reverend Myung Sun

Moon, his "moonies," and his political arm, CAUSA, as well as Elizabeth Clare Prophet of the Church Universal and Triumphant, espousing anti-Communist aims and promoting other conservative political goals.

Military officers are active in both Moon's and Prophet's organizations. Sometimes these officers are lured in by what appears to be the lofty goals of New Age leaders. For example, Major General Daniel Graham was a guest on Prophet's national television program, aired during her church services, promoting a space defense system for the U.S.A. Moon is reported to have contributed money to help the U.S.-backed contras in Nicaragua who are fighting the entrenched pro-Marxist, anti-Christian dictatorship of that country.[31]

The First Earth Battalion: Satan's U.S. Army Elite

Among the most dangerous of New Age groups in the Army is the First Earth Battalion, a special new type of military unit founded by Army Lieutenant Colonel Jim Channon. The training and operations manual used by this group is crammed full of occult symbols. Channon's foundling group has received a lot of favorable attention in military circles, but the concept has not been fully adopted as yet.

David Spangler, one of the top New Age strategists and spiritual leaders, is highly commendatory of Lt. Col. Channon and his First Earth Battalion. He has been quoted as saying:

> One might not expect the military to be a scene of New Age activity, but it is. Among the military men who are exploring a holistic world view and its implications for the military is Army Lieutenant Colonel Jim Channon. Soldiers in this special group would be trained not only in the usual martial arts but also in other forms of conflict resolution and in spiritual disciplines. They would be "warrior monks" whose main mission would be to create harmony out of conflict by using techniques from meditation to force of arms, from ecological skills to humanistic psychology.[32]

Spangler notes that "Channon envisions the philosophy and training of this battalion as *being open to anyone, civilian or military.*"[33] In Channon's First Earth Battalion Manual, we read:

Those who strive after the truth . . . are known as warriors. They are capable. They get the job done. . . . The First Earth wants the action orientation of the Warrior tempered with the patience and sensitivity and ethics of the monk. *These are the soldiers who have the power to make Paradise. Why go for anything else?*[34]

Lt. Colonel Aquino and the Temple of Set

Without being able to read Jim Channon's mind, we can only ponder about his comment that his New Age-trained soldiers (and civilians) "have the power to make Paradise." I have my suspicions about the type of paradise that such men would establish, and my suspicions are not at all pretty.

My skepticism seems to have a valid foundation if recent events even partially explain the revolution occuring inside the Armed Forces. Only a few months prior to my writing this section, I received a phone call from a dedicated Christian woman in Denver, Colorado, whose efforts are aimed at exposing underground New Age activities in society. She asked me what I knew about a U.S. Army Lieutenant Colonel Michael Aquino.

"Nothing," I replied. "I recall the name vaguely, but that's all."

"Well, his name keeps mysteriously coming up in my research of New Age activities in the Armed Forces," she said, "but we can't find out much about him."

I dismissed our conversation from my mind as I had what seemed to be a zillion things I was working on, including this book. But within weeks, as I watched a network TV news show one day suddenly the news reporter began to describe a U.S. Army Lieutenant Colonel based in California. According to the news report, this officer had been accused of the sexual abuse of a child. The officer was said to be the head of a satanic, Egyptian Mystery Religion church in San Francisco named the Temple of Set. Allegedly scores of children were sexually abused at the Presidio childcare center in San Francisco and even transported to the Temple of Set, where they were used in occult rituals of the most disgusting variety. The Army officer's name: Michael Aquino.

This news report inspired me to look more closely into the activities of Lt. Col. Michael Aquino. Subsequently I have discovered that he is a twenty-year veteran Army officer who now openly leads the Temple of Set in San Francisco. This is the successor to the Church of Satan, founded by Anton LaVey. Lt. Col. Aquino has proclaimed himself the High Priest of Satan.[35]

Aquino has made no attempt to hide his activities as a satanist from the U.S. Army hierarchy. Yet he is allowed to remain on active duty as an officer polluting the minds of the men under him.

As a former career officer myself, having proudly served for over twenty years in the U.S. Air Force, I can only cry out in protest when I consider the degradations our young men and women in uniform must suffer and endure. What has happened to the conscience of our military leaders when men like Aquino are permitted to serve in positions of authority in our Armed Forces?

History records that Set (also Seti) was the angry and malevolent Egyptian god of thunder and lightning and war. Set was one of the three gods/goddesses of the unholy trinity of deities that first originated in ancient Babylon. So again we discover connections with Mystery Babylon, the Harlot Religion, in the midst of our U.S. Armed Forces.

Witches in Uniform

As we've seen, the First Earth Battalion and the circumstances surrounding the Temple of Set are only two of many instances of New Age occultism in our military. In Europe, where over 350,000 U.S. troops are stationed, it is not unusual to read classified ads in the official overseas newspaper for the Armed Forces, *The Stars and Stripes,* inviting new servicemen arrivals to join established witches' covens and satanic sects.

Recently the news wires carried stories about witches and pagans demanding representation by their own Wicca and pagan chaplains within the Armed Forces Chaplain Corps. Eventually these spiritually demented military worshipers of Lucifer will get the rights they demand, as will the homosexuals. The federal courts, with so many New Agers, secular humanists, and liberals sitting on the bench, will see to it.

Already the U.S. military in 1987 opened its ranks to Buddhist chaplains. This marked the first time a religious group outside of Christianity or Judaism has been represented by chaplains in the U.S. Armed Forces.[36] The floodgates will now be opened so that Lucifer can minister to our men and women in uniform.

Shock Troops from Hell

Just as we are seeing the startling discovery of New Age soldiers of darkness within our own uniformed services, Adolf Hitler also had a special type of soldier who led the way in conquest. *Storm troopers,* they were called. Parachuted in with a *blitzkrieg* wave, shock troops were used to surprise, terrify, demoralize, and rapidly overcome the enemy. New Age propaganda is even now paving the way for a future brigade of shock troops, who are to be led in their missions by the New Age "Christ." Foster Bailey of the Lucis Trust referred to this new type of religious warrior in his revealing treatise *Things to Come.*

> We have been admonished in times past not to be hearers of the word only, but to be doers also. Now we are admonished not to be doers only but to be cooperators with the [New Age] Christ also. Thus we can become part of the now forming inner group which has been called "Christ's own people." *This special group, in training now, is the spiritual shock troop of the coming Aquarian age.*[37]

To be a soldier in this elite band of spiritual shock troops and to thus cooperate with the New Age "Christ" is, says Bailey, "exhilarating, even exciting. There is joy in it and greatly increased usefulness."[38]

What's more, Bailey tells us that total obedience, regardless of personal doubt, is required of a shock troop. "A disciple who is a cooperator with the Christ is not eager to protect himself from error."[39] No, a man or woman who accepts membership in this most elect of militias must forge ahead in obedience to the "hierarchy":

> It is far better to go all out . . . than to shrink from the possibility of being partly wrong. A real disciple is willing to take a chance in spiritual work. The higher the hurdles the lighter we should sit in the saddle.[40]

A *militant spirit*—that's what is required of the true New Age believer. "Indians on the warpath," is how one New Age writer characterizes the spirit required to usher in the Age of Aquarius. Dane Rudhyar offers the term *"aggressiveness."*[41] New Age author Ron Hagart endorses this term when he writes:

> One could say we're a race of rather aggressive mystics. Aggressiveness is demanded from us these days; how else can we begin to reverse Humanity's slide toward doom?[42]

Another military term that New Age leaders frequently use is *mobilization*. Mobilization, they are saying, is needed if the New Age is to succeed in its ambitious quest for world dominance. John Randolph Price has spoken of the beginnings of a new *spiritual offensive*: "Millions are strategically located throughout the world, ready for the new spiritual offensive."[43]

His militaristic fervor, and his support of such New Age doctrines as pantheism ("oneness") and reincarnation and karma ("the creative law of cause and effect"), are vividly apparent in Price's pronouncement that:

> The New Thought movement has gathered great momentum and the *true believers* in the inseparable oneness of God and man and the creative law of cause and effect are now stepping forth from every religion on earth and are moving onto the staging area.[44]

John Randolph Price is adamant in his insistence that New Agers must become activists. They must always understand their role in the implementation of the "Divine Plan."[45] Price has already "enlisted" millions in his own messianic venture: the Planetary Commission and its WORLD HEALING MEDITATION. Excitedly and with great emotional appeal, he stirs up mob psychology by assuring his listeners:

> Yes, we have entered the New Age, but now we have the responsibility, the obligation to create the *civilization* of the

Aquarian Age. That's our purpose, our mission, yours and mine. That's why we are here.

Yes, the salvation of the world does depend on you.[46]

Sally Fisher, a militant New Yorker who conducts New Age health seminars in which visualization and related techniques are employed, epitomizes the attitude of the average New Age disciple. Asked why she planned to participate in a Gay March on Washington, the nation's capitol, she explained:

> It is almost our obligation as enlightened beings to spread this light around. . . . If we truly follow the path we find it leads out into the world. . . . I think we should all go from our churches, temples, ashrams, and healing circles to the streets.[47]

A Tendency to Violent Acts

Fisher was part of a demonstration in Washington in June 1988 that resulted in her arrest by police.[48] While she and other New Age activists may not initially intend to commit violence as part of their "obligation" to bring in a new society, their vulnerability to a satanic spirit of cruelty and brutality leaves them wide open.

The New Age practice of occult meditation leaves the individual in a semiconscious trance state and easily susceptible to influence by demonic spirits. Christopher Hyatt describes the process of Eastern Meditation as "emptying oneself out: a spiritual laxative."[49] Once you've emptied your mind, it can be quickly filled up by unholy spirits. That's what demon possession is all about.

Once the person is indwelt by demons, he or she becomes like putty in their master's cruel hands. When he gives the order for them to take to the streets, they will obey. When the demon spirit whips up an attitude of violence and unrepressed hostility, it must be ventilated.

Satan's New Age followers will one day soon ventilate that hostility against the People of Light, God's people: born-again Christians. Jose Arguelles, head of the New Age's Harmonic Convergence, has spoken of a coming "purification period" in which the "people's army of earth" will "destructure civilization" and dismantle the present world economy. This army is to be made up of "super-humans" whose minds are linked up with "spirit guides" from another dimension.[50] In truth, these will be New Age warriors taking direct orders from demons. Warriors who curse the light. They will be Soldiers of Darkness.

ELEVEN

Cursing the Light

Be ye, therefore, followers of God, as dear children. . . .
For ye were sometimes darkness, but now are ye light in
the Lord; walk as children of light.   (Ephesians 5:1, 8)

Such disciplines as witchcraft, sorcery, devil worship,
and the rest . . . if properly used could help people. . . .
We have been given a black eye long enough by ignorant
and superstitious people. . . .   (Rev. Roger C. Hight,
Pastor, New Age Assembly Church,
Corpus Christi, Texas)

The only thing Satan despises more than the light of a born-again Christian is the flashingly brilliant and majestic light of God Himself. If we can clearly understand this inescapable fact, we can then better comprehend Satan's hideous, black Plan to totally eliminate every vestige of Christianity off the face of the earth. We can also comprehend why he plans to require that his Mark be placed on the foreheads or right hands of *his* people. By this physical sign, the people of darkness—Satan's disciples—will be easily distinguished from God's holy people: the men, women, and children of light.

Satan and the people of the lie curse the light. They cannot wait for the Christian period to end. Vera Alder, in her stunning book *The Initiation of the World,* sums up the New Age view by boastfully proclaiming that the Jesus era, the "Age of Ignorance" as she terms it, is ending. The Age of the Christians, says Alder, was astrologically the Piscean Age. It is now over, finished. A brighter New Age is dawning.

187

The Piscean Age, as you know, lasts two thousand or so years, as do the other zodiacal signs. Its inception marked the beginning of the Christian era. It is passing out of manifestation now, as the new Aquarian Age is coming in.[1]

Alder, whose writings have made her a respected and highly esteemed name in New Age circles, characterizes the Piscean (Christian) person as an immature, racially inferior species content with religion "in its simplest, most childish and unexplained form." Scornfully, she remarks that this Christian subhuman "dislikes bringing his mind to bear upon any new conception. He is," she adds, "as a child before his Maker . . . still completely tuned into the mental outlook of the Age of Ignorance."[2]

The two thousand years of the Christian era are also described by Alder as the "Black Age," a time of bleak winter when the divine work of true spiritual leaders languished because of humanity's blindness and stupidity. Finally, she says, it is ending and a Golden Age of spring is on the horizon, replete with the promise of godhood and prosperity for New Age man. Alder announces that this World Initiation "will be the key event that launches mankind into this bright new era of greatness."[3]

Are Christians Parasites?

Colin Wilson, a popular science fiction writer from Great Britain whose works are greatly admired by occultists and other New Agers, thinly veils the general contempt by those in the New Age for Christians in his novel, *The Mind Parasites*. In his book, Wilson tells the story of a leader who discovers that human consciousness has been victimized, dragged down, and held back by a strange parasite that has been feeding on men's collective minds for centuries. This unwelcome parasite saps mind power and keeps men at a lower level of ability and consciousness. But those who become aware that they are victimized by these parasites quickly realize that they can get rid of them. By ridding themselves of these dangerous mind parasites, people become free human beings endowed with enormous power.[4]

Marilyn Ferguson, author of the powerfully persuasive *The Aquarian Conspiracy*, uses these same concepts to describe how seekers can acquire great powers. They must first rid themselves of the parasites that plague their minds if they are to become transformed into wondrous New Age beings:

> Just so, our natural power is sapped by the parasites of the centuries: fear, superstition, a view of reality that reduces life's wonders to creaking machinery. If we starve these parasitic beliefs they will die.[5]

How do we destroy the parasites? Ferguson relates that a number of "Aquarian conspirators" have done so by giving up such negative ideas as "conventional Christianity" and "religious dogma."[6] New Age spiritual experience consists of "knowing without doctrine," she insists. Spirituality means that we must accept the profane as well as the sacred, for even if we start by studying what is sacred, "the sacred takes you back to the profane."[7]

Does this mean that Bible doctrine—the doctrine and gospel given man by Jesus Christ—is to be discarded for what is, in effect, profanity? Evidently this is exactly what Ferguson has in mind. "Doctrine," she claims, "is second-hand knowledge. Stand above [doctrine], pass on and be free. . . . This is the transmission of knowledge through direct experience."[8]

Freedom is what New Agers desire most—freedom from judgment and freedom from the conviction of their sins. This is why L. Ron Hubbard, founder of Scientology, claimed that his New Age teachings were "the road to absolute freedom."

Of more malignant proportions is this cryptic comment by Alice Bailey's spirit guide, Djwhal Khul: "Only he who is free can control and utilize those who are prisoners."[9] It does not take much imagination to comprehend what this statement means. Djwhal Khul, the so-called Tibetan Master, says that the bringing in of the New Age by destructive means and by the initiation of mankind is at the very heart of his teachings: it is the "Great Work" ordained by the Ascended Masters.[10]

Satan's Mystical Religion vs. God's Truth and Example

Satan's spirituality is based on direct experience—the experience of rejecting God's doctrine and replacing it with the rush of excitement that follows mystical experiences. Ferguson and other New Age authorities call for a radical type of spirituality which excludes doctrine. They sponsor a religion of, "if it feels good, do it!"

Satan's religion does indeed have the diabolical, ecstatic power to make us feel good through experiencing his foul but often disguised presence. "Forget the Bible," he seductively suggests. "Forget doctrine . . . relax and *know* that *I* am your master . . . embrace me, *experience* me."

Clearly Lucifer's New Age leaders hate the Bible, God's book of doctrine and truth. They know that the Bible is the handbook, the constant guide and reference source for practicing Christians. The seething anger and resentment of Satan for God's Word proceeds from his diseased mind and is instilled in the minds of his human followers. Accordingly, New Age leaders labor ceaselessly to defeat both the Bible and the devout men and women who believe in it as the unvarnished and perfect Word of Almighty God.

The faithful Christian saved by the grace of God is, to Satan, a constant reminder that Jesus Christ has won the victory. This is cause enough for his furious intemperance and hatred toward us. Meanwhile, to the followers of Satan, the born-again Christian is a sharp-edged reminder that without Jesus Christ their lives are bankrupt and empty, that their sins are unforgiven. As New Age author Marilyn Ferguson admits, the key to the New Age generation is its unwillingness to accept guilt.[11] Unfortunately, she and others in the New Age see this as a virtue rather than a vice.

Today's unbelievers in Jesus Christ desperately want freedom from guilt. They seek a religion that is not judgmental, one in which every man does his own thing, unburdened by conscience. The New Age says to the unbeliever, you are god, there are no rules, you be the judge of right and wrong, you and you alone are the lawgiver. This is exactly what a reprobate person living in sin craves hearing.

No one is guilty. We are all innocents. (Leo Buscaglia, *Personhood*)

I got my truth. I can't use anybody else's. . . . You are all beautiful. You are God. That is it, baby. (Terry Cole-Whittaker, *Magical Blend* Magazine)

The High Religion has nothing to do with sin, only the spiritual development of man. (John Randolph Price, *Superbeings*)

You are the supreme being. . . . there isn't any right/wrong. (Carl Frederick, *Playing the Game the New Way*)

I have my truth. You are welcome to your truth. (Mafu, a demon entity channeled by Penny Torres)

Along comes the Christian to convince the New Ager of the Truth. Without uttering a word, the Christian who walks in Truth is a living light, a testimony to the New Ager that sin is a reality and that God hates sin. The Christian testimony is that there is only one God, the great I AM, who sits on a heavenly throne.

What's more, the Christian bears witness to the Word of God, the *only* Bible. This witness is a sharp rebuke to the permissive, anything goes, immoral lifestyle of the New Age. It confirms to the New Age devotee the harsh reality that there is indeed one sovereign God who makes the rules, who solely decides what is right and what is wrong. It sets forth the Truth they dread to hear: that God shall someday be their judge. And what a judge, for He holds the keys to eternal joy *or* to everlasting damnation.

No wonder the New Age man or woman whose heart is hardened and made callous by Satan despises the people of God. The light of God shining in the lives of Christians makes transparent the hidden works of the Devil and illuminates his evil blueprint for chaos. Satan has therefore passed the word down to his New Age leadership: the Christian light must be extinguished; it is a torch that must be snuffed out if his Plan is to succeed.

The Drumbeat of Hatred

To vanquish God's light in the world, Satan maintains through his New Age disciples a constant drumbeat of hatred and hostility toward the people of the true God. His theologians and teachers write books and lengthy articles in New Age journals and magazines denouncing Christian fundamentalists for their

separativeness, their intolerance, their immaturity, and their ignorance. New Age spokesmen make appearances at every forum
imaginable, at corporate meeting halls, at New Age conferences
and symposia, and they have instant, almost unlimited access to
the media. Always their message is the same: all religions lead to
God *except* that of the Christian fundamentalists.

Biblical Christians are today the most despised and persecuted minority on Planet Earth. This persecution is often most
keenly experienced in the supposed "Christian" countries of the
West—in the United States and West Germany, where the vanguard of the New Age World Religion is making such tremendous strides, and in Great Britain, which is now undergoing a
dramatic occult explosion. The tempo of the drumbeat of hatred
is increasing. Someday battle drums will sound a piercing shriek
of chaotic decibels against the men and women who are contending for the faith once delivered to Christ's apostles (see Jude
3).

Should Christians Be Put Away?

To the New Age hierarchy, the Christian is thoroughly evil and is
at the root of all the world's problems. Benjamin Creme, for
example, identifies those who oppose the New Age "Christ," the
Lord Maitreya, as members of the "black lodge." Christians who
hold fast to Jesus as *the* Christ are disparaged as spiritually
bankrupt, as "the Lords of materiality." Their punishment for
not bowing down to Lord Maitreya, Creme warns, is that they
will be "sealed off to their own domain."[12] In other words, they
will be *put away* once the kingdom of the Lord Maitreya materializes.

Creme has remarked that even though the New Age cause
has come under fire from "Christian fundamentalist groups, nevertheless, their opposition will not delay Maitreya's coming. He
is invulnerable." All we are witnessing, says Creme, is the "last
ditch stand of the old order."[13]

Christians also come under harsh criticism in the writings of
Dane Rudhyar, New Age author of the book *The Occult Preparations for a New Age.* Rudhyar carefully outlines how the
present world system will end, being replaced by a "New Civilization" which exalts the occult. In Rudhyar's view, Christianity
has been defective almost from its inception because early Chris-

tians in the early centuries A.D. rejected gnosticism and failed to stress unity with the Ancient Wisdom.[14] Scathingly he writes:

> Christianity lost its collective Soul because it repudiated all that had been the spiritual tradition of Asia and Egypt in an attempt to focus man's attention on the New Christ Revelation. . . . The emotion-rousing dogma of salvation by divine atonement for an original sin perverted the entire pattern of cosmic evolution and induced a wholesale neurotic sense of guilt.[15]

Rudhyar complains that because of the perversion of Christians in insisting on the revelation of Jesus Christ, "the Old Traditions were forced in most places to go underground and to hide what remained of the spiritual harvest of the past cultures of mankind."[16]

What "spiritual harvest of the past cultures" does Dane Rudhyar lament the loss of? Traveling back in time to the era of Paul and other first-century Christians, we find the "noble" traditions of the Greeks who practiced infanticide and rampant homosexuality. We also find the human sacrifices of the Babylonians and the Canaanites who threw their children into the fires to appease the gods. We further discover the temple prostitution of Rome, Pergamos, and Corinth.

I could, of course, go on and on. The fact is, the wickedly unrighteous "Old Traditions" which Rudhyar and other New Age occultists are now reviving as twentieth-century religious rituals *were what Jesus came to destroy.* His desire was and is that man practice instead a holy lifestyle, that we emulate the Father and lead lives of purity, joy, and richness of the Spirit. The holy goals of Jesus Christ are diametrically opposed to those promoted today by the New Age, and this is why Christians are being portrayed as the "bad guys" by New Age religionists.

Are Christians Paranoid Idiots?

Thus, we should not be surprised to discover Timothy Leary, the ex-Harvard professor and 1960s "King of the LSD counter-culture," being resurrected in the late 1980s as a New Age authority. Predictably, Leary is lashing out these days at Christians of what he derisively calls "the Calvinist persuasion." Such persons he describes as "psychopathic, paranoid . . . weird."[17] Accusingly, he states:

> Many problems we face today are caused by fundamentalist religion—Middle East crises, terrorism, the current war-like atmosphere based on fanaticism—people who totally believe in their own cause. . . . This is the familiar position taken by . . . the right wing Christian, etc.[18]

The Hindu gurus who have been so enthusiastically greeted in the United States since the days of the Beatles make little effort to hide their utter contempt and hatred for Bible-believing Christians. They come preaching love, freedom, and tolerance, and New Age disciples swoon at their every utterance. But every one of these men of Satan soon reveal themselves as haters of Jesus Christ and His people. One of the most prominent of the many gray-bearded "man-gods," a liar who has captured tens of thousands of Americans in his net of deceit, teaches that men not of the New Age consciousness are "retarded" and "idiots."[19] Fundamentalist Christians, he says, will not make it to paradise:

> The fundamentalist Christians are the worst Christians. They are the most fanatic people. They believe that Christianity is the *only* religion; all other religions are wrong, and that the whole world should be turned toward Christianity. . . . These are very primitive ideas.[20]

His followers believe Rajneesh Bhagwan to be God. Yet this guru is evidently so high on drugs and debauchery that he cannot separate illusion from reality. On one occasion, he seriously told his rapturous listeners that President Ronald Reagan's best friend was a chimpanzee. Evidently this had some relationship with the fact that as a Hollywood actor President Reagan had once starred in a movie with a chimpanzee.[21]

Confused—and perhaps delirious—the Rajneesh claimed that the chimpanzee was Reagan's only friend and that on the first day after the President was elected, he took the chimpanzee for a walk at the beach. According to the guru, Ronald Reagan had this problem primarily because "He is a fundamentalist Christian."[22]

Even after his U.S. debacle, with his Ashram—his New Age community in Oregon—folding amidst documented charges of corruption, Rajneesh continues to enchant and captivate thousands of New Agers. In fact, he still has among his German, American, and British followers a prepondeance of higher educated, affluent people. They would not be considered stupid by contemporary standards but as intelligent, thoughtful individuals. If a bearded and robed Hindu guru can delude and convince these people to believe his babblings, think of what impact *the real Antichrist* will have when he appears and begins his campaign on Planet Earth.

Another, more intellectually respectable New Age authority who seems to relish attacking Christians is psychologist Robert Anton Wilson, who has authored such ungodly and irreverent books as *The Illuminati Papers, Sex and Drugs,* and *Cosmic Trigger.* In a recent interview he roundly denounced Christian fundamentalists:

> Fundamentalism is a stage of innocence or arrogance where you don't realize the creative role your own brain plays in the reality tunnels you perceive. Sophistication consists in understanding your role as a co-creator of your reality.
>
> To me, fundamentalism of all sorts is conducive to stupidity and interferes with the proper functioning of intelligence, creativity, joy, and having a good time.[23]

Wilson, who frankly and proudly admits, "I've been a heretic all my life," recently published a book, *The New Inquisition,* that accuses Christian fundamentalists of being extremists. To correct this, he believes that the more enlightened people of the planet might have to rise up and put a stop to it: "I think the 1990s are going to bring back the kind of radical change we experienced back in the 1960s."[24]

Are Christians Superstitious and Immature?

Roger C. Hight, pastor of the New Age Assembly Church in Corpus Christi, Texas, would no doubt warmly agree with Wilson. If the New Age person is to achieve his divinity and to tread the "Path to the Rainbow," Hight believes, the tenets of Christian fundamentalism must be discarded. Hight preaches that man is himself "God," and that there is no personal, sovereign God to whom we can turn.[25] Professing a belief that psychic and occult powers are part of the natural laws of the universe, Hight avidly recommends that man practice occult and magical techniques, explaining:

> Under the natural laws of the universe, man can, if he so chooses, invert a law to a negative use! So, such disciplines as witchcraft, sorcery, devil worship and the rest, although falling under negative use, *properly used, could help people.*
>
> The word occult has been given a most sinister meaning for the last two thousand years; but, in all honesty, there is nothing sinister or forbidden about the word.[26]

Hight criticizes people—presumably Christians—who would deny the use of sorcery and other occult methodology to Aquarian men of goodwill. Characterizing such people as superstitious and immature, he indignantly writes:

> We have been given a black eye long enough by ignorant and superstitious people, and I pray most heartily that during this, the Aquarian Age, people will mature, understand the Laws that govern their being, and begin to live by them so that the race consciousness will reach a state whereby Heaven and Earth shall become one.[27]

In Hight's angry statement, we find just one of the reasons why the New Age so despises and hates the sincere Christian. Christians well-versed in their Bible are uncompromising in their conviction that the occult is of the Devil and defiles any who dabble in it. Likewise, Biblical Christians reject the mixing of Christianity with Eastern religions and mysticism. This, too, makes the Christian an object of scorn and derision to New Agers.

Ruth Montgomery, whose many books about her communications with the unseen spirit world have repeatedly hit the best-seller charts, is just one of the New Age teachers upset because true Christians reject the malignant practice of necromancy, or communication with spirits. Montgomery, through her spirit guides, makes her displeasure clear when she says of Christian fundamentalists:

> So many are ignorant, with closed minds and little education, that they fail to realize the close relationship between the ancient Eastern religions and that which Christ brought to the world: They fail to understand that we are all one. . . . Unless they can accept that basic premise they will continue along their bigoted, ever narrowing path that leads to nowhere.[28]

The error of Christian fundamentalists will be finally put to rest, Montogomery relates, around the year 2000 when the world goes through a momentous period of chaos, disruption, suffering, and cleansing. She says that "walk-ins" and extraterrestrials (defined by Christians as "demons") will supervise this purification of the planet. The result of all this chaos will be the defeat of the obstinate Christian believers and the establishment of a joyous New Age millennium:

> The rift between Christian fundamentalists and spiritually minded New Agers will . . . be erased. . . . at which time the population will be so decimated that the survivors, helped by walk-ins and extraterrestrials will realize the wisdom of all pulling together for the good of everyone. There have always been religious confrontations and wars fought in the name of religion. The New Age, the millennium, will see an end to that strife, at least for a thousand years.[29]

The Singling Out of Christian Fundamentalists

Ruth Montgomery would vehemently deny that she hates Christians, even though she has reiterated over and over that Christian fundamentalists and others who can't fit in will have to die physically and pass into spirit. Their death, she reveals, will allow the majority to get busy at building the blessed New Age Kingdom.[30]

New Age leaders wickedly enjoy making distinctions among Christians. Those who willingly accept New Age doctrines and who agree to take the initiation and Mark to be given the world are "good" and will be spared from the suffering and chaos shortly to transpire. However, those Christians who doggedly stick to their "erroneous" belief that Jesus is the only Christ and that His Way is the only way are unfit candidates for New Age citizenship. These stubborn Christian malcontents are sneeringly lableled "fundamentalists," as if this were a dirty word.

Recently, on a secular radio talk show in Austin, Texas, I debated Benjamin Creme, the forerunner for Lord Maitreya, the false New Age "Messiah." After several minutes of patiently listening to this demon-possessed man praising his Lord Maitreya, my turn came. I effectively refuted every point Creme had made, pointing out the Bible's admonition that anyone who denies that Jesus Christ is *the one and only Christ* is of the Antichrist. Exasperated and breathing fire, Creme furiously accused me of being a "Christian fundamentalist." It was one of the few statements he made during the entire two-hour interview that I could agree with wholeheartedly.

In Chicago, where I made a personal appearance on the most popular secular talk show in that city, the outspoken host began the interview by looking squarely at me while thumbing through the pages of my book, *Dark Secrets of the New Age*. Resolutely he declared: "It looks to me as though you're some kind of "Christian fundamentalist fanatic." My response was immediate. With a wide and engaging smile, I enthusiastically exclaimed, "Praise the Lord!"

Should there be a stigma attached to unabashedly defending the Word of God and contending earnestly for the Christian faith? God forbid! A *Christian fundamentalist* is simply what the term indicates: a person who believes in and has patterned his or her life after the *fundamentals* of the gospel. A Christian fundamentalist believes in the Bible as the inerrant, perfect Word of God. He or she confesses Jesus as personal Lord and Savior. Baptist, Methodist, Assembly of God, Presbyterian, Pentecostal, Lutheran . . . you can't put a denominational tag on a Christian fundamentalist.

In truth, every born-again believer in Jesus Christ is either a Christian fundamentalist or they've gone off into error. This is why I am so proud to be called by this term. I constantly ask

God to make my life an example of joy, love, peace, and goodness so that others will, through my light, aspire likewise to be "Christian fundamentalists." My desire is that no one perish, but that all will accept God's grace and His perfect gift of eternal salvation. This blessed hope typifies all Christian fundmentalists.

Satan and his ungodly New Age teachers cannot stomach men and women who confess Jesus Christ and refuse to buckle under to the pressure of the world. So he brands Christian fundamentalists (whom I will hereafter in this book identify simply as "Christians") as dangerous and evil. In fact, New Agers preach, Christians are the *only evil* there is.

Satan's New Age teachers would have the world believe that *all* religions are holy and that *all* paths lead to God. As we've seen, even the sleaziest and most despicable of practices and beliefs are wrapped by the New Age in clean white linen. For example, we note the remarkable enthusiasm in the New Age for the occult.

The Pagan Attack on Christianity

Among the many New Age teachers who openly spout venom against Christians are those who practice witchcraft, who worship nature, the earth and the cosmos as pantheistic gods, and who, as radical feminists, are promoting a Mother Goddess religion.

Monica Sjoo and Barbara Mor are among the latter. In their ungodly book *The Great Cosmic Mother,* subtitled *Rediscovering the Religion of the Earth,* they advocate sins of the flesh while attacking Christians as patriarchical, moralistic, and narrow:

> The fundamentalists have confused—and have attracted many confused people—with their . . . moralistic God. . . . The American fundamentalist preachers and politicians are working very hard to make "humanism" a dirty word. This is the result of their Bronze Age religious heritage, in which every day, fleshly, earthly reality had to be demonized in order to make "spirit" the property of a few.
>
> True humanism, primal spirituality, and the energy of evolution must join together in a conscious force, to tell the truth about God. The truth is that "God" is not in a book—

"holy," golden or otherwise. . . . God is the universe. We are all now living inside the body of God.[31]

Sjoo and Mor contend that a Christianity that believes in a personal Father God, sin, guilt, and suffering "must be repudiated." Arrogantly and blasphemously they suggest that any religion that believes these things is a "vampire machine" that keeps itself empowered by "eating our human energies and our souls." They say that Christianity should be replaced by a "global spirituality" that recognizes humanity's needs as sexual beings and as an evolving species. What is necessary is to cast a spell over the world, to honor such magical "natural" religions as that of the witches and the Earth Goddess.[32]

Few realize the hold that modern witchcraft and other pagan religions have on the New Age. The New Age has its roots in the ancient Babylonian religion, and that was a religion of paganism, witchcraft, and the occult. Today witches come dressed in trendy black fashionable dresses and make the rounds of television talk shows. Their philosophies (such as pantheism: all is God) are even being taught in public schools, and—incredibly—in some "Christian" churches. Yet their beliefs and practices have changed little over the past two thousand years. Witches, who love to describe theirs as the Old, High Religion, as the Ancient Wisdom, or as the Religion of the Earth, still fervently hate Christians and everything that Christians stand for. Their father, Satan, has not changed, and neither have they.

On command of their hellish master, the New Age pagans are on the offensive against Christians. We are *the* enemy, says pagan advocate Margot Adler.

The fundamentalist impulse—coupled with the inevitable rise of apocalyptic millennialism as we approach the year 2000—is, along with nuclear war, the most dangerous peril facing the human race. Most fundamentalists . . . are at war with the diversity of life and ideas. . . .

Perhaps most dangerous, most fundamentalists do not believe this world, this earth, these bodies we inhabit, are holy. Since they see this world as sinful and this time as evil, they seek only a world that comes after.[33]

The Holiness of God

In one respect, Adler hits the nail on the head. Christians see only God, *not* the world, as holy. He exclusively is holy, for "all have sinned and come short of the glory of God" (Rom. 3:23). Moreover, Paul told us that we who are Christ's, as well as all of creation, await the redemption that surely lies in store at Jesus' Second Coming (Rom. 8:22, 23).

To pagans, indeed to all who profess involvement in the New Age religion, this is absolutely unacceptable. I do not know of even one New Age leader who would argue with Adler when she remarks:

> The world is holy. Nature is holy. The body is holy. Sexuality is holy. The mind is holy. The imagination is holy. You are holy. . . . Thou art Goddess. Thou art God.[34]

This, then, is the crucial distinction between the tenets of Christians and those of New Agers. Every person in the New Age, knowingly or unknowingly, worships Satan. Christians exalt a *holy God;* New Agers profess that *all is God*. Clearly there can be no compromise between these two opposing views. Fundamental Christianity is non-negotiable. The Truth cannot be bargained away for the sake of the false unity of a global spirituality. God is not a bargaining chip. He is Lord! Period.

Though some New Age leaders shrewdly attempt to mislead on this point, they well recognize the utter incompatibility of Christianity and the New Age World Religion. They anxiously await the day when the New Age Messiah-King arrives to punish Christians and to relegate the God of the Bible to the junk-heap of human history. No wonder one New Ager, Tom Williams, a priest with the paganistic Church of All Worlds in St. Louis, Missouri, has wishfully commented:

> Someday, people may speak of the last two thousand years as the "Christian Interlude."[35]

Jesus' Kingdom Will Be Everlasting

Jesus' Kingdom, the New Age will discover, is not an interlude. It will be everlasting. Someday the deceivers of the New Age will be forced to bow down on their knees before the Most High God, Jesus the Christ. On that eventful Day of Judgment they will certainly be forced to confess the vast difference between darkness and light. As they fearfully and with trepidation and trembling look upon the King of Kings, they perhaps shall remember the words that Jesus once gave His disciples:

> I am the light of the world; he that followeth me shall not walk in darkness, but shall have the light of life. (John 8:12)

TWELVE

Call Not Evil Good

Woe unto them who call evil, good, and good, evil; who put darkness for light, and light for darkness. . . .

(Isa. 5:20)

I am the devil and yet I am God.

(Jaqui Holt, *Life Times*)

I n the closing days of World War II, American and British soldiers who liberated the remaining Jews from Nazi concentration camps could scarcely believe their eyes. The horrors of the ovens and the stench of rotting human corpses almost overwhelmed their senses. How can this be, some asked in amazement; how is it possible that human beings can be trained and motivated to commit such heinous crimes?

In the following months, those questions were partially answered. Hitler and his satanic-led associates had carefully prepared the minds of the murderers. He had pumped them up into believing they were a superior race akin to gods. Their victims were said to be members of a lower race, deserving of their fate. What the murderers were doing was not evil but necessary and good. Perhaps even holy.

If the Nazi overlords could easily convince these men to willingly commit such unspeakable atrocities, how much more effective will a future Antichrist be in convincing his New Age "Soldiers of Darkness" to perpetuate equally evil acts? We have already seen that the New Age disciple is under the delusion that he is a member of a new race of superbeings. He is god. His adversaries, Biblical Christians, are racially inferior, ignorant, unsophisticated, and dangerous to world peace and unity. They are "evil." Worse, the Christians are a threat and an obstacle to the New Age Kingdom.

Is Life Just a Movie?

The New Age doctrines of evolution, karma, and reincarnation furnish all the rationale needed to justify the murder of Christians so that their "negative" influence is removed from the planet. These doctrines teach that every person is an evolving god who is a member of one of several evolving races. The person's good and bad acts must, through karma, be reconciled and balanced as he evolves toward godhood. In the process, he reincarnates again and again as he travels on his journey, or path, to eventual divinity.

In the New Age view, to torture or to kill a person may be an act of God, necessary to *help* the individual balance out his karma. He can be reincarnated in the next life as a more conscious and advanced being. Maybe even as a god! Life is seen as *maya,* or illusion—it's all unreal anyway, so no hurt has really been done. There is no death. We are all just recycled again and again, over and over. This is the reason why the wheel is a popular New Age symbol. It denotes the never-ending cycle of reincarnation and rebirth.

This absurd belief takes on monstrously enlarged proportions when we hear New Age leaders preach that evil really doesn't hurt or damage anyone because life is, after all, *just a movie.* It's all just a dream in our heads. Gurdjieff's theory, for example, contends that "Life, from the period of adolescence, is the unconscious unrolling of a film that has been wound up in us."[1] Shakti Gawain (the surname means "Goddess" in Hindu religion), author of the 500,000-copy best-seller *Creative Visualization,* tells an interviewer, "I am learning to view my life as a fascinating and adventurous movie."[2]

How insensitive and unfeeling! Surely Satan has dulled the senses of these so-called "teachers of the New Age." Tell the father of a hapless young girl whose nude, battered, lifeless body has just been found in a desolate field somewhere, victim of a fiendish attack, that "it's all just a movie, a fascinating cinematic adventure." Explain to a brokenhearted, middle-aged woman in tears because her faithless husband has left her for a younger woman that it's just the "unconscious unrolling of a film," mere illusion: evil doesn't really exist.

It doesn't take too brilliant a mind to recognize the horror inherent in such repugnant doctrines. Yet, New Age leaders have been able to convince tens of millions of the "truth" of such Satanic doctrines as human evolution to godhood, the existence of "good" and "bad," inferior and superior races, and the laws of karma and reincarnation.

Satan has taken over the minds of these people and warped their thinking processes. They are like animated robots and zombies, zealously anxious to please their master lest they not receive their reward: godhood and the divine powers godhood bestows. I call this The Great Brain Robbery: it is nothing less than the closing of the conscience. To comprehend its astonishing proportions, let's examine the lies Satan has taught his New Age followers about three important realities: the nature of evil, the nature of pain and suffering, and the nature of death.

Evil Does Not Exist

Who is God? The New Age says he is both the creator and the destroyer, a combination of good and evil. He is both holy, and he is the devil. "I am the devil and yet I am God," goes one bit of New Age prose.[3]

But, New Age leaders quickly add, this is all a dream, for reality is this: there is *only good* in the world. The Universal Mind, or "God," merely creates in our human minds the *illusion* of evil. The Force does so to help us learn lessons on our way to becoming gods. Evil is really just some kind of cosmic joke.

Jack Underhill, editor of the influential *Life Times* magazine, epitomizes the commonly accepted New Age concept of evil when he writes:

> There is no Devil, no Beezelbub sniffing over the delectable sulphurous bubbles of boiling cauldrons of hellfire and damnation. . . . We understand Good better when we have met intimately with what is called Evil.[4]

Satan, Underhill rosily assures his readers, is not a real, existent being, nor is he a dark angel who rebelled against God.

Instead, he is "the part of us that refuses to recognize that we are the innocent children of a loving and unconditionally supporting God that never judges us and always finds us beautifull."[5] Yes, no matter what evil the New Ager commits, it's all just beautiful, all part of the glorious work involved in perfecting ourselves.

> When God gave us free choice He gave us freedom from being judged. . . . The New Agers know that there is no wrong path, no bad way, no failure, no evil, no Devil, only *us* with complete free choice to find our way back to God in any way we choose, and to grow in the experience. Satan is no more than God seen through cheap glasses.[6]

But . . . we might ask Underhill . . . But there is all the evil we see on the TV news and read in the daily newspaper. What about *that* evil? Confidently, reassuringly comes the reply: the people who are murdered, raped, robbed, victimized asked for it! Before they ever entered this particular incarnation, they decided what would happen to them during this life. As Underhill says:

> There are no victims at any level of life. We are the masters of our own destinies, the co-creators with the universe of all we bring into these lives.[7]

The Rasping Voices of Demons

New Agers are rapturously listening to the whispering, inner voices of their devils, voices that lyingly deny the very existence of evil. New Age literature, seminars, and sermons are permeated with the rasping voices of these parasite demons. These agents of evil use spirit channeling, automatic writing, and seances to speak to the world at large.

Seth, a demon who has dictated many best-seller books to his human counterpart, Jane Roberts, has said: "There is no authority superior to the guidance of a person's inner self. The universe is of good intent only. Evil and destruction do not exist."[8] This may seem an extreme and unholy doctrine to God-fearing Christians, but it has great appeal in the New Age. Each year a huge crowd gathers in Austin, Texas, from all over the world for the annual Seth International Conference.

Shakura, yet another demon spirit who comes cloaked as a wise entity from beyond, seductively suggests:

All is good. The only thing evil is in the mind and even that is good. . . . Suffering, heartbreak, sickness and death are all opportunities to wake up. Especially death.[9]

The demon visitor Soli tells listeners: "There is no such thing as good and evil."[10] Meanwhile, a perverted dark angel who comes disguised as the Archangel Michael accuses Christian fundamentalists of fostering the error of both believing God to be a real person and believing in the reality of evil forces:

The baby soul tends to be fundamentalistic in its religious beliefs. Personification of the godhead is strongest in this cycle. The immature soul believes in the forces of evil.[11]

The only thing that's truly evil is to believe in evil, some in the New Age teach. For example, William Warch, in his primer for New Age beginners, *The New Thought Christian,* insists that to believe in evil is very harmful to one's own self-esteem:

The belief that you are bad, a form of evil, distorts your vision and self-esteem. This belief will enable you to produce negative results in your world. . . . You are made up of the same stuff God is, and that is nothing but Good. You are Good. You are not evil. No one is evil.[12]

No one is evil? We could profitably ask Warch some probing questions. For example, what about the mass murderers? The repressive monsters? What of the vile dictator Idi Amin, who fed hundreds to crocodiles and massacred thousands in Uganda just a few years ago? What of the Argentine military dictatorship that ordered the Army to thrust young victims into the sea from helicopters? What of the men running the torture chambers of prisons in Iran, where young women reportedly are raped, pregnant women are beaten until they miscarry, and the imprisoned opponents of the country's harsh Islamic rulers frequently have their feet and stomachs scorched with hot irons? Are these men not evil?

Warch, who is well-known in New Age circles as a member of the executive board of the International New Thought Association, is prepared to provide us the pat New Age answer. "No one is evil," he repeats. "People often judge others as evil because they don't understand motives."[13]

Were Judas and Hitler Divine?

If "no one is evil," what about someone with as tarnished a reputation as Judas Iscariot? Surely this was an evil man, and surely his betrayal of Jesus was a supremely evil act. *Wasn't it?* Well . . . no, not according to the New Age. G. I. Gurdjieff, the late Russian mystic whose philosophy has been adopted for use in Pacific Bell Telephone seminars and is now taught in Unity and other churches, believed that Judas was "the most conscious of the disciples, and the one who rendered the greatest service."[14]

We have received reports from a reliable source that one New Age church actually teaches its congregation to meditate and pray to Judas as "god of light." Judas, we were told, is exalted by these New Agers because it is he who helped Jesus work out Jesus' karma!

If all is God, how can Judas or anyone else be bad? Thus Mafu, a spirit who speaks through the mouth of Penny Torres, one of the top-drawing New Age spirit channelers, instructed an audience of admirers: "Those entities whom you judge to be bad . . . of course, they are not, they are God."[15]

Does this mean that Hitler was divine or, astonishingly, that Lucifer himself is divine? Yes, reply the New Age "theologians." Even they. Again, it's all a matter of motive, we are told. Thus, John White, Director of Education for the Institute of Noetic Sciences, a California-based research organization headed by Apollo 14 astronaut Edgar Mitchell, states that Karl Marx, Adolf Hitler, and Mao Tse-tung each "in his own way mobilized resources and took steps to establish what he thought of as a better world."[16]

Benjamin Creme got straight to the point when he was asked if Hitler's soul is "perfect." Creme responded, "Yes, of course. Like every other soul, Hitler's is divine."[17] Creme maintains that Hitler was an occultic medium who was a high-placed New Age "initiate of the second degree." However, Hitler back-slid and must now work off his karma before he can advance.[18]

And Lucifer, the Devil, is he also divine? The demon Ramtha, so acclaimed for his New Age wisdom, speaking through J. Z. Knight, the Seattle, Washington woman who has gained international fame as a spirit channeler, assures us he is: "In Lucifer lies divinity," Ramtha insists.[19] This demon also suggests that if we cannot accept this "truth," then perhaps we need to awaken, change our perception, and quit being so judgmental.

Amazingly, even though he spouts such nonsense as this, Ramtha is venerated as an all-knowing, perfect Master and is literally worshiped by tens of thousands of New Agers. Best-seller books he has dictated to his possessed subject, J. Z. Knight, are available in Waldenbooks and B. Dalton bookstores, and his videos are brisk sellers too. One lady, a secretary in a large, highly regarded and well-known law office with seventy-two in-house attorneys, has confided to my wife, Wanda, that every day during the lunch break, employees of the firm gather in the conference room to view Ramtha on video. They take notes and discuss his teachings much as do Christians at a group Bible study.

Let Go and Let Satan

My voluminous research proves conclusively that demons like Ramtha are at the root of every New Age teaching. I have yet to discover a single New Age cult, organization, or church that was not founded by a demon or demons. Without exception, I have found that it was demons who first gave their human contact the idea, the inspiration, or the command to set up the group. Often the very structure, goals, and organizational blueprint for daily operation were detailed, and the leadership of the group selected by the demon overlords. This should not be surprising since the New Age teaches that one's "higher self," "inner voice," spirit guide, or the "Christ within" (not Jesus!) is always right and is always to be obeyed.

New Agers are taught to let go and let their inner "god"— the Self or the Universal Mind or Force—take over. Total, absolute surrender to the higher intelligence is the password. Matthew Fox best expressed this by commenting on the advice of his mystic spirit guide, the heretical German priest, Meister Eckhart, who lived in medieval days:

> Meister Eckhart confessed that "he prayed God to rid me of God." One must recognize the importance of letting go in this radical way . . . if one is to befriend the dark . . . if anywhere lies sheer abandon.[20]

Pledging Allegiance to the Devil

Befriend the dark? Sheer abandon? Is that what the New Age stands for? The startling answer is *yes*. Satan has devised a strategy that is working like clockwork. That strategy is to call good evil, and evil good. New Agers are buying into this strategy simply because they have no discernment. Once a person rejects Jesus Christ, his mind is opened and becomes vulnerable and receptive to the awful alternative. These people have become mere pawns of the Devil, to whom they must give all allegiance.

The first step in pledging allegiance to the Devil is for the individual to acknowledge the "rightful place" that sin has in their lives. Paul told us to put on the whole armor of God to withstand temptation and sin. But Satan seductively teaches that sin is not necessarily to be avoided:

> We also need to let sin be sin for a while to allow sin its rightful and instructive place in our own and others' lives. . . . Too much armor, too heavy defences, too thick walls prevent the vulnerability of our consciences.[21]

Once a New Age student is willing to accept the lie that sin has "a rightful and instructive place in our own and others' lives," he or she is ready to recite the second stanza of "I pledge allegiance to the Devil." In this phase of instruction, the deluded student is taught the positive power and value of *evil*. Evil is presented to the individual by the Devil's agents as something to be embraced in its darkness, even cherished as something holy, and considered praiseworthy and of "God."

The New Age idea of evil is best expressed by Matthew Fox's friend from beyond, Meister Eckhart:

All things praise God and bless God. Evil too praises God.[22]

Fox also teaches his followers at his Institute for Creation-Centered Spirituality that God resides in the depths and in the darkness, and there we must go if we are to commune with him:

> We sink into the depths and in this depth we find God, who dwells especially in the depths and in the dark.[23]

Matthew Fox's statement that God dwells in the dark is an abominable lie easily refuted by Scripture. But this spiritually sick Dominican priest is not content merely to utter this blasphemy, for he goes on to declare that entering the darkness is a good thing. "The very act of entering darkness, to befriend it," Fox says, "becomes a profoundly healing event."[24]

The New Age has no cure for the evil that fills the columns of our daily newspapers and explodes about us in the recesses of today's world. The New Age seeks no cure. Its response is to heartily recommend that man *embrace evil and befriend it.* Says Dr. Martin Groder, a psychiatrist and business consultant in Chapel Hill, North Carolina: "The only way to deal with your dark side is to take it out to lunch. Once you acknowledge it, your evil demon may actually turn out to be your best friend."[25]

How does one take his dark side "out to lunch"? Groder provides one rather shocking example. He tells of a troubled, guilt-ridden man who came to him confessing to enormous thoughts of incest toward his own daughter. The psychologist advised him to tell other men friends of these feelings. Then he would discover that all men have such thoughts and his guilt would promptly vanish.[26]

Groder confidently states that if you take his advice and make your dark side—your evil demon—your best friend, you are on your way to liberation! "This is part of the liberating and extremely rewarding process of discovering who you are," he writes.[27] Any discerning Christian can tell the person who follows this tragic advice that he will not become liberated. He will instead be swiftly taken in spiritual bondage and become a tool of the Devil.

You Can Do Anything . . . You Are God!

The willingness of the New Ager to accept and embrace evil is an inevitable by-product and unavoidable result of possession by demonic forces. These forces accept the New Ager as he is. They do not require him to improve no matter how great his faults. You are what you are, they say, and in fact, if you want to, you can go ahead and be worse! You can do anything you want, no matter how callous, no matter how sick. *You are God.*

The rejection of evil as an active and insidious force is the ultimate denial of reality. It leads the new Ager blindly onward to become a selfish and narcissistic nonperson. He is transformed into a possessed entity who spouts terms like "peace," "love," and "forgiveness" as if they are empty concepts exercised in a vacuum. Devoid of the true *agape* love that only Jesus Christ can bestow, New Age disciples are given a weak substitute, a type of spiritual Kool-aid, by their own master: Satan, the Lord of This World.

The positive affirmation below, recommended by John Randolph Price as meditation for New Age spiritual seekers, is just one example of this valueless spiritual Kool-aid:

> I am a delightful child of God. My spirit is God being me in the absolute. My soul is God being me in expression. . . . I am God being me! . . . I dismiss all thoughts of right and wrong. . . . I no longer hold any unforgiveness toward MYSELF. I rise above all feelings of guilt, and I am free to love myself as never before. . . . My love for ME, MYSELF, the I that I am, knows no bounds. I AM LOVE. I AM LOVE. I AM LOVE.[28]

A careful, Scriptural analysis of this blasphemous, self-centered and immoral affirmation, typical of many propounded in the New Age, leaves a Christian shocked and almost at a loss for words. The person who expresses and believes this affirmation, yet claims to be a Christian is easily seen as either a deceiver or else one who has been deceived. Even a five-year-old trained by loving Christian parents knows that he cannot "dismiss all thoughts of right and wrong." He knows that he cannot by himself "rise above all feelings of guilt"; and the well-adjusted five-year-old knows full well, even at that early age, that he is not "God." The true God of the Bible instills such knowledge within so that almost from the crib, every person has inside his soul a longing to serve a greater God, the only God, the great I AM of the Scriptures.

Walking as Children of Light

We have seen how both *sin* and *evil* are considered in the New Age to be of positive value, even as holy attributes. Regrettably, such twisted beliefs lead to yet a third conclusion on the part of those who have bought into the New Age lie: *Darkness must be affirmed as good and embraced with enthusiasm.*

Now before I discuss this horrendous New Age teaching, I believe it is important we set forth God's Word. In stark contrast to the doctrines the New Age World Religion is fostering, the Bible regards sin, evil, and darkness as abominations of the Devil to be strictly avoided by Christians. It is ludicrous for a Christian, or anyone in their right mind for that matter, to maintain that sin, evil, and darkness can be entered into without harsh consequences.

"What communion hath light with darkness?" asks 2 Corinthians 6:14. The answer rings loud and clear: *Absolutely none.* Paul adjures us in Ephesians 5:1 and 8, "Be ye, therefore, followers of God, as dear children. . . . For ye were sometimes darkness, but now are ye light in the Lord; walk as children of light." Further, the Scriptures remind us that we are to "have no fellowship with the unfruitful works of darkness, but, rather, reprove them" (Eph. 5:11).

Sin is of the darkness, and it is surely an atrocity before the Lord to make light of sin or to teach that sin is ultimately harmless, or worse, holy. Jesus, we read in Galatians 1:4, "gave himself for our sins, that he might deliver us from the present evil world, according to the will of God and our Father."

What does God think of sin? It is so abhorrent an affront to His holiness that His Scriptures tell us that "the wages of sin is death." But, continues that same Bible passage, "the gift of God is eternal life through Jesus Christ our Lord" (Romans 6:23). What must we do to avoid the penalties of sin? The unequivocal, forthright answer is found in 1 John 1:9, 10:

> If we confess our sins, he is faithful and just to forgive us our sins, and to cleanse us from all unrighteousness.
>
> If we say that we have not sinned, we make him a liar, and his word is not in us.

Though the New Age would attempt to uplift evil as beneficial, God's Word, the Bible, is clearly to the contrary. "Abstain from all appearance of evil" (1 Thess. 5:22), we are commanded. In Romans 12, we are further instructed to "abhor that which is evil, cleave to that which is good" (v. 9). And we are led to resist and to overcome evil with good: "Be not overcome of evil, but overcome evil with good" (v. 21).

Elegantly and with power, the Old Testament gives us instructions on the choices we are to make if we are to receive eternal life. "See, I have set before thee this day life and good, and death and evil" (Deut. 30:15). "Therefore," the Scripture warns, "choose life, that both thou and thy seed may live" (v. 19).

Embracing the Darkness

In the New Age World Religion, light and darkness are said to be two complementary sides of the same coin. They are like two colors that sometimes bleed and blend together to create a unified, if mixed, design. New Age ministers encourage their flocks literally to wallow in darkness and not to be afraid of the dark. Their religion is one of opposites complementing each other, of yin and yang intertwining, of black and white meeting and embracing. Darkness and light are not two qualities, or two lifestyles, to keep separate. They are both to be experienced and appreciated as valuable learning tools as the person journeys toward self-empowerment and divinity.

Matthew Fox, the Dominican priest whose concept of "creation-centered spirituality"—worshiping the creation, not the Creator—seems to have taken the New Age world by storm, is an enthusiast of embracing the darkness. To him we can attribute the great blasphemy of equating God with darkness. Fox also preaches that making contact with darkness is to contact God Himself:

God is superessential darkness and to make contact with the darkness is to make contact with the deepest side of the Godhead.[29]

Fox also contends that a person cannot grow spiritually *unless* he dwells in the darkness: "Growth of the human person takes place in the dark. Underground. In subterranean passages. There . . . God alone works."[30]

Even the most immature of Christians can recognize this as a lie. Fox, in speaking of dark, underground, subterranean passages, is in truth painting a vivid picture of hell. *Sheol,* the Hebrew word for hell or hades, is what Fox envisions: a pit, ditch, or underworld place of darkness and despair. This is where Satan and his demons will live and where humans will writhe in agony and pain. In the New Testament the word *Gehenna* is used, a term describing the place of the final sufferings of the wicked and unrepentant.

The Old Testament (see Psa. 6:5; 88:4; Isa. 38:18; Job 29:26) reveals the utter horror of this underground abode of evil. Its most dread reality is that those who are cast there are without hope of communication with God. Fox and his New Age counterparts must surely find great satisfaction in leading people to believe just the opposite: that this place of evil is where God dwells and where He can be found.

Where Can God Be Found?

The Bible tells us that when a person cries out for God, professes a belief in His Son Jesus Christ, repents of his sins and commits himself to serve Christ, something very wonderful and priceless is *added* to his life. He becomes filled with the Holy Spirit and his mind is renewed.

How different, unfortunately, is the New Age concept regarding rebirth or transformation. Fox, for instance, refers readers to Meister Eckhart's dictum: "God is not found in the soul by adding anything but by a process of subtraction."[31]

In the New Age, transformation is said to come about when you shed your "outmoded" belief in a greater, personal God outside yourself and accept instead that an inner journey to darkness will magically make *you* a god.

Some in the New Age even teach that we must not covet the light, but must seek after more darkness by going deeper into ourselves through meditation. Rainer Maria Wilke, who has said we must love and accept the "dragons" within, suggests that we go deeper into the darkness until we eventually discover the roots of our existence.[32] Wilke's God is not the God of the Bible, a point that becomes dynamically clear when she states:

> No matter how deeply I go down into myself my God is dark and like a webbing made of a hundred roots that drink in silence.[33]

Wilke's thought that God is dark and resembles a webbing made of a hundred roots that drink in silence is sick and depressing. One can easily imagine the horror and dread terror of becoming entwined and entrapped in an octopus-like network of roots deep beneath the earth somewhere in a dark passageway of evil. To Wilke, such phraseology is lyrically beautiful. To the Christian who knows God as the wondrous being of light whom no man has seen, who sits on a majestic throne in heaven, Wilke's comments constitute dark poetry.

The New Age teachers laugh at our revulsion and apprehension. They profess to be unafraid of the darkness and what it represents, and they cynically scorn those who would withdraw from the dark. Matthew Fox lambastes people of the light with the rhetoric that, "We have become afraid of the dark. Afraid of no light . . . *We whore after more light*."[34] Better it would be, says Fox, if we were filled "with wonder and gratitude and praise for what amazing things can happen in the dark."

> For example, we all began in the dark. Our loving parents presumably conceived of us in the dark nights of their lovemaking. We ought to celebrate that dark sacrament of marriage's most intimate moments with more sensuality and honesty than we do.[35]

Just as could be expected of a heretical priest who is into nature/earth worship and who teaches that Eve's act of disobedience in the Garden was not original sin but "original blessing,"

Fox insists that "darkness and sensuousness need to be taught and appreciated."[36]

How tragic a teaching! Who would have ever believed just a few years ago that wicked men would rise up to lead a new, dynamically growing worldwide religious movement based on the principles that "darkness and sensuousness need to be taught and appreciated"? Worse, who could have foreseen the advent of a New Age World Religion that embraces evil and denies sin while boasting of its spirituality and godlike attributes? This is unadulterated satanism designed to bring man to the very threshold of utter chaos and debauchery.

How important it is that as Christians we recognize that the day of the Beast and his Mark is imminent and that Jesus could come at any time:

> And that, knowing the time, that it is high time to awake out of sleep; for now is our salvation nearer than when we believed. The night is far spent, the day is at hand; let us therefore cast off the works of darkness, and let us put on the armor of light. (Romans 13:11, 12)

Understanding Evil

In Salado, Texas this year, some 1200 theologians, philosophers, historians, editors, ministers, psychiatrists and professors gathered to attend a three-day symposium called "Understanding Evil."[37] They debated and discussed every form of evil, from a child pulling the wings off a housefly to Hitler's death camp at Auschwitz. They confronted slavery and the Inquisition and the Holocaust. They delved into the AIDS crisis, studied child abuse, and contemplated on the modern names of evil: Hitler and Manson and Stalin and Pol Pot.

Rollo May, the New Age psychiatrist, and M. Scott Peck, the celebrated New Age author of *The Road Less Traveled*, were there, as well as historian J. B. Russell.

What astounding new knowledge or hopeful information came out of this historical gathering? Regrettably, none. A *Chicago Tribune* reporter present said there was much talk, little resolution, and no solutions.[38] Finally Bill McKay, a man who had come for help because he has the responsibility of running a center for disturbed teenagers, became frustrated. Repeatedly he asked speakers to define "evil." "We've got kids who are potential Charles Mansons," he said in a questioning voice filled with anguish. "These kids have no conscience, we don't know how to deal with them." He never did get an answer.[39]

These learned men, gathered from all over the globe, had no answers because they did not know God. They did not know His Word. His Word tells us that His Son, Jesus Christ, came "to destroy the works of the devil" that we might live. His Word tells us that God is light and there is no darkness in Him, that to find that light we must go outside of ourselves and seek Him. This is God's solution for evil. It is the only answer there is. And it is a magnificient answer!

Tragically, millions of New Agers do not recognize evil though it brutally confronts, envelops, and seizes them. We recall that Pontius Pilate looked Jesus squarely in the face and asked, "What is truth?" Remarkably, Truth was right there in front of him, unrecognized in the person of the Christ.

Who Waits in the Dark?

Far more grievous than Pilate's error is that of today's New Agers. They do not ask of Jesus, what is Truth?, but instead seek it within the depths of their own being.

They know and readily admit that it is the darkness they seek, for without God as their hedge of protection, they are drawn to the darkness as a moth is drawn to a flame. Once they taste the darkness, they are hooked, because the darkness is the place where Satan dwells. They have trespassed into *his* territory. Thus, Miriam Starhawk, in her *Dreaming the Dark,* confesses:

> The depths of our beings are not all sunlit; to see clearly we must be willing to dive into the dark, inner abyss and *acknowledge the creatures we may find there.*[40]

Just what *creatures* do New Agers find and acknowledge in the dark, inner abyss within? Their name, unquestionably, is legion. Their master is Satan. They want you to believe that they are not evil, that there is no evil, that all is good. That is their smooth lie.

In Salado, Texas, at the symposium on "Understanding Evil,"

perhaps the most poignant and chilling statement was that of *Texas Monthly* magazine editor Gregory Curtis. Perceiving that the many "experts" at the symposium could shed no light at all on what evil is and what is its source, Curtis sagely concluded:

> What we have to fear in the 20th Century is evil that does not know itself, that is, in fact, convinced it is good. How could the Holocaust have happened? The answer is, *they believed.*[41]

PART FOUR

Who Can Escape the Mark of the Beast?

THIRTEEN

All Hail the New Age Messiah!

*For there shall arise false Christs, and false prophets,
and shall show great signs and wonders, insomuch
that, if it were possible, they shall deceive the very elect.
Behold, I have told you before.* (Jesus the Christ,
Matthew 24:24, 25)

*My face is known to a growing number of brothers, but
My Name for the present must remain undisclosed. In
this way, my Secret can be maintained.* (Lord Maitreya,
the "New Age Christ,"
Messages from Maitreya)

We know from Bible prophecy that a great but supremely evil world leader will arise on earth. He will be far more powerful and more demonically inspired than perhaps any man who has ever lived. He will be the Antichrist, the Beast with the number 666.

The Antichrist will seize world political and economic power, and all of humanity will honor and obey him, except those who are chosen by Jesus Christ. These will resist and be killed. Their obliteration will greatly simplify matters for the Beast. Without the restraining power of the Holy Spirit (see 2 Thessalonians 2), he will move quickly to establish a One World Religion and a One World Government.

The Bible of the Christians and the Jews will surely be revised and "objectionable" passages—for example, those that refer to Jesus—will be removed. The churches will all be unified in doctrine and ritual. The Image to the Beast will be set up in Christian churches and in all temples as a focal point for world religious unity. This Image will also remind mankind that the "Christ" of the Aquarian Age has come and that it is he who rules the planet.

The awful truth is that the New Age "Christ" bears no resemblance whatsoever to the Christ witnessed by Peter, John, James, Thomas, and the other disciples—Jesus Christ, whose acts while on earth were recorded in the Gospels. Instead the "Christ" of Aquarian man will be the "son of perdition" prophesied by Paul in 2 Thessalonians 2. The New Age "Christ" will be filled spiritually with the poisonous and thoroughly evil nature of Satan. He will be Satan's man: the imposter king who comes as one of the horsemen of the Apocalypse—the rider of the white horse (Rev. 6).

New Age authorities make this point very clear: The new Age "Christ" is *not* the same as the Christian Christ. As Foster Bailey has scornfully snapped:

> "The expectation of the return of a great world teacher, a divine planetary avatar, is universal." However: The Christian doctrine that he (the Christ) comes as a Christian to save us from hell and for some distant judgment date is a hangover from humanity's childhood days. He does not come to save us. . . .
>
> The churchmen of Christianity have imprisoned the Christ in their own separative religious organizations to such an extent that one might think God loved only Christians. The word Christ is a name in the Hierarchy for the holder of an all-embracing world-wide divine leadership. . . . He is not at all limited to Christianity."[1]

The Personality and Powers of the Antichrist

What manner of man will the Antichrist be? What horrible satanic powers will he wield? The Bible reveals the answers.

He Comes as a Liar!

Daniel prophesied that the Antichrist will have a "fierce countenance" and that he will "understand dark sentences":

And in the latter time . . . when the transgressors are come to the full, a king of fierce countenance, and understanding dark sentences, shall stand up. (Dan. 8:23)

When the Bible says the last-days ruler will understand dark sentences, it refers to his uncanny ability to deliver powerfully evil speeches that have dark meaning and contain untruth after untruth. He will undoubtedly hold audiences spellbound.

He Shall War Against the People of God

The Antichrist will not be reluctant to take on Christian believers and destroy them:

And his power shall be mighty, but not by his own power; and he shall destroy wonderfully, and shall prosper, and practice, and shall destroy the mighty and the holy people. (Dan. 8:24)

. . . his heart shall be against the holy covenant; and he shall do exploits. (Dan. 11:28)

He Will Corrupt the People Through Flatteries

"You are a god. You are perfect." This is the essence of the New Age lie. How very flattering to actually be called a god or goddess!

"You are all-powerful!" Another New Age lie, but again, so appealing, so flattering. No wonder Bible prophecy forewarned us:

And such as do wickedly against the covenant shall be corrupt by flatteries. . . . (Dan. 11:32)

He Will Establish Himself as the Master of a "World Mind"

The Antichrist will consolidate all earthly power under his dictatorial control. Evidently the governing of the world will be divided up into ten regions or kingdoms, each led by a king whose master is the Antichrist:

> And the ten horns which thou sawest are ten kings, who
> have received no kingdom as yet, but receive power as kings
> one hour with the beast. These have one mind, and shall give
> their power and strength unto the beast (Rev. 17:12, 13).

"One Mind"—a One World Mind. This is the ultimate goal of the Beast of Satan.

He Will First Declare a God of Forces

The Antichrist will institute a planetary religion in which a God of Forces is exalted. This is already the New Age god, and so this declaration of the Antichrist will be cheered by humanity. Actually, in worshiping the vague and nebulous "God of forces," the New Ager can worship any imaginary god he chooses. All are part and parcel of the "Force" thought to permeate our universe. In effect, in the New Age kingdom, any deity can be worshiped except the personal God of the Holy Bible. What the deluded New Agers do not always know is that all gods other than Jesus Christ are proxies for the Devil.

> And the king shall do according to his will. . . . Neither shall
> he regard the god of his fathers. . . . But in his estate shall he
> honor the God of forces. . . . Thus shall he do in the most
> strong holds with a strange god, whom he shall acknowledge
> and increase with glory; and he shall cause them to rule over
> many. . . . (Dan. 11:36-39)

Note the word "them," indicating the many gods that may be worshiped in the New Age.

He Will Eventually Declare Himself to Be "God"

Not content with being a mere World Teacher or political leader, the Antichrist will eventually (after a three and a half year reign—see Daniel 8:8-14) put away all pretense and declare himself to be "God." The New Agers worldwide who worship tens of thousands of different gods and goddesses will one day suddenly be ordered to cease their worship of all but the "One

Great God," who is the New Age "Christ." The false prophet of the Beast will supervise this unification of all worship.

What a shock to the millions of people who first believed the lie that they would have the liberty and license to worship whom and what they desired in their own imaginations. The screws will be tightened by a jealous World Ruler!

> . . . and he shall exalt himself, and magnify himself above every god, and shall speak marvelous things against the God of gods, and shall prosper till the indignation be accomplished; for that which is determined shall be done. (Dan. 11:36)

He Will Cause All to Worship Satan as Lord

The plot thickens and worsens. "In worshiping me as your God, you are actually worshiping Satan. He is my lord, and he is your lord. Bow down to my image, for it is also his image. I am the Son of Satan." This will be the fateful announcement that shall someday ring in the ears of a world groaning from demonic attack and lacerated by sin and corruption.

And like automatons, the people of earth will do as they are told. Without hesitation. For the Mark either on their forehead or their right hand signifies their allegiance to the Beast.

> And they worshiped the dragon which gave power unto the beast; and they worshiped the beast, saying, Who is like unto the beast? Who is able to make war with him? (Rev. 13:4)

What an unholy road to hell Satan will have caused the people of earth—all except for the Christians—to travel. First, he assures them that they are their own god. Then he teaches them to conjure up in their vain imaginations images of false gods and goddesses who will serve them and help them learn to become all they can become as the gods they are. Then he dramatically switches gears and announces that the New Age "Christ" alone is God. Finally comes the shocker of shockers: all along it was Satan himself whom they were worshiping!

Likely, in that day the voice of Satan will proceed from the mouth of his Antichrist on earth. He will be heard to solemnly state:

> With whose voice do I speak? I speak with my own, but whose voice is that? Am I God? Am I a christ? Am I a being come to you from the dwelling places of the Infinite? I am all these things, and more. . . . I wish to present to you, therefore, the revelation of man's destiny, for behold! I have placed my seal upon this planet.[2]

Sound unbelievable, even preposterous, to you? Then consider this: the above statement has already been uttered. David Spangler, one of the New Age's most famous and highly regarded teachers and "theologians," recorded this very quote in his revealing book *Revelation: The Birth of a New Age.* Who uttered it? According to Spangler, this was the pronouncement of "John," a marvelous spirit from beyond.

Spangler says that it is John, also known as "Limitless Love and Truth," who will separate the wheat from the chaff, sending Christians and other New Age unbelievers to another dimension where they will be more happy and where they will be reeducated. Meanwhile, on earth the New Age "Christ" can move ahead in building his magnificient Kingdom.[3]

He Will Come as a Miracle-worker

We are seeing today an explosion in signs, wonders, and miracles. The New Age press constantly is reporting healings, miraculous psychic powers, and prophecies coming to pass. The Christian community is also seeing a huge increase in signs and wonders ministries; but so often, the faith healers and miracle-workers bring with their marvelous works heretical doctrines that bear no fruit.

While God certainly can heal wounded bodies and while there is no miracle He cannot perform, we must always be on guard against *lying* signs and wonders. If *anyone* comes performing miracles and demonstrating signs and wonders, let him give Jesus Christ all the credit. And let his ministry be based solely on the preaching of the cross and on the gospel "once delivered unto the saints" (Jude 3). Otherwise, he is a miracle-worker of Satan. He may even be the Antichrist or his false prophet, for the Bible prophesies that after the Holy Spirit, the Restrainer, is lifted by God:

> . . . then shall that wicked one be revealed. . . . Even him whose coming is after the working of Satan with all power and signs and lying wonders. And with all deceivableness of unrighteousness in them that perish, because they received not the love of the truth, that they might be saved. (2 Thess. 2:8-10)

Clearly, the New Age Antichrist and his prophet will be empowered by Satan to perform these lying signs and wonders that shall deceive the whole world. It will not be by his own power but by a greater power (Dan. 8:24). His powers will derive from his practice of satanism, sorcery, and witchcraft, which occultists have always grouped under the term "the craft":

> And through his policy also he shall cause craft to prosper in his hand. . . . (Dan. 8:24, 25)

He Will Come Disguised as a Peacemaker

The whole world hungers for peace. One influential New Age group, Global Forum, recently editorialized, "The human race must find solutions to the problems that menace its very existence. *People will do anything that needs to be done when it comes to the issues of life and death.*"[4]

The Antichrist will demonstrate to the world that he is a sterling man of peace. He will shed tears over the war dead, deliver impassioned pleas for peace before the United Nations General Assembly, and jet from nation to nation forging peace treaties. One day he will proudly boast that world peace is assured, and the masses will acclaim him as a savior.

Yet, the Bible reveals that his will be a false peace. "For when they shall say, Peace and safety, then sudden destruction cometh upon them, as travail upon a woman with child, and they shall not escape" (1 Thess. 5:3).

Only the return of Jesus Christ will insure world peace. But until He comes agin, let no one deceive you. There will be wars followed by wars until one day this entire planet is enveloped by the mushroom clouds of atomic weapons and blood runs like the rivers. This is prophesied in Joel, Ezekiel, Daniel, and Revelation, and it will occur.

Listen to these words of Jeremiah and meditate on the truth of God's Word:

> Then said I, Ah, Lord God! Behold, the prophets say unto them, Ye shall not see the sword, neither shall ye have famine, but I will give you assured peace in this place.
>   Then the Lord said unto me, The prophets prophesy lies in my name. I sent them not, neither have I commanded them, neither spoke unto them; they prophesy unto you a false vision and divination, and a thing of nought, and the deceit of their heart. (Jer. 14:13, 14)

He Shall Rule Over All the World

The New Age Antichrist will have a planetary domain. This will be just what Djwhal Khul, the Lucis Trust's spirit guide, and so many other demons as well as human New Age leaders have long sought:

> We need . . . the political synthesis of a World Federation with the . . . World Brain . . . We need also a planetary way of life, a planetary ethics and a planetary way of feeling to supply the powerful drive we shall require for the great tasks that lie ahead of us.[5]

The drive to create a One World Order is in high gear. The two superpowers, the U.S.A. and the U.S.S.R., are both reeling like drunks from the blows of Satan. While the New Age is making huge strides in America and the West, in the Soviet bloc there is a literal tidal wave of New Age occultism overflowing the land.

Until now, the Communists have always held to the view that Christianity and religion would slowly disappear as communism met the spiritual and material needs of the masses. The Soviets have fought to close churches and have persecuted true

Christian believers. But now an amazing transformation is occurring. Religion is again given the green light in Russia. Religion, mind you. Not Christianity.

Mikhail Gorbachev, the Soviet Communist Party leader, is surely the most shrewd strategist of Satan the Kremlin has ever known. He recognized that the spiritual void of his people demanded to be filled. So now he comes to the rescue, bringing occultism and New Age doctrines to the Soviet people and encouraging mystical and psychological practices and beliefs.

Foreign observers are startled to discover that for the first time ever, Soviet television carries programs about psychic and mind powers. The Soviet citizen now reads information once expressly prohibited in the press and in magazines—for example, interviews with psychics and fortune-tellers, astrological forecasts, and strange and bizzare tales of mysterious events and magical feats. Meanwhile, the Soviet defense establishment spends millions studying and researching how Eastern mysticism and the occult can be harnessed for the military.[6]

Mikhail Gorbachev, New Age Man of Peace or Deceiver?

It is reported that Soviet leader Gorbachev threw his support behind the Harmonic Convergence of August 16-17, 1987, when hundreds of thousands of New Agers meditated worldwide to invoke and usher in a New Age Kingdom.[7] Gorbachev has stated again and again what New Agers love to hear—that the world desperately needs a "higher consciousness" and world unity, without Jesus Christ of course.[8]

As Gorbachev has put it: "We are all passengers aboard one ship, the Earth, and we must not allow it to be wrecked. There will be no second Noah's ark."[9]

Secretary Gorbachev has even called for a World Brain to help solve the world's mounting problems: "The United Nations should set up a world 'brain trust' of scientists, politicians and even church leaders to help solve global problems."[10]

To put his New Age preaching into action, Gorbachev is sending Soviet delegates to a global New Age Convocation called The Global Spiritual and Parliamentary Forum on Human Survival, to meet in Oxford, England in 1988.[11] About forty nations will send delegates, and Gorbachev wants to let the world know that he is solidly behind this first-step movement to set up an ongoing "Council of Wise Persons." Gorbachev issued this announcement:

> A world consultative council under the U.N. auspices uniting the world's intellectual elite would be globally beneficial.[12]

In Moscow in 1987, Secretary Gorbachev and his Soviet Communist Party hosted a gala New Age peace festival, entitled World Congress for Peace, Equality and Development in a Nuclear-Free Environment by the Year 2000. A U.S. New Age delegation attended. Miss Hunter Campbell, one of those participating, recalls: "There was one moment in the conference when Soviet leader Mikhail Gorbachev began crying when he was presented with a crystal globe. Half the women there started crying too, and it was one of those moments in my life when I thought, 'Yes, the world works.' "[13]

Werner Erhard, founder of est, is now conducting New Age seminars in Russia for Soviet managers and Communist Party officials, while Esalen, the New Age think-tank in California, has begun a Soviet-American Exchange Program. One official Soviet visitor sent to the U.S.A. by Gorbachev was recently quoted in a prominent New Age magazine as expressing the prevailing Soviet view that "The Force is God. But it's a Cosmic God."[14] There was little doubt in his mind that communism and the New Age religious, social, political, and economic philosophies perfectly dovetail.

Mikhail Gorbachev set forth his own New Age views in the astonishing book *Perestroika: New Thinking for Our Country and the World*. So many New Agers, liberals, and Communist sympathizers bought this book that, published in the U.S., it hit the *New York Times* Bestseller List in 1987 and 1988.

In the book, Gorbachev parroted the standard New Age lie of Satan, declaring that the drive for world peace "can and must rally mankind and facilitate the formation of a *global consciousness*." A global consciousness is simply a New Age synonym for a One World Mind. Gorbachev also called for a "world-wide revolution" so that mankind would have a "new way of thinking." This revolution, he added, must "begin in the mind." In addition, there must be "universal values," said Gorbachev, "to take advantage of man's spiritual capital."[15]

The demonically inspired Soviet chief called for a "restructuring" of the whold world, to include "a new world economic order."[16]

Is Soviet leader Mikhail Gorbachev really a devout New Ager, or is he shrewdly using the New Age to secretly promote the Kremlin's plans for world domination? Actually it does not matter. Either way he and his fellow Communists are dancing to the tune of Satan. Once a New Age World Order is firmly entrenched, communism will find itself just one pillar supporting the great world superstructure held firmly in the grip of the Beast.

All Is Ready

All the chips are falling in place. All the world's religions are merging. The apostate Christian church is largely abandoning its faith in Jesus to foster this world unity. Meanwhile, a One World Government and One World Economic System are on the horizon. As Norman Cousins, prominent New Age leader and president of the World Federalist Society, has trumpeted, "World government is coming. In fact, it is inevitable. No arguments for it or against it can change that fact."[17]

Two Earth-shattering Events to Come

Cousins, regrettably, is correct. The whole world is going New Age. But the changeover will not be complete until two momentous, earth-shattering events transpire: first, there is to be a rapture out of this world of God's people; and second, all the rest of the world will receive an invitation. This won't be just another plain vanilla-type invitation. This will be an invitation to become a full-fledged partner with the dark forces of this planet—an invitation to receive the Mark of the Beast.

We are on the very threshold of the satanic inauguration of all mankind. The Luciferic Initiation is at hand. Come one, come all, for this is your passport for a one way trip. To hell.

FOURTEEN

Passport to Hell: The Great Luciferic Initiation of All Mankind

And I looked and, behold, a pale horse, and his name that sat on him was Death, and Hell followed with him. And power was given unto them over the fourth part of the earth, to kill with sword, and with hunger, and with death, and with the beasts of the earth. (Rev. 6:8)

The choice is: do you wish to become a natural Christ, a universal human, or do you wish to die?

(Barbara Marx Hubbard, *Happy Birth Day Planet Earth*)

Someday in the not-too-distant future—most New Age leaders pinpoint the year 2000—every person on earth will be given a choice. Either we accept the Mark of the New Age World Leader and worship his image, or we are killed.

The Bible warns that accepting his Mark will save your mortal life but doom you to eternal hell (Rev. 14:9-11). Yet, the Scriptures reveal that all but those who believe on and are saved by Christ Jesus will take the Mark and undergo a Luciferic Initiation. Why? Because they will believe the Lie.

Paul prophesied in 2 Thessalonians 2 that after the Antichrist is come and after he declares himself to the world as God, the vast majority will be given a strong delusion by God. They will believe in this horrid world leader and eventually worship him as God. And they will accept his Luciferic Initiation, because they first rejected the Truth, which is Christ Jesus. Paul tells us that these people "received not the love of the truth, that they might be saved":

> And for this cause God shall send them strong delusion, that they should believe a lie, that they all might be damned who believe not the truth, but had pleasure in unrighteousness. (2 Thess. 2:10-12)

We learn, then, from Bible prophecy the ultimate destiny of these masses of unsaved people. They will believe the lie and be damned for all eternity. But just how will the New Age Antichrist convince these people to take his Mark and be initiated into the Mystery of Iniquity? And more poignantly, what is to be the fate of the Christians, Jews, and other New Age unbelievers who refuse initiation?

Initiation of the World . . . in Group Formation

New Age citizens will not have to worry about how they are going to get to the churches, synagogues, and temples to be initiated and given the Mark. In the New Age, individual salvation is considered an outmoded Christian concept. Universal love, unity, and group consciousness are the ideals for the New Age. Thus, Benjamin Creme has explained that people will be initiated in *group formation*:

> We are entering the "crisis of love." This is the experience which the human race faces as it enters that period when it will, as a whole . . . take its place in the Kingdom of Souls.
> During the Aquarian Age, the aim of the Christ, Maitreya, the Hierophant at the first two initiations, will be to initiate millions of people in group formation, into the Hierarchy. . . . Vast numbers will take the first and some will take the second initiation. This is an extraordinary event to be happening on a mass scale. It shows the success of the evolutionary Plan as it is envisaged by the Lord of the World, Sanat Kumara, or Shamballa, and carried out by his agents, the planetary Hierarchy.[1]

Evidently the "Lord of the World," Sanat, whom Christians know as Satan, will conduct mass initiation ceremonies throughout the world. They will be held shortly following the declaration of the New Age "Christ" that he alone is God and that all must worship his image in their churches and temples. This will be what Benjamin Creme calls the "Day of Declaration." "It will be," he states, "an experience for the whole of humanity—humanity will be faced with a choice and make the decision to reject gross materialism."[2]

By "reject gross materialism," Creme refers to the New Age idea that all the world's goods and riches must be redistributed to the "have not" countries and peoples.[3] Creme calls this "sharing," but what it really boils down to is Communist-like dictatorial control over the world economies. The One World Government will control all currencies, and no one can buy or sell unless he has the Mark or the number or the name of the Beast. This will be the fiat of the New International Economic Order.

Like Creme, Djwhal Khul and Alice Bailey also speak of a coming great mass initiation of mankind. Khul also speaks of being initiated in group formation as he sounds the clarion call that man should abandon his goal of individual salvation and surrender to the group will:

> The world goes forth to the initiates of the future: Lose sight of self in group endeavor. Forget the self in group activity. Pass through the portal to initiation in group formation and let the personal life be lost in the group life.[4]

How alien to Christianity, which teaches the uniqueness of man and individual responsibility to God. Yet, the demand by New Age leaders for a dissolving of individual identity is common among cult groups. Cult leaders do not want man to think for himself, nor do they want him to trust in God or God's Word. Surrender your will to the leadership, they implore. Merge your spirit with the group. Become part of the One.

Group Initiation: A Sound-and-Light Spectacular

The mass initiation ceremonies will be full of pageantry and pomp. They will undoubtedly be colorful sound-and-light spectaculars, rivaling the most gaudy of today's satanic rock concerts. Demonic tongues will be in evidence as the crowds work themselves into feverish ecstasy.[5]

Satanic symbols will be prominently displayed on the altar and walls, and celebrants will be expected to visualize and focus all their mental energies on these symbols. Geoffrey Hodson reveals that people might even gather in large groups and form symbols with their bodies—stars, triangles, and pentagrams— invoking the spirits to visibly descend to earth in fleshly form.[6]

Elizabeth Clare Prophet's writings suggest that participants will sing out and chant praises to the pentagram (five-pointed satanic star) and other images that represent the false New Age god:

> Glory to the flame! . . . Glory to the five-pointed star
> whereby all mankind learn the testing of Cosmos' secret rays![7]

There might well be human sacrifices made, as incredible as that would be. The brutality on television and in movies and the astonishing sacrificing of animals and even babies by today's satanists and witches are paving the way. Human sacrifice is, in the warped New Age view, symbolic of birth and rebirth in the cycles of reincarnation. Death is considered easy and desirable.[8]

All Hell to Break Loose

I strongly believe that after the Day of Declaration, all the religions of the earth will begin to offer the initiation and Mark in their respective churches, synagogues and temples. This will be what Djwhal Khul has termed "enforced initiation"[9] and Matthew Fox has called the "New Pentecost, a New Creation, a spiritual awakening that all the world's peoples and all the world's religions might share in."[10]

At that point, all hell will break loose as the Christians, Jews, and some hard-core Moslem fundamentalists who refuse to deny Allah, their God, rebel. Ruthless suppression will follow those who adamantly refuse to admit their own "divinity" and stubbornly resist taking the Mark of unity. Some Christians and other rebels will probably go underground, much as did the Jews and resistance fighters against the Nazis in Europe of World War II. They will be hunted down, however, and destroyed one-by-one by the police and specially commissioned "earth missionaries." A few may be put into special concentration camps, both for slave labor purposes and to show to the world the possibilities for reeducation and rehabilitation provided by the benevolent dictator, the New Age "Christ."[11]

The New Age "Christ" will call these killings "dislocations" and the imprisonment in concentration camps "relocations." Indeed, this veiled terminology is already in use among New Age leaders. Barbara Marx Hubbard, for example, has declared:

> Christ-consciousness and Christ-abilities are the natural inheritance of every human being on Earth. When the word of this hope has reached the nations, the end of this phase of evolution shall come. All will know their choice. All will be required to choose.
> There will be mighty dislocations and magnificient relocations. . . . All who choose not to evolve will die off; their souls will begin again within a different planetary system which will serve as kindergarten for the transition from self-centered to whole-centered being.
> The kindergarten class of Earth will be over.
> Humankind's collective power is too great to be inherited by self-centered, infantile people.[12]

So we see the clear outlines of the New Age doctrine that only the spiritually advanced can survive. Only those who embrace world unity and humanity as One, excluding Jesus Christ as *the* way, are fit to live. Christian believers are to be murdered and sent back to "kindergarten" in some other planetary system. Christianity is heretical. It leads to separativeness. Thus it is self-centered and not amenable to unity.

We as Christians cannot be allowed to exist because we, like cancerous cells, must be cut out of the world organism:

> Just as any cell, once cancerous, can infect the whole body with destructive growth, every human in the body of humanity can destroy the whole. This cannot be. This will not be.[13]

There must be a "radical cleansing" of the planet, New Age leaders teach. Take Benjamin Creme, for example. He threatens that those who remain adamant in refusing to join in the World Initiation will find themselves in the minority and have to "withdraw from this life."[14] Either accept the New Age, he solemnly states, or face the alternative.

And just what is Creme's alternative? "The alternative," he warns, "is annihlation."[15]

Revealed: The Secret of Secrets

What will *initiation* involve? For one thing, it will mean the physical taking of the Mark either on the forehead or on the right hand. But this will merely signify a chilling event that *will have already taken place in the spiritual realm*. That event is the acceptance by the initiate—the candidate for the Mark—of Lucifer as lord.

Thus will the great Secret of Secrets, the Mystery of Iniquity, be revealed in the New Age temples. Lucifer is the one whom all the world has been serving all along. Having rejected the Truth, all who have received the Mark will be given over entirely to a reprobate mind. Their lot is with Lucifer, their master. Their "Christ" is his earthly representative.

New Age leaders have for more than a decade now—ever since they were allowed to go public in 1975—admitted that it is Lucifer, the Solar God and Solar Logos, whom the New Age serves. David Spangler, for instance, has stated:

> Christ is the same force as Lucifer. . . . Lucifer prepares man for the experience of Christhood. (He is) the great initiator. . . . Lucifer works within each of us to bring us to wholeness, and as we move into a New Age . . . each of us in some way is brought to that point which I term the Luciferic Initiation . . . for it is an invitation into the New Age.[16]

Spangler is not lying. He is simply defining the "Mystery of Iniquity." Lucifer *is* the one who brings the New Age disciple to wholeness and unity—with *him*. He is the initiator who invites mankind into the New Age.

New Age occultist Edouard Schure confirms Spangler's confession but in a much more direct way. He describes Lucifer as finally triumphant and victorious both in heaven and on earth. The New Age "Christ" will then signal to Lord Lucifer that the

New Age Kingdom is in place and welcome him and his angels to come and reign. There will be rejoicing on earth and in the spiritual world that the forces apposing Lucifer are finally vanquished:

> Lucifer, having regained his star and his diadem, will assemble his legions for new works of creation. Attracted by his flaming torch, celestial spirits will descend . . . and he will send these messengers from unknown spheres to earth. Then the torch of Lucifer will signal "From Heaven to Earth!"— and the . . . (New Age) Christ will answer "From Earth to Heaven!"[17]

Dane Rudhyar touches upon the coming sudden declaration that Lucifer will be Lord of the New Age in his enlightening book *Occult Preparations for a New Age.* He suggests that the world may at first find itself disoriented and even shocked to discover what is happening. Eventually, however, all except believing Christians will accept Lucifer as their god, for they will realize that all along Sanat Kumara, whom they worshiped in the New Age as lord, was really Satan in disguise. Rudhyar himself intimates that Sanat is Satan when he remarks, "The interesting anagrammatic relationship between the terms Sanat and Satan is no doubt a most revealing symbolic indication."[18]

Rudhyar mentions that in the days to come "Fallen Angels" might become rehabilitated and honored once again by mankind. He also poses the idea that at this crucial point in time, man will be forced by "divine Fire" to choose between masters. Rudhyar's preference, of course, is that man choose the occult "Path."[19]

So Lucifer is no longer the hidden god of the New Age. Rudhyar, Spangler, Khul, Hubbard, and other New Age leaders are revealing more secrets than ever before. Theirs is today an open conspiracy, led behind the scenes by demons.

Why then is the whole world still confused about the Luciferic roots of the New Age? In part this confusion comes about as a result of the New Age's absurd contention that, though Lucifer is lord, he is not Satan. Satan is said to be a figment of the Christian imagination—a destructive thought-form created by hostile Jews centuries ago that now deserves to be discarded on the junk-heap of history. Lucifer is not Satan. Lucifer is a good angel.

Following the fateful Day of Declaration, however, all humanity will discover that there *is* a Satan, and he is so evil, so despicable, and so hideous that we can scarcely imagine his true characteristics. They will discover, too, that Satan and Lucifer are one and the same. This is what the New Age is now concealing. This is the secret lie of New Age teachers—what they blasphemously term the "Mystery of the Ages":

> The hour for the ancient mysteries has arrived. . . . These ancient Mysteries were given to humanity by the Hierarchy . . . hidden in numbers, in ritual, in words, and in symbology; these veil the secret. . . .
>
> It is these Mysteries which (the New Age) Christ will restore upon His reappearance, thus reviving the churches in a new form, and restoring the hidden Mystery. . . .
>
> The Mystery of the Ages is, through the reappearance of the Christ, on the verge of revelation. . . .[20]

People to Believe the Lie

It would seem that a doctrine that holds up Lucifer as God would not be popularly received. But keep in mind that the Holy Spirit who now restrains Satan will in days to come no longer be limiting the Devil's powers. The world will be sent the *strong delusion;* people's minds will be clouded and deluged with filth and impure thoughts. Visualization, meditation, and other consciousness-altering techniques will have made the vast majority susceptible to demonic imagery and possession. *The world will be insane!*

Under these extreme circumstances, people will believe the most ridiculous of lies. Recently we have seen this to be the case among New Agers who worship Hindu gurus such as the Rajneesh Bhagwan, wear crystals around their necks to bring in the "powers" and "forces," channel supposed spirits from the dead, and even sacrifice animals and babies to Satan. The world is already shaken, but there's more quivering and rocking to come.

> Maitreya will shake doctrines loose and destroy all dogmas that become stumblimg blocks to his kingdom to take us by

the hand to lead us into the new dispensation. The path is not narrow like the fundamentalist believes, but it has been widened for everybody that wants to enter in.[21]

So we see the New Age declaring that the path is wide. Jesus Christ is thus called a liar by the New Age, for it was He who testified in Matthew 7:13, 14 that *wide and broad is the path to destruction:*

> Enter in at the strait gate; for wide is the gate, and broad is the way, that leadeth to destruction; and many there be who go in that way; Because strait is the gate, and narrow is the way, which leadeth unto life, and few there be that find it.

Jesus once rhetorically asked, when I return, will there be found on earth any who believe in the Faith? He knew the path that lay ahead for mankind, and He knew that the great majority would choose disobedience and sin rather than submit to a loving but sovereign God.

The Bible prophesies that as the end of the age nears, things will get worse and worse, with men deceiving and being deceived. Unrighteousness, inhumane acts, and cruelty will abound and grow in intensity until finally the whole earth explodes in a furious killing and bloodletting climax. In a sense, the New Age is right: the way *has* been widened for everybody.

PART FIVE

A Victorious Crown for the King of Kings

FIFTEEN

The Glorious Return

*For as the lightning cometh out of the east, and shineth
even unto the west, so shall also the coming of the Son
of man be . . . and they shall see the Son of man
coming in the clouds of heaven with power and great
glory.* (Matthew 24:27, 30)

*The Day of Declaration will occur when humanity,
through its representatives, invites Him to speak to
mankind. . . . They would have to be very sure that
Maitreya was indeed the World Teacher, Christ, or
Messiah before they would invite him to address the
world.* (Benjamin Creme,
Maitreya's Mission)

W hat a magnificient God we have who believe on Him and His Word! The Bible
describes His majestic and glorious re-
turn. Never has there been a day and a moment as there will be
then. The sun will be darkened, and the moon will not give its
light; the stars will fall from heaven, and the powers of the
heavens will be shaken. Then Jesus Christ will be seen arriving in
the clouds of heaven with power and great glory. A mighty
trumpet will sound, and the angels will gather up the elect "from
the four winds, from one end of heaven to the other (see Matthew 24:31).

Revelation 19:11-16 describes this fantastic turn of events
when Jesus shall come to set up His millennial Kingdom on
earth. His return, which will occur immediately after the great
and chaotic Tribulation period, is described in this manner:

And I saw heaven opened, and behold, a white horse; and he that sat upon him was called Faithful and True, and in righteousness he doth judge and make war.

His eyes were like a flame of fire, and on his head were many crowns; and he had a name written, that no man knew, but he himself.

And he was clothed with a vesture dipped in blood; and his name is called The Word of God.

And the armies that were in heaven followed him upon white horses, clothed in fine linen, white and clean.

And out of his mouth goeth a sharp sword, that with it he should smite the nations, and he shall rule them with a rod of iron; and he treadeth the winepress of the fierceness and wrath of Almighty God.

And he hath on his vesture and on his thigh a name written, KING OF KINGS, AND LORD OF LORDS.

The Fall of the Beast

At Christ's return the Bible does not mince words about the fate of the Beast, the false prophet of the Beast, and the remaining inhabitants of earth who are not saved:

And the beast was taken, and with him the false prophet that wrought miracles before him, with which he deceived them that had received the mark of the beast, and them that worshiped his image. These both were cast alive into a lake of fire burning with brimstone.

And the remnant were slain with the sword of him that sat upon the horse, which sword proceeded out of his mouth; and all the fowls were filled with their flesh. (Rev. 19:20, 21)

The Pale Substitute "Christ" of the New Age

In stark contrast to the Bible's description of the events to come regarding the return of Jesus Christ, the New Age "Christ" is shown to be a weak and pitiful substitute for the real Christ of heaven. Satan and his New Age leadership know that they cannot duplicate the fantastic, all-glorious appearance of Jesus, so they are already busy creating excuses in advance.

New Age leaders can't imitate Jesus' mind-boggling coming in the clouds with all power and glory, so they claim that their "Christ," the Lord Maitreya, *has already appeared* on Planet Earth. Benjamin Creme says that the New Age "Christ" is now in London living in a Pakistani community, though he has not as yet revealed his identity to everyone:

Maitreya the Christ has been in London since July, 1977. He lives as an ordinary man concerned with modern problems—political, economic, and social.[1]

Creme further says that Lord Maitreya came silently from "Shamballa" and took up residence in London.[2] This certainly does not fit the prophetic picture of the Bible.

Maitreya will soon declare himself World Teacher, Creme maintains. He will come on all the world's television screens simultaneously, miraculously interrupting all scheduled broadcasting. He will speak and be heard by everyone in their own native language.[3]

But *when* will he appear? It's at this juncture that the New Age really begins to quibble and make excuses. After his embarrassment over announcing in 1982 that Maitreya would appear to the world within a few short months, Creme now says that *the Aquarian "Christ" cannot come until all the world's media invite him!*

The Day of Declaration will occur when humanity, through its representative, invites him to speak to mankind. . . . They would have to be very sure that Maitreya was indeed the World Teacher, Christ, or Messiah before they would invite him to address the world.[4]

How pitiful a false "Christ" is this Lord Maitreya. God's timetable prevails, and Benjamin Creme and his cohorts know it. Only when God is ready for the Tribulation period to unfold will this New Age "Christ" step forward on the world scene. Even then, we do not know if the Beast of Revelation will be Maitreya or another false "Christ" of the New Age.

What we should realize, however, is that Jesus Christ, the

only God there is, the God of Gods and Lord of Lords, does not delay His coming because man has not yet invited Him to speak on TV! God alone knows the day and the hour, but nothing man does can speed or slow His Son's return. He is sovereign and His will shall be done.

Are You Ready for His Return?

The most important question in the universe is this: When Jesus returns, will you be ready? Do you know where *you* will spend eternity?

All that I have written in this book can be summed up in this one statement: Jesus is Lord; He promised us He would be with us always and that He would return in the last days to reign and rule.

Yes, Satan also has a Plan. In following that Plan, he will gladly enlist you in his New Age army and give you his Mark.

But if you choose to side with Satan and refuse to accept God's gracious free gift—the sacrifice on the cross of His Son, Jesus, for your sins—your life will become more and more miserable with each passing day. And your ultimate fate will be death.

If you are not today a Christian, if you have not yet called on the Lord, repented of your sins and asked forgiveness, and if you have not asked Jesus to come into your heart and keep you for eternity, my prayer is that you will do so. He loves you and awaits your invitation.

For God so loved the world, that he gave his only begotten Son, that whosoever believeth in him should not perish, but have everlasting life. (John 3:16)

FOOTNOTES

Chapter 1: The Gathering Fury

1. Marilyn Ferguson, *The Aquarian Conspiracy: Personal and Social Transformation in the 1980s* (Los Angeles: J. P. Tarcher, Inc., 1980).

2. Jose Arguelles, interviewed by John-Alexis Viereck, *Meditation,* Summer 1987, Vol. II, No. 3, pp. 6-19. Also see Antero Alli, "A Post-Convergence Interview with Jose Arguelles," *Magical Blend,* Issue 18, 1988, pp. 17-20.

3. *Ibid.*

4. *Ibid.*

5. See *New Age Monitor,* May-July, 1986, pp. 2, 3 and *Windstar,* Winter 1987/Spring 1988. J. Peter Grace was one of the featured speakers at the Windstar Foundation's "Choices for the Future" symposium, June 12-14, 1987. For an excerpt of one of his presentations see *Choices and Connections '88-'89* (Boulder, Colo.: Human Potential Resources, Inc., 1987), pp. 435, 436, 472.

6. See Cliff Kincaid, "More Wisdom from Ted Turner," *Human Events,* August 2, 1986, p. 14; and Dave Price, "Broadcaster Ties Survival to 'New Age' President," *The Denver Post,* June 15, 1986, p. 2-B.

7. European royalty is being used by Satan to promote New Age concepts. *New Age Journal* in 1987 reported on Queen Elizabeth and the Royal Family's support of holistic health. HRH Princess Juliana of The Netherlands is a member of The Planetary Citizens and other globalist organizations, and Prince Philip is now preaching the population control doctrine to audiences.

8. Kathleen Hayes, "Hart Puts 'New Ideas' Above Personal Morals, Ethics," *NRI Trumpet,* January 1988, pp. 1, 3.

9. *Ibid.*

10. George P. Schultz, "World Needs to Realign Thinking to the New and Future Age," *Forum, the Sunday Oregonian,* January 3, 1988, p. B-3.

11. See Donald Keys, *Earth at Omega* (San Anselmo, Calif.: Planetary Citizens/Branden Press, 1985) p. 61.

12. Reports of the conversion of Soviet leader Mikhail Gorbachev are coming in from all fronts. I refer you to evangelist J. R. Church's excellent newspaper *Prophecy in the News,* February 1988, p. 16; also see *NRI Trumpet,* January 1988; "Soviet-American Citizens' Summit," special report by the Center for Soviet-American Dialogue, 14426 NE 16th Pl., Bellevue, WA 98007; and the *Omega Letter,* February 1988. The most striking confirmation comes direct from Gorbachev himself in his book, *Perestroika, New Thinking for Our Country and the World* (New York: Harper & Row, 1987).

13. Bernard Gittelson with Laura Torbet, "Are You a Little Bit Psychic?," *Redbook,* October 1987, pp. 76, 78, 80.

14. "What Is the Personal Growth Aspect of the New Age?," *Changes,* January-February 1988, p. 25.

15. *Ibid.*

16. Marla Donato, *Chicago Tribune* reporter, "Welcome to the Dawning of Another New Age," distributed by New York Times Syndication, and printed in *Washington Times,* December 28, 1987, p. E-1.

17. Marla Donato, "Welcome to the New Age," *Chicago Tribune,* November 4, 1987, pp. 13, 16, 18.

18. Virginia Smith, "Oprah Winfrey Reveals Secret of Her Incredible Success," *Examiner,* July 14, 1987, p. 29.

19. "The Tower of Babel," *Magical Blend,* Issue 15, 1987, p. 1.

20. *Ibid.*

21. Michelle Smith and Lawrence Pazder, M.D., *Michelle Remembers* (New York: Congdon & Lattes, Inc., 1980), p. 259.

22. *The New Group of World Servers* (New York: World Goodwill, an activity of the Lucis Trust).

23. *Ibid.,* p. 7.

24. *Ibid.,* pp. 2-4.

25. Benjamin Creme, *Messages from Maitreya the Christ* (Los Angeles: Tara Center, 1980), p. 30.

26. Matthew Fox, *Original Blessing: A Primer in Creation Spirituality* (Santa Fe, N.M.: Bear & Company, 1983), p. 305.

27. Letter and special report from Lucis Trust, Autumn 1987.

28. Barry McWaters, *Conscious Evolution: Personal and Planetary Transformation* (San Francisco, Calif.: Evolutionary Press, 1982), pp. 113, 114.

29. John Randolph Price, *The Planetary Commission* (Austin, Texas: Quartus Books, 1984), p. 69.

30. P. S. Cuddy, "Transformation Toward New Age Synthesis," *Distant Drums,* March 1986, p. 8.

31. *Ibid.*

32. *Ibid.*

33. *Ibid.*

34. Foster Bailey, *Things to Come* (New York: Lucis Publishing Company, 1974), p. 114.

35. Alice A. Bailey, *The Labours of Hercules* (New York: Lucis Publishing Company, 1982), p. 203.

36. Barbara Marx Hubbard, *Happy Birth Day Planet Earth!* (Santa Fe, N.M.: Ocean Tree Books, 1986), p. 32.

37. Bailey, *Things to Come,* p. 39.

38. *Ibid.,* p. 16.

39. Commission Update (report), Planetary Commission for Global HEALING, Austin, Texas, March 1988, p. 4.

40. *Ibid.*

Chapter 2: **The Mark**

1. Eklal Kueshana, *The Ultimate Frontier* (Chicago, Ill.: The Stelle Group, 1963) pp. 44-48.

2. Earl Paulk, *Held in the Heavens Until* . . . (Atlanta, Ga.: Dimension Publishers, 1985). Other teachers who today preach what is called "Dominion Theology," "Reconstructionism," "Restoration Theology," "Kingdom Now Theology," and similar man-made philosophies and dogma also believe that Jesus either will not or cannot return until mankind has somehow prepared the way by setting up an earthly kingdom. These un-Biblical philosophies are not in accordance with Bible prophecy as revealed in Revelation 19—22 and elsewhere.

3. Whitley Strieber, *Communion* (New York: Beech Tree Books, William Morrow, 1987).

4. *Ibid.,* p. 126.

5. *Ibid.*

6. *Ibid.,* p. 122.

7. *Ibid.,* pp. 83, 107.

8. *Ibid.,* p. 131.

9. See *Hebrew Greek Key Study Bible,* compiled and edited by Spiros Zodhiates, Th.D. (Chattanooga, Tenn.: AMG) and *Vine's Expository Dictionary of New Testament Words* (Oliphants, Ltd., 1940).

10. "Contactee: Firsthand," *California UFO,* January/February 1987, p. 29.

11. See Albert Churchward, *The Signs and Symbols of Primordial Man* (London: George Allen and Company, Ltd., 1913), pp. 72, 73, 324.

12. S. Angus, *The Mystery Religions* (New York: Dover Publications, 1975; originally published 1925 in London), p. 90.

13. *Ibid.*

14. Kathryn Paulsen, *The Complete Book of Magic and Witchcraft* (New York: Signet, New American Library, 1980).

15. *Ibid.*, p. 17.

Chapter 3:   **Mystery Mark of the New Age**

1. Maurice Nicoll, *The Mark* (Boston: Shambhala, 1985).

2. *Ibid.*, see pp. 6, 27-29, 50, 185-191.

3. *Ibid.*, p. 211.

4. Ads for ASTARA offering their booklet "Finding Your Place in the Golden Age" appeared in numerous New Age publications in 1987 and 1988.

5. See Elizabeth Clare Prophet, *Saint Germain on Prophecy: Coming World Prophecy* (Livingston, Mont.: Summit University Press, 1986) pp. 4, 5.

6. Mark L. Prophet and Elizabeth Clare Prophet, *Lord of the Seven Rays: Mirror of Consciousness* (Livingston, Mont.: Summit University Press, 1986) p. 242.

7. *Ibid.*

8. Edmund Harold, *Focus on Crystals* (New York: Ballantine Books, 1986), pp. 22-25.

9. *Ibid.*

10. Mark L. Prophet and Elizabeth Clare Prophet, *Lord of the Seven Rays: Mirror of Consciousness,* p. 265.

11. *Ibid.,* p. 239.

12. *Ibid.,* pp. 238, 239.

13. *Enter the Aquarian Age Through the Teachings of the Ascended Masters,* advertising brochure, Church Universal and Triumphant.

14. *Ibid.*

15. See *Vine's Expository Dictionary of New Testament Words,* p. 331 and the *Hebrew Greek Key Study Bible,* edited by Spiros Zodhiates, Th.D., p. 70 of Greek Lexicon.

16. Alice Bailey, *The Rays and the Initiations* (New York: Lucis Publishing Company, 1960).

17. *Ibid.,* p. 23.

18. *Ibid.*

19. *Ibid.,* p. 24.

20. *Ibid.*

21. Geoffrey Hodson, *The Hidden Wisdom in the Holy Bible,*

Vol. I (Wheaton, Ill.: The Theosophical Publishing House, 1967), p. 208.

22. Alice Bailey, *A Treatise on Cosmic Fire* (New York: Lucis Publishing Company, 1964), p. 696.

23. Elizabeth Clare Prophet, *My Soul Doth Magnify the Lord* (Livingston, Mont: Summit University Press, 1986).

24. Reported widely throughout the Catholic media, these visitations are said to be continuing.

25. Rev. Martin Rumpf, "Apparitions at Marienfried, Germany," *Divine Love* magazine, Issue No. 33, 2nd Quarter, 1971.

26. *Ibid.*

27. Murry Hope, *Practical Egyptian Magic* (New York: St. Martin's Press, 1986), p. 45.

28. See Alice Bailey, *A Treatise on Cosmic Fire;* Kuthumi and Djwal Kul, *The Human Aura* (Livingston, Mont.: Summit University Press, 1986), pp. 143, 144, 178-186; and Barbara Walker, *The Woman's Encyclopedia of Myths and Secrets* (San Francisco: Harper & Row, 1983), p. 14.

29. Geoffrey Hodson, *The Hidden Wisdom in the Holy Bible,* Vol. I, p. 140.

30. *Ibid.*

Chapter 4: **His Number Is 666**

1. Alice Bailey, *The Rays and the Initiations,* p. 79.

2. *Ibid.*

3. *Ibid.*

4. *Ibid.*, p. 79.

5. *Ibid.*, p. 80.

6. *Ibid.*, p. 81.

7. Alice Bailey, *A Treatise on Cosmic Fire.*

8. *Ibid.*, p. 914.

9. *Ibid.*, p. 991.

10. Sir John Sinclair, *The Alice Bailey Inheritance* (Wellingborough, Northamptonshire, England: Turnstone Press Limited, 1984), p. 103.

11. *Ibid.*

12. Harriette and F. Homer Curtiss, *Coming World Changes* (Albuquerque, N.M.: Sun Publishing Company, 1981).

13. *Ibid.*, p. 89.

14. *Ibid.*, pp. 90, 91.

15. *Ibid.*, 89.

16. *Ibid.*, pp. 90, 91.

17. *Ibid.*, p. 109.

18. Vera Alder, *When Humanity Comes of Age* (New York: Samuel Weiser, Inc., 1972).

19. *Ibid.*, p. 39.

20. Benjamin Creme, *Messages from Maitreya.*

21. *Ibid.*, pp. 18, 19.

22. Geoffrey Hodson, *The Hidden Wisdom in the Holy Bible,* Vol. I, p. 145.

23. *Ibid.*

24. *Ibid.*, p. 148.

25. *Ibid.*

26. J. E. Cirlot, *A Dictionary of Symbols,* second edition (New York: Philosophical Library, 1971), p. 233.

27. See *Choices and Connections '88-'89,* pp. 249, 250.

28. Barbara Walker, *The Woman's Encyclopedia of Myths and Secrets,* pp. 400-401.

29. *Ibid.*

30. *Ibid.*, pp. 450, 451.

31. Patrizia Norelli-Bachelet, *Symbols and the Question of Unity* (Wassenaar, Holland: Servire Publishers, 1974).

32. Alice Bailey, *The Labours of Hercules,* p. 115.

33. *Ibid.,* p. 115, 116.

34. Sir John Sinclair, *The Alice Bailey Inheritance,* p. 103.

35. Alice Bailey, *The Labours of Hercules,* p. 119.

36. *Ibid.*

37. *Ibid.*

38. Barbara Walker, *The Woman's Encyclopedia of Myths and Secrets,* pp. 8, 895-898, 935, 936.

39. Manly P. Hall, *The Secret Teachings of All Ages* (Los Angeles, Calif.: The Philosophical Research Society, Inc., 1928), p. CII.

40. Patrizia Norelli-Bachelet, *Symbols and the Question of Unity,* pp. 108, 112.

41. Alice Bailey, *The Labours of Hercules,* p. 185.

42. Vera Alder, *The Initiation of the World* (York Beach, Me.: Samuel Weiser, Inc., 1972), p. 109.

43. *Ibid.*

44. Barbara Walker, *The Woman's Encyclopedia of Myths and Secrets,* p. 14.

45. Alice Bailey, *A Treatise on Cosmic Fire.*

46. J. J. Hurtag, *The Keys of Enoch* (Los Gatos, Calif.: The Academy for Future Science, 1977, revised 1982), p. 391.

47. *Ibid.*

Chapter 5: **The Unholy Worship of the Symbols of Oppression**

1. Dick Sutphen, "Symbol Therapy," *Master of Life*, Issue 37, 1988, p. 31.

2. See the full-page ad by New Age Activists in *Psychic Guide*, September-November 1986, p. 5.

3. Albert Churchward, *The Signs and Symbols of Primordial Man*, p. 309.

4. Barbara Walker, *The Woman's Encyclopedia of Myths and Secrets*, p. 1016.

5. Sir John Sinclair, *The Alice Bailey Inheritance*, p. 75.

6. Two Disciples, *The Rainbow Bridge* (Danville, Calif.: Rainbow Bridge Productions, 1981), pp. 199, 200.

7. Sir John Sinclair, *The Alice Bailey Inheritance*, p. 75.

8. *Ibid.*, pp. 172, 173.

9. Benjamin Creme, *Maitreya's Mission* (Amsterdam: Share International Foundation, 1986), p. 46.

10. H. P. Blavatsky, *Isis Unveiled*, Vol. II (Pasadena, Calif.: Theosophical University Press, reprinted 1976), p. 31.

11. John Barela, *Antichrist Associates and Cosmic Christianity* (Broken Arrow, Okla.: Today, The Bible and You, 1986), pp. 168-170.

12. Two Disciples, *The Rainbow Bridge,* p. 73

13. *Ibid.*

14. *Ibid.,* pp. 99, 100.

15. *Ibid.,* pp. 196-200.

16. Alice Bailey and The Tibetan Master, Djwhal Khul, *Ponder on This* (New York: Lucis Publishing Company, 1971), p. 142.

17. Alice Bailey, *The Reappearance of the Christ* (New York: Lucis Publishing Company, 1948, 5th paperback edition, 1984), p. 84.

18. Whitley Strieber, *Communion,* p. 251.

19. Edmund Harold, *Focus on Crystals,* p. 115.

20. M. Scott Peck, "The Road Less Traveled," *Life Times,* Fall-Winter 1986, p. 22.

21. *Ibid.*

22. Sir John Sinclair, *The Alice Bailey Inheritance,* p. 118.

23. *Ibid.*

24. Patrizia Norelli-Bachelet, *Symbols and the Question of Unity,* pp. 124, 125.

25. *Ibid.*, pp. 124-126.

26. Georgette G. Bremmer, "200 Study Personalities at Church," *Acorn*, Westlake Village, California, 1987.

27. Sr. Maria Beesing, The Rev. Robert J. Nogosek and the Rev. Patrick H. O'Leary, *The Enneagram: A Journey of Self Discovery* (1984).

28. Helena Blavatsky, *The Secret Doctrine*, Vol. I: *Cosmogenesis* (Calif.: Theosophical University Press, 1888).

29. "Becoming Sun-Like," *The Beacon*, July-August 1986, p. 289.

30. Geoffrey Hodson, *The Hidden Wisdom in the Holy Bible*, Volume I, pp. 54, 55.

31. Barry McWaters, *Conscious Evolution*, p. 126.

32. Ken Carey, *Vision* (Kansas City: Uni*Sun, 1985), p. 13.

33. Edouard Schure, *From Sphinx to Christ* (San Francisco: Harper & Row, 1982), p. 229.

34. Buryl Payne, "Peace Events," *Magical Blend*, Issue 17, 1987, p. 55.

35. Group Avatar, "The Cosmic Moment Has Arrived," *The Quartus Report*, #11, Vol. V, 1986, p. 10.

36. "Jesus and Kuthumi" (Elizabeth Clare Prophet), *Corona Class Lessons* (Livingston, Mont.: Summit University Press, 1986), p. 403.

37. *Ibid.*, p. 64.

38. Arthur C. Clarke, *2010: Odyssey Two* (New York: Ballantine, 1982).

39. Joseph Campbell, "Day of the Dead Lecture," *Magical Blend,* Issue #16, 1987.

40. Alexander Hislop, *The Two Babylons* (Neptune, N.J.: Loizeaux Brothers, 1916), p. 226.

41. Corinne Heline, *The New Age Bible Interpretation,* Old Testament, Vol. I (Santa Monica, Calif.: New Age Bible & Philosophy Center, 5th Edition, 1985), pp. 364, 365.

Chapter 6:   **Beauty and the Beast**

1. Alice Bailey, *Initiation, Human and Solar* (New York: Lucis Publishing Company, 1951), p. 165, 166.

2. John Barela, *Antichrist Associates and Cosmic Christianity,* p. 178.

3. See Manly P. Hall, *The Secret Teachings of All Ages;* Kathryn Paulsen, *The Complete Book of Magic and Witchcraft;* and Paul Huson, *Mastering Witchcraft* (New York: Perigee Books, 1980).

4. Rudolf Koch, *The Book of Signs* (New York: Dover Publications, Inc., 1955), p. 6.

5. Manly P. Hall, *The Secret Teachings of All Ages,* p. CIV.

6. Wade Davis, *The Serpent and the Rainbow* (New York: Warner Books, 1987).

7. Elemire Zolla, *The Androgyne: Reconciliation of Male and Female* (New York: Crossroad Publishing Co., 1981), p. 57.

8. Two Disciples, *Rainbow Bridge.*

9. *Ibid.,* p. 218.

10. *Ibid.,* pp. 85, 86.

11. *Ibid.,* p. 86.

12. Benjamine Creme, *Maitreya's Mission,* p. 51.

13. "Jesus and Kuthumi" (Elizabeth Clare Prophet), *Corona Class Lessons,* p. 53.

14. Mark and Elizabeth Prophet, *The Science of the Spoken Word* (Colorado Springs, Colo.: The Summit Lighthouse, 1974), pp. 67, 68.

15. *Ibid.,* p. 77.

16. Robert Anton Wilson, *Cosmic Trigger: Final Secret of the Illuminati* (Phoenix, Ariz.: Falcon Press, 1977), pp. 73, 74; also see David Solomon, *LSD* (New York: Putnam, 1964) and Laura A. Huxley, *This Timeless Moment* (Millbrae, Calif.: Celestial Arts Publishing, 1975).

17. James W. Sire, *The Universe Next Door* (Downers Grove, Ill.: InterVarsity Press, 1976), p. 167.

18. *Ibid.,* p. 168.

19. Vera Alder, *The Initiation of the World,* pp. 46, 47.

20. Corinne Heline, *New Age Bible Interpretation*, New Testament, Vol. 6 (Santa Monica, Calif.: New Age Bible & Philosophy Center, 5th edition, 1984), p. 227.

21. Robert Keith Spenser, *The Cult of the All-Seeing Eye* (Hawthorne, Calif.: The Christian Book Club of America, 1964), pp. 5-17.

22. *Ibid.*, p. 13.

23. *The Book of the Goddess Past and Present*, edited by Carl Olson (New York: The Crossroad Publishing Company, 1986), pp. 42, 43.

24. Murry Hope, *Practical Egyptian Magic*, p. 45.

25. See Barbara Walker, *The Woman's Encyclopedia of Myths and Secrets* and Alice Bailey and The Tibetan Master, Djwhal Khul, *Ponder on This*, pp. 408, 409.

26. *Ibid.*, p. 410.

27. J. J. Hurtag, *The Keys of Enoch*, p. 508.

28. *Ibid.*

29. *Ibid.*

30. *Ibid.*, p. 512.

31. Alexander Hislop, *The Two Babylons*, p. 87.

32. Patrizia Norelli-Bachelet, *Symbols and the Question of Unity*, p.4.

33. A. S. Raleigh, *Occult Geometry* (Marina del Rey, Calif.: De-Vorss and Company, Publishers, 1981, originally published 1932 by The Hermetic Publishing Company), pp. 10, 11.

34. Albert Churchward, *The Signs and Symbols of Primordial Man,* p. 325.

35. Jenny Dent, *God Loves Us All,* Vol. 1 of the Spiritual Teaching for Children Series (New Lands, Liss, Hampshire, England: The White Eagle Publishing Trust, 1982), p. 8.

36. Aleister Crowley is greatly admired by occultic New Agers. Such books as *Sex and Magick* by Crowley are best-sellers in New Age bookstores.

37. Bent Corydon and L. Ron Hubbard, Jr., a.k.a. Ronald DeWolf, *L. Ron Hubbard: Messiah or Madman?* (Secaucus, N.J.: Lyle Stuart, Inc., 1987).

38. Elizabeth Clare Prophet, *Saint Germain on Prophecy,* p. 217.

39. *Ibid.,* p. 219.

40. J. H. Brennan, *The Occult Reich* (New York: The New American Library, 1974), pp. 85, 86.

41. Albert Churchward, *The Signs and Symbols of Primordial Man,* pp. 187, 224.

42. A. S. Raleigh, *Occult Geometry,* p. 29.

43. *Ibid.,* pp. 29-34.

44. *Ibid.,* p. 31.

45. *Ibid.*

46. Alice Bailey, *The Rays and the Initiations*, pp. 362, 492. Also see "The Jewel in the Lotus," *Choices and Connections '88/'89*, p. 554.

47. Werner Keller, *The Bible as History* (New York: Bantam Books, 1982), pp. 303, 315.

48. Leo F. Buscaglia, *The Way of the Bull* (New York: Fawcett Crest, Ballantine Books, 1973).

49. Alexander Hislop, *The Two Babylons*, pp. 114, 215, 241-243, 252-255, 264, 270, 319.

50. Barbara Walker, *The Woman's Encyclopedia of Myths and Secrets*, p. 780.

51. Odell Shepard, *The Lore of the Unicorn* (New York: Harper Colophon Books, 1979), pp. 238, 240.

52. See "Ramtha, a Voice From Beyond," *Newsweek*, December 15, 1986, p. 42; and "And Now, the 35,000-Year-Old-Man," *Time*, December 15, 1986, p. 36.

53. Texe Marrs, *Dark Secrets of the New Age* (Westchester, Ill.: Crossway Books, 1987), p. 95.

Chapter 7:   **Satan's Design to Seduce the Mind**

1. Alice Bailey, *The Destiny of the Nations* (London, England: Lucis Press, Ltd., 3rd paperback edition, 1982), p. 19.

2. *Ibid.*, p. 120.

3. Foster Bailey, *The Spirit of Masonry* (New York: Lucis Publishing Company, 1957), p. 59.

4. *Ibid.*

5. For example, see Werner Keller, *The Bible as History;* Alexander Hislop, *The Two Babylons; Halley's Bible Handbook,* 24th edition (Grand Rapids, Mich.: Zondervan, 1965); and Ralph Woodrow, *Babylon Mystery Religion* (Riverside, Calif.: Ralph Woodrow Evangelistic Association, 1981).

6. S. Angus, *The Mystery Religions,* p. 45.

Chapter 8:   **The Image That Lives . . . and Speaks!**

1. Perhaps the most ungodly books I have come across are those by Morton T. Kelsey, which attempt to introduce the symbology of psychiatrist Carl Jung to a wider Christian audience. Such books by Kelsey include *Myth, History and Faith: The Remythologizing of Christianity* (New York: Paulist Press, 1974) and *Prophetic Ministry: The Psychology and Spirituality of Pastoral Care* (New York: Crossroad, 1982).

2. For excellent discussions of the dangers of Jungian psychology, inner healing, and visualization of symbols and images, see Dave Hunt, *Beyond Seduction* (Eugene, Ore.: Harvest House Publishers, 1987), Don Matzat, *Inner Healing: Truth or Deception?* (Eugene, Ore.: Harvest House Publishers, 1987), and Martin Bobgan, *Psychoheresy* (Santa Barbara, Calif.: Eastgate Publishers, 1987).

3. Morton Kelsey, *Myth, History and Faith: The Remythologizing of Christianity,* p. 118.

4. Morton Kelsey, *Prophetic Ministry: The Psychology and Spirituality of Pastoral Care.*

5. Robert Anton Wilson, *Cosmic Trigger: Final Secret of the Illuminati,* p. 72.

6. Robert Leichtman and Carl Japikse, "Tuning Into Divine Archetypes," *Magical Blend,* February-April 1988, pp. 37-40.

7. *Ibid.,* p. 38.

8. *Ibid.,* pp. 39, 40.

9. Benjamin Creme, *Transmission-Meditation* newsletter, Tara Center, Hollywood, California, May 1986, p. 3.

10. J. David Stone, *Spiritual Growth in Youth Ministry* (Group, 1985), p. 70.

11. William Wolff, *Psychic Self-Improvement for the Millions* (Bell Publishing, 1969), pp. 15, 30, 34, 59-61, 63, 80-84.

12. Foster Bailey, *The Spirit of Masonry,* p. 59.

13. Norman Vincent Peale, "No More Stress or Tension," in *Plus: The Magazine of Positive Thinking,* May 1986, pp. 22, 23. Norman Vincent Peale seems to have become more New Age and pro-occult with each passing year. In 1987 he strongly endorsed a book by Harold Sherman, *The Dead Are Alive,* which un-Biblically claimed that we could—and should—communicate with spirits from beyond. Peale's endorsement on the front cover of this book, published by Ballantine Books, stated, "A masterpiece! Could be the greatest of all Sherman's great books. I hope it will be widely read."

14. Joseph Chilton Pearce, *Magical Child Matures* (New York: Bantam Books, 1986).

15. *Ibid.*, p. 187.

16. Whitley Strieber, *Communion*, p. 152.

17. *Ibid.*, p. 106.

18. *Ibid.*, p. 251.

19. *Ibid.*, p. 215.

20. J. J. Hurtag, *The Keys of Enoch*, pp. 204, 207.

21. *Ibid.*, p. 340.

22. *Ibid.*, pp. 204, 207, 275.

23. *Ibid.*, p. 242.

24. *Ibid.*, pp. 296, 297.

25. *Ibid.*, p. 241.

26. *Ibid.*, pp. 238, 241.

27. *Ibid.*, pp. 238, 301.

28. *Ibid.*, p. 241.

29. *Ibid.*, pp. 296, 300.

30. *Ibid.,* p. 276.

31. *Ibid.,* p. 534. Also see pp. 271, 272, 276.

32. *Ibid.,* pp. 275, 276, 533-540.

33. *Ibid.,* p. 539.

34. *Ibid.,* p. 275.

35. *Ibid.,* pp. 170, 242.

36. *Ibid.,* pp. 552-553.

Chapter 9: **Marked for Extinction: A Death Sentence for Christians**

1. Christopher Hyatt, "Undoing Yourself," by Antero Alli, *Magical Blend,* Issue #16, 1987, p. 22.

2. Djwhal Khul, channeled through Alice Bailey, "Food for Thought," *Life Times,* Winter 1986-87, p. 57.

3. John Randolph Price, *Practical Spirituality* (Austin, Tex.: Quartus, 1985), p. 19.

4. Ruth Montgomery, *Threshold to Tomorrow* (New York: Fawcett Press, 1982), pp. 195-208.

5. Maharishi Mahesh Yogi, *Inauguration of the Dawn of the Age of Enlightenment* (Fairfield, Ia.: Maharishi International University Press, 1975), p. 47.

6. Christopher Hyatt, "Undoing Yourself," by Antero Alli, *Magical Blend*, Issue #16, 1987, pp. 20-22.

7. *Ibid.*, p. 22.

8. *Ibid.*

9. J. H. Brennan, *The Occult Reich*, pp. 40-47, 53-56.

10. Caroline M. Myss, "AIDS: Passageway to Transformation," *Life Times*, Vol. 1, No. 4, 1982-87.

11. John Randolph Price, *The Planetary Commission*, pp. 27, 28.

12. Ruth Montgomery, interview in *Magical Blend*, Issue 13, 1986, p. 23.

13. Ruth Montgomery, *Threshold to Tomorrow*, pp. 206, 207.

14. *Ibid.*

15. John Randolph Price, *The Planetary Commission*, p. 163.

16. John Randolph Price, *The Quartus Report*, Report No. 11, Volume V, 1986.

17. John Randolph Price, *Practical Spirituality*, pp. 15-21.

18. *Ibid.*

19. Djwhal Khul, channeled through Alice Bailey, "Humanity," *Life Times*, Winter 1986-87, pp. 71, 72.

20. *Ibid.*

21. *Ibid.*

22. *Ibid.*

23. David Spangler, *Revelation: The Birth of a New Age* (Middleton, Wisc.: Lorian Press, 1976), pp. 163, 164.

24. *Ibid.*

25. Matthew Fox, *Original Blessing,* pp. 262, 263.

26. For example, see Vera Alder, *The Initiation of the World.* Willis Harmon, Stanford University scientist and an ardent New Ager, and former astronaut Edgar Mitchell have founded an institution called The Institute of Noetic Sciences to study New Age man (homo noeticus).

27. See Moira Timms, *Prophecies and Predictions: Everyone's Guide to the Coming Changes* (Santa Cruz, Calif.: Unity Press, 1980), pp. 125, 126, 276, 277, 289; and LaVedi Lafferty and Bud Hollowell, *The Eternal Dance* (St. Paul, Minn.: Llewellyn Publications, 1983), p. 153.

28. F. Homer Curtiss and Harriette Curtiss, *Coming World Changes,* p. xii.

29. *Ibid.,* p. xi.

30. Alice Bailey, *Education in the New Age* (New York: Lucis Publishing Company, 1954), p. 111, 112.

31. *Ibid.,* 112.

32. J. J. Hurtag, *The Keys of Enoch*, p. 332.

33. *Ibid.*

34. *Ibid.*, p. 173.

35. *Ibid.*, pp. 173, 332, 418-422.

36. *Ibid.*, p. 317.

37. *Ibid.*

Chapter 10: **Soldiers of Darkness**

1. Benjamin Creme, *Messages from Maitreya*, pp. 42, 87.

2. *Ibid.*, p. 26.

3. *Ibid.*, p. 36.

4. *Ibid.*, pp. 76-82.

5. *Ibid.*

6. *Ibid.*, p. 36.

7. Elizabeth Clare Prophet, *The Great White Brotherhood in the Culture, History, and Religion of America* (Los Angeles, Calif.: Summit University Press, 1975) p. 220.

8. *Ibid.*, p. 221.

9. *Ibid.*, p. 137.

10. *Ibid.*

11. *Ibid.*

12. *Ibid.*, pp. 137-140.

13. *Ibid.*, p. 140.

14. *Ibid.*, p. 139.

15. *Ibid.*, p. 140.

16. Donald Keys, *Earth at Omega* (San Anselmo, Calif.: Planetary Citizens/Branden Press, 1985), pp. 143, 144, 146.

17. *Ibid.*, p. 130.

18. *Ibid.*, pp. 115, 116.

19. *Ibid.*

20. Edouard Schure, *From Sphinx to Christ,* pp. 83-86. Also see the Hindu Vedic scriptures, especially the *Bhagavad-Gita.*

21. See Alice Bailey, *The Reappearance of the Christ* (New York: Lucis Publishing Company, 1948) and Benjamin Creme, *The Reappearance of the Christ and the Masters of Wisdom* (London: The Tara Press, 1980).

22. Neil Cohen, "A Message From the Heart," *Life Times,* Vol. 1, Winter 86-87, pp. 43, 44.

23. *Ibid.*

24. Group Avatar, "The Cosmic Moment Has Arrived," *The Quartus Report,* No. 11, Vol. V, 1986, p. 10.

25. Alice Bailey, *Problems of Humanity* (New York: Lucis Publishing Company, 1947), p. 166.

26. Alice Bailey, *Ponder on This,* pp. 141-143. Also see Alice Bailey, *The Reappearance of the Christ,* pp. 31-34.

27. "Commission Update," The Planetary Commission for Global Healing, Austin, Texas, Summer 1987, p. 4.

28. John Randolph Price, *Practical Spirituality,* pp. 15-21.

29. "Trying to Dig up Root of All Evil," *Chicago Tribune,* October 18, 1987, Section D.

30. "Commission Update," The Planetary Commission for Global Healing, Austin, Texas, March 1988, p. 2.

31. For example, see Victor Sandoval, "Committee to Defend Constitution Front for Korean Cult Leader Moon," *Spotlight,* July 29, 1985, p. 5; "The Moonies and the Christian Right," *Mother Jones,* January 1986; "Moon's Followers Recruit Christians to Assist," *Christianity Today,* June 14, 1985; and "Evidence Points Toward Col. North Tie to Rev. Moon," *San Francisco Examiner,* July 20, 1987, p. A-4.

32. David Spangler, *Emergence: The Rebirth of the Sacred* (New York: Delta/Merloyd Lawrence, Dell Publishing, 1984), p. 122.

33. *Ibid.*

34. *Ibid.*

35. "The Second Beast of Revelation: Claims of Satanism and Child Molesting," *Newsweek,* November 16, 1987.

36. "Chaplains' Ranks Are Opened to Buddhists," *Los Angeles Times,* October 27, 1987, Part I, p. 27.

37. Foster Bailey, *Things to Come* (New York: Lucis Trust, 1974), p. 109.

38. *Ibid.,* p. 108

39. *Ibid.,* pp. 108, 109.

40. *Ibid.*

41. Ron Hogart, "Astrology Seen," *Magical Blend,* Issue 18, 1988, p. 72.

42. *Ibid.*

43. John Randolph Price, *The Planetary Commission,* p. 32.

44. *Ibid.,* p. 46.

45. *Ibid.,* p. 69

46. *Ibid.,* p. 20.

47. Sally Fisher, quoted in *Magical Blend,* Issue 18, 1988, p. 36.

48. *Ibid.*

49. Christopher Hyatt, "Undoing Yourself," by Antero Alli, *Magical Blend,* Issue 16, 1987, p. 21.

50. John-Alexis Viereck, interview with Jose Arguelles, "Earth Speaks: The Great Return, August 16-17," *Meditation,* Summer 1987, Vol. II, No. 3, pp. 6-19, 50.

Chapter 11: Cursing the Light

1. Vera Alder, *The Initiation of the World,* p. 245.

2. *Ibid.*

3. *Ibid.,* pp. 138, 139.

4. Colin Wilson, *The Mind Parasites* (Berkeley, Calif.: Wingbow Publishers, a division of Book People).

5. Marilyn Ferguson, *The Aquarian Conspiracy,* p. 193.

6. *Ibid.,* p. 377.

7. *Ibid.,* p. 379.

8. *Ibid.,* p. 377.

9. Alice Bailey, *Ponder on This,* p. 4.

10. *Ibid.,* p 5.

11. Marilyn Ferguson, *The Aquarian Conspiracy,* p. 398.

12. Benjamin Creme, *Maitreya's Mission,* p. 99.

13. *Ibid.,* pp. 123, 124.

14. Dane Rudhyar, *Occult Preparations for a New Age* (Wheaton, Ill.: The Theosophical Publishing House, 1975).

15. *Ibid.*, p. 26.

16. *Ibid.*, p. 27.

17. Timothy Leary, quoted in *Magical Blend,* Issue 13, 1987.

18. *Ibid.*

19. For inside information about the travesty that Bhagwan Shree Rajneesh perpetrated on his followers, I recommend three revealing books: *The Ultimate Game: The Rise and Fall of Bhagwan Shree Rajneesh* by Kate Strelley with Robert D. San Souci (Harper & Row, 1987); *Bhagwan: The God That Failed* by Hugh Milne (St. Martin's Press, 1987); and *The Golden Guru: The Strange Journey of Bhagwan Shree Ranjneesh* by James Gordon (The Stephen Greene Press, 1987).

20. *Ibid.*

21. *Ibid.*

22. *Ibid.*

23. Robert Anton Wilson, "The New Inquisition," *Meditation,* Winter 87-88, p. 27-29.

24. *Ibid.*

25. Rev. Roger C. Hight, *Path to the Rainbow* (Oklahoma City, Okla.: Gonders & Associates Publishers, 1975).

26. *Ibid.*, pp. 67, 69.

27. *Ibid.*, p. 69.

28. Ruth Montgomery, *Ruth Montgomery, Herald of the New Age* (Garden City, N.Y.: Doubleday Publishers, 1986), p. 264.

29. *Ibid.*, p. 265.

30. Ruth Montgomery, *Threshold to Tomorrow.*

31. Monica Sjoo and Barbara Mor, *The Great Cosmic Mother: Rediscovering the Religion of the Earth* (San Francisco: Harper & Row Publishers, 1987), pp. 419, 420.

32. *Ibid.*, pp. 420, 421.

33. Margot Adler, *Drawing Down the Moon* (Boston: Beacon Press, 1979), p. viii.

34. *Ibid.*, p. ix.

35. Tom Williams, quoted by Margot Adler, *Drawing Down the Moon,* p. 283.

Chapter 12: **Call Not Evil Good**

1. C. S. Nott, *Teachings of Gurdjieff: A Pupil's Journal* (York Beach, Me.: Samuel Weiser, Inc., 1962), p. 212.

2. Shakti Gawain, "Living in the Light," *Life Times,* Winter 86-87, p. 12.

3. Jaqui Holt, *Life Times*, Vol. 1, No. 3, p. 19.

4. Jack Underhill, "Some New Age Myths and Truths," *Life Times*, Vol. 1, No. 3, p. 9.

5. *Ibid.*

6. *Ibid.*

7. Jack Underhill. "I Fought the Law and the Law Won," *Life Times*, Vol. 1, No. 4, p. 88.

8. Promotional flyer, "1987 International Seth Seminar," Austin Seth Center, Austin, Texas. Also see Jane Roberts, *The Seth Material* (Englewood Cliffs, N.J.: Prentice-Hall, 1970) and other "Seth" books.

9. Shakura, "What Does 'Awakening' Mean?," *Life Times*, Winter 86-87, Vol. 1, No. 2, p. 38.

10. Soli, *Life Times*, Vol. 1, No. 1, 1986.

11. Chelsea Quinn Yarbro, "Messages From Michael," *Life Times*, Winter 86-87, Vol. 1, No. 2, p. 7.

12. William Warch, *The New Thought Christian* (Marina del Rey, Calif.: DeVorss & Company, 1977), p. 57.

13. *Ibid.*, p. 56.

14. C. S. Nott, *Teachings of Gurdjieff: A Pupil's Journal*, p. 214.

15. Michele L'Ecuyer, "Mafu," *Life Times*, Vol. 1, No. 2, Winter 86-87, p. 81.

16. John White, "The Second Coming: A New Age View of an Ancient Myth," *New Frontier*, December 1987, p. 15.

17. Benjamine Creme, *Maitreya's Mission*, p. 159.

18. *Ibid.*, pp. 159, 193, 194, 204, 209.

19. "Channels, The Latest in Psychic Chic," *USA Today*, January 22, 1987, p. D-1.

20. Matthew Fox, *Original Blessing*, p. 137.

21. *Ibid.*, p. 102.

22. *Ibid.*, p. 213.

23. *Ibid.*, p. 162.

24. *Ibid.*

25. Martin Groder, "Evil Thoughts: Understanding Your Dark Side," *Bottom Line*, October 15, 1986, p. 9.

26. *Ibid.*, p. 10.

27. *Ibid.*, p. 9.

28. John Randolph Price, *The Planetary Commission*, p. 139.

29. Matthew Fox, *Original Blessing*, p. 137.

30. *Ibid.*, p. 135.

31. *Ibid.*, pp. 132, 133.

32. Rainer Maria Wilke, quoted by Matthew Fox, *Original Blessing*, p. 133.

33. *Ibid.*

34. *Ibid.*, p. 135.

35. *Ibid.*

36. *Ibid.*, p. 24.

37. "Trying to Dig Up Root of All Evil," *Chicago Tribune*, Section D, pp. 1-3, October 18, 1987. Also see Becky Knapp, "The Shadow of Evil," *Austin American-Statesman*, October 16, 1987, p. C-8.

38. *Ibid.*

39. *Ibid.*

40. Miriam Starhawk, *Dreaming the Dark: The Spiral Journey: A Rebirth of the Ancient Religion of the Great Goddess* (New York: Doubleday, 1979), p. 19.

41. Gregory Curtis, quoted in "Trying to Dig Up Root of All Evil," *Chicago Tribune*, Section D, pp. 1-3, October 18, 1987.

Chapter 13:   All Hail the New Age Messiah!

1. Foster Bailey, *Things to Come*, pp. 116, 117.

2. David Spangler, *Revelation: The Birth of a New Age*, p. 150.

3. *Ibid.*, p. 156.

4. *Omega-Letter*, North Bay, Ontario, Canada, February 1988, p. 15.

5. Alice Bailey, *Education in the New Age*, vi-vii.

6. Texe Marrs, *Rush to Armageddon* (Wheaton, Ill.: Tyndale House Publishers, 1987), pp. 145-154.

7. *NRI Trumpet*, Aurora, Colorado, July 1987, p. 1.

8. Mikhail Gorbachev, *Perestroika: New Thinking for Our Country and the World*.

9. *Omega-Letter*, North Bay, Ontario, Canada, February 1988, p. 11.

10. *Ibid.*, p. 10.

11. *NRI Trumpet*, Aurora, Colorado, January 1988, p. 12.

12. *Ibid.*

13. Marla Donato, *Welcome to the Dawning of Another New Age*, p. E-2.

14. S. W. Virato, "An interview with Igor Mikhailusenko, Soviet Poet," *New Frontier*, November 1987, p. 15, 43, 44.

15. Mikhail Gorbachev, *Perestroika: New Thinking for Our Country and the World*.

16. *Ibid.*

17. Norman Cousins, quoted by Cliff Kincaid, "Ted Turner's Global Tomorrow," *Human Events,* August 10, 1985, p. 12.

Chapter 14: **Passport to Hell: The Great Luciferic Initiation of All Mankind**

1. Benjamin Creme, *Maitreya's Mission,* p. 154.

2. *Ibid.,* p. 179.

3. *Ibid.,* pp. 111, 129.

4. Alice Bailey, *The Externalization of the Hierarchy,* pp. 413, 414.

5. Demonic tongues can be traced all the way back to Babylon. Demonic tongues are prevalent today in Hindu ashrams and in the New Age. Seth International, an Austin, Texas-based organization whose followers study the writings of the spirit guide Seth recently (Spring 1988) conducted three seminars on how to speak in demonic tongues.

6. Geoffrey Hodson, *The Brotherhood of Angels and Men* (Wheaton, Ill.: The Theosophical Publishing House, 1982), p. 86.

7. Elizabeth Clare Prophet, *The Great White Brotherhood in the Culture, History and Religion of America,* p. 163.

8. For a shocking exposé of human sacrifice in today's world, I refer you to *Satan's Underground* by Lauren Stratford (Eugene, Ore.: Harvest House, 1988).

9. Djwhal Khul, quoted by the Two Disciples, *The Rainbow Bridge*.

10. Matthew Fox, *Original Blessing*, p. 305.

11. The U.S. Government already has in place a system of camps for emergency use, some ostensibly prepared for an extraordinary infusion of immigrants from Latin America. These camps, run by the U.S. military, could easily be used by a future Antichrist-run government.

12. Barbara Marx Hubbard, *Happy Birth Day Planet Earth*, p. 17.

13. *Ibid.*, p. 19.

14. Benjamin Creme, *Maitreya's Mission*, p. 128.

15. *Ibid.*

16. David Spangler, *Reflections on the Christ* (Findhorn, Scotland: 1978), pp. 44, 45.

17. Edouard Schure, *From Sphinx to Christ*, pp. 283, 284.

18. Dane Rudhyar, *Occult Preparations for a New Age*, pp. 23, 24.

19. *Ibid.*

20. Alice Bailey, *The Reappearance of the Christ*, pp. 121-123.

21. Benjamin Creme, quoted by Pauline Griego MacPherson, *Can the Elect Be Deceived?* (Denver, Colo.: Bold Truth Press, 1986), p. 84.

Chapter 15: The Glorious Return

1. Benjamin Creme, *Maitreya's Mission*, p. 3.

2. *Ibid.*, p. 4.

3. *Ibid.*, pp. 14, 16.

4. *Ibid.*, p. 8.

For More Information

Texe Marrs and Living Truth Ministries offer a newsletter about Bible prophecy, the New Age Movement, cults, the occult challenge to Christianity, and other important topics.

If you would like to receive a free copy of this newsletter or wish to have information about other books and tapes by Texe Marrs, please write to:

Texe Marrs
Living Truth Ministries
8103 Shiloh Court
Austin, TX 78745